IMPLAUSIBLE BELIEFS

in the *Bible*, *Astrology* and *UFOs*

ALLAN MAZUR

Transaction Publishers

New Brunswick (U.S.A.) and London (U.K.)

Library of Congress Catalog Number: 2007047846
ISBN: 978-1-4128-0677-0
Printed in the United States of America

Library of Congress Cataloging-in-Publication Data

Mazur, Allan.
    Implausible beliefs : in the Bible, astrology, and UFOS / Allan Mazur.
        p. cm.
    Includes bibliographical references and index.
    ISBN 978-1-4128-0677-0 (alk. paper)
        1. Belief and doubt. 2. Irrationalism (Philosophy) 3. Bible—
    Evidences, authority, etc. I. Title.

BD215.M39 2008
121'6—dc22

                                                2007047846

"The true-believer syndrome merits study by science. What is it that compels a person, past all reason, to believe the unbelievable? How can an otherwise sane individual become so enamored of a fantasy, an imposture, that even after it's exposed in the bright light of day he still clings to it—indeed, clings to it all the harder?"
—M. Lamar Keene, spiritualist and fraud, 1976

Contents

Acknowledgments

I thank the following people for critically reading part or all of the text or for providing assistance or advice: Michael Barkun, Matt Coulter, Daniel Gilbert, Winifred Golden, Ian Hamilton, Larry Hatch, Irving Louis Horowitz, Samuel Jackson, Theodore Kemper, Stephen Maisto, Roger Masters, Julie Mazur, Ulrich Mueller, Michael Nauer, Matthew Nisbet, Robert Sheaffer, Craig Spaeth, Rodney Stark, Matthew Tribe, and James Watts. This does not imply that any of them agree with all statements made here.

Portions of chapter 3 were published in *Politics and the Life Sciences* and *Science* (Mazur 2004, 2007a). An adaptation of chapter 4 appeared in *The Skeptical Inquirer* (Mazur 2007b).

Part 1

Implausible Beliefs

1

Why Are We So Gullible?

People should be free to believe whatever they want. On the other hand, we expect university students to understand that the value of π = 3.14..., not 3.0; that the world is round, not flat; that Earth orbits the sun once a year and is not the center of the universe; that our planet is billions of years old, not 6,000; that humans have lived on it for hundreds of thousands of years, having evolved from earlier primate species; and that the Grand Canyon is far older than the alleged era of Noah's flood. These are facts, not seriously open to scientific dispute.

There are, in addition, purely subjective values, wholly without scientific basis, that have become so broadly accepted in the modern world that few object to their inclusion in the United Nations' Universal Declaration of Human Rights: All humans are born free and equal in dignity and rights, without distinction of any kind, whether by race, sex, religion, national or social origin, or on the basis of the country or territory to which a person belongs. All people have the right to freedom of religion, or to change religions, either alone or with others, and to practice their religion. No one shall be subjected to torture or to cruel or degrading punishment. Slavery in any form is prohibited. Marriage shall be entered into only with the free and full consent of the intending spouses; men and women are entitled to equal rights during marriage and at its dissolution. Everyone has the right to recognition everywhere as a person before the law, and any individual charged with a penal offense should be presumed innocent until proven guilty.

None of these moral positions is implied by a full and literal reading of the Bible or the Koran, which, to the contrary, have been cited to justify exactly the opposite positions. The only way to bring the corpus of holy writings into line with modern Western morality is to selectively ignore or radically reinterpret passages that condone if not require enslavement, racism, wholesale slaughter, collective guilt, polygamy and sexual inequality, and the stoning or burning to death of people who promote other religions.

The Literal Bible and Other Implausible Beliefs

Why do so many educated, intelligent Americans believe the Bible is the inerrant word of God, literally word for word? Why do we accept so many other implausible beliefs – about UFOs, abduction by space aliens, the accuracy of horoscopes?

For most of Judeo-Christian history, the exact wording of scriptures was not of great interest to most followers because they could not read. Those who could knew that the hand-copied writings then in circulation contained errors and deviated from one another. In the second century CE, the pagan critic Celsus complained that Christians changed their texts at will, and his Christian opponent Origen acknowledged the great number of differences among the manuscripts. Pope Damasus was sufficiently concerned about variant wordings that in 382 CE he commissioned his secretary, Jerome, to produce a standardized translation of the New Testament in Latin. Working for twenty years, Jerome compared numerous texts in Hebrew, Aramaic, Latin, and Greek before settling on his own version, later known as the Vulgate Bible, the first book printed by Gutenberg and to this day the official text of the Roman Catholic Church.

The Vulgate solidified a canon that had evolved over the first four centuries of the Christian era. It included four gospels from among many circulating at the time. Some writings were excluded because they were inconsistent with orthodox doctrine as it had developed. The recently restored and authenticated Gospel of Judas, for example, wholly reverses the standard view of Judas Iscariot as treacherous betrayer. Here he is portrayed as the most trusted of the original disciples, asked by Jesus to instigate the chain of events that would free the Spirit of Christ from its physical constraints (Kasser et al. 2006).

Aware of divergences in theme and wording even within the canon, the Catholic position was, and continues to be, that the Bible is properly understood in the context of the apostolic tradition, and the Church alone can pronounce the meaning of scripture and its dogmas. When Martin Luther led the Protestant Reformation, he opposed this idea, dismissing the authority of the corrupt Catholic hierarchy and insisting that faith could be based solely on reading the Bible. This dispute revived interest in the accuracy of the Testaments, that is, the degree to which the now-printed book – known to be a copy of older copies, whose originals and earliest copies are all lost – exactly reflected the words of the first writers. Scholars of the seventeenth century, comparing extant New Testament writings, located tens of thousands of variations, and far more are known today.

Most variations are trivial errors in copying, but sometimes the copyist, whether purposively or not, changed the meaning of the text. Professor Bart Ehrman of the University of North Carolina raises several questions that are answered differently depending on which New Testament manuscript is consulted:

> Was Jesus an angry man? Was he completely distraught in the face of death? Did he tell his disciples that they could drink poison without being harmed? Did he let an adulteress off the hook with nothing but a mild warning? Is the doctrine of the Trinity explicitly taught in the New Testament? Is Jesus actually called the "unique God" there? Does the New Testament indicate that even the Son of God himself does not know when the end will come? The questions go on and on, and all of them are related to how one resolves difficulties in the manuscript tradition as it has come down to us.

Ancient manuscripts of the New Testament also take different positions on the nature of Christ, the role of women in the church, and the treachery of the Jews (Ehrman 2005: 208).

Extant copies of the Gospel of Matthew may contain variations intended to reconcile Jesus's paternal lineage with his mother's virginity. Because the earliest Christians were all Jews, it was important to show that Jesus fulfilled Old Testament expectations for a messiah, including descent from King David. Matthew opens with a genealogy of Jesus, giving each father-to-father link from Abraham through King David and finally through "Joseph, the husband of Mary, of whom Jesus was born" (1:16). This mention of Mary is an anomaly, the only female in the lineage. Did Matthew modify an earlier genealogy, creating an "in-law link" to preserve descent from King David in a way that is consistent with virgin birth?[1]

Joseph intended to break his engagement when he learned his intended wife was pregnant, but an angel assured him that the child was conceived by the Holy Spirit, and this occurred to fulfill words spoken by the Lord though the prophet Isaiah: "Look, the virgin shall conceive and bear a son" (Matthew 1:23). But Isaiah (7:23) is misquoted. His Hebrew word *alma*, meaning "young woman" without any implication of virginity, is replaced in Greek translation by *parthenos*, which can mean either a young woman or a virgin (Schowalter 1993). That is not to say that the doctrine of virgin birth is the result of a mistranslation, but that one cannot trust a literal word-for-word reading of the Bible.

The traditional English Bible is the King James Version of 1611. So many serious defects were known by the mid-nineteenth century that a full revision was published in 1901. The twentieth century saw many newer English translations, each claiming improvements over prior work. No doubt the process will continue. But since all original sources and the earliest copies are lost, there is no way to unequivocally determine the words or meanings of the first writers, or to resolve inconsistencies that appear in today's best translations. Mark writes that Jesus was crucified the day *after* the Passover meal was eaten (14:18-43, 15:25), but John says he died the day *before* (19:14). After Jesus's birth in Bethlehem, according to Luke, Joseph and Mary returned to Nazareth (2:39), but according to Matthew they fled to Egypt (2:13-14). Paul says that after his conversion on the road to Damascus he did *not* go to Jerusalem to see those who were apostles before him (Gal. 1:16-17), but Acts says that he *did* go to Jerusalem after leaving Damascus (9:26). Which if any of these choices is the inerrant word of God?

Since the nineteenth century, Americans have been among the most literal of Bible believers. According to the General Social Surveys, administered from 1984 to 2006, 34 percent of American adults feel "The Bible is the actual word of God and it is to be taken literally, word for word" (http://sda.berkeley.edu/archive.htm). Fundamentalist religiosity is enmeshed in U.S. politics and Middle East politics. It is the basis of America's present "God war," pitting Dan Brown's mega-selling *The Da Vinci Code* and Richard Dawkins's *The God Delusion* against the phenomenally successful *Left Behind* series by Tim LaHaye and Jerry Jenkins. It is the basis for attempts to undermine the teaching of evolution in high school.

In this most technologically-advanced nation, why do so many people profess beliefs that are contradicted by science and logic? There is no point limiting the question to religion. We get a broader fix by asking why so many Americans believe other implausibilities as well. For that reason I compare biblical literalism to belief in astrology, and to faith that flying saucers are visiting our world from deep space. Half of Americans think there is some truth to astrology, a credulousness that has extended to the White House. Nancy Reagan, fearful after the assassination attempt on her husband, regularly consulted astrologer Joan Quigley about fortuitous timing of President Reagan's affairs. The Reagans had dealt with astrologers for years before reaching Washington (Reeves 2005).

Most believers in the implausible are normal, lawful citizens, but there is a dark side we cannot ignore. The attack of September 11, 2001, was the work of fanatic Islamists, motivated by literalist interpretations of the Koran. In 1994 Timothy McVeigh, protesting government limits on public access, trespassed into Area 51, the restricted Air Force installation near Las Vegas, rumored to be the repository for crashed UFOs. The next year he bombed the Murrah Federal Building in Oklahoma City, killing 168 people. On both occasions McVeigh was acting on his deep belief in arcane conspiracy theories and government cover-ups. Awaiting execution, he watched the movie *Contact*, about communication with space aliens, six times in two days (Barkun 2003; Michel and Herbeck 2001).

Religious Tolerance

The United States has from its outset been tolerant of diverse religions. But how tolerant should one be of suicide bombers who believe they are going to paradise? Mohammed Atta, leader of the 9/11 hijackers, wrote to his colleagues a letter found in his luggage:

Continue to pray throughout this night. Continue to recite the Koran.... Purify your heart and clean it from all earthly matters.... The time of judgment has arrived. Hence we need to utilize those few hours to ask God for forgiveness... From there you will begin to live the happy life, the infinite paradise. Be optimistic. The prophet was always optimistic....

Everybody hates death, fears death. But only those, the believers who know the life after death and the reward after death, would be the ones who will be seeking death....

Keep a very open mind, keep a very open heart of what you are to face. You will be entering paradise. You will be entering the happiest life, everlasting life....

Check all of your items – your bag, your clothes, knives, your will, your IDs, your passport, all your papers. Check your safety before you leave.... Make sure that nobody is following you.... Make sure that you are clean, your clothes are clean, including your shoes....

In the morning, try to pray the morning prayer with an open heart. Don't leave but when you have washed for the prayer. Continue to pray....

When you enter the plane: Oh God, open all doors for me. Oh God who answers prayers and answers those who ask you, I am asking you for your help. I am asking you for forgiveness. I am asking you to lighten my way. I am asking you to lift the burden I feel....

God, I trust in you. God, I lay myself in your hands. I ask with the light of your faith that has lit the whole world and lightened all darkness on this earth, to guide me until you approve of me. And once you do, that's my ultimate goal....

There is no God but God. There is no God who is the God of the highest throne; there is no God but God, the God of all earth and skies. There is no God but God, I being a sinner. We are of God, and to God we return.

Like the United States, Israel too asserts tolerance for other religions. Between 1948 and 1967, when Jordan occupied the Old City of Jerusalem, Jews were blocked from access to the Western Wall of Herod's Temple, the holiest site in Judaism. After winning control of the Temple Mount in the Six Day War, Israel guaranteed Muslim access to the Dome of the Rock and the Al-Aqsa Mosque, together the third holiest site in Islam, which lies literally atop the Western Wall. Yet at the same time, Jewish fundamentalists insisted that God gave them everlasting possession of all the land between the Nile and Mesopotamia. For decades after 1967, this was a major justification for Israeli occupation of Gaza and the West Bank, home to millions of Palestinians.

Both Jewish and Muslim governments support schools that promote nationalistic assertions from the Bible or the Koran. These governments pursue policies that contradict the UN Declaration of Human Rights but are consistent with religious scriptures. Muslim and Jewish governments discriminate even against co-religionists of a different denomination than is in power. In Israel, rabbis of Reform or Conservative denominations are not officially recognized and cannot perform marriages. The Muslim world is rife with denominational discrimination, most obviously the antipathy between Sunnis and Shiites.

None of this is unusual from an historic perspective. Traditional societies recognized no separation between their own religion and their political order, so the governments of the Middle East, indeed many of today's Third World and predominately Catholic nations, tread a well-worn road paved with religion-based laws. Even the atheistic behemoths of the twentieth century, the Soviet Union and China, imposed their ir-religion on their polities. It was post-Enlightenment Holland, the United States, and France that fell out of step by allowing either full toleration of non-established sects or full separation of church from state, doctrines that more or less spread among the industrial democracies.[2]

What are the limits of religious tolerance? Surely there *are* limits, as there are restraints on freedom of speech, which disallow a shout of "fire" in a crowded theater, or libeling a living person, or inciting a riot, or threatening the assassination of a president. The United States or individual states have occasionally imposed religious restrictions, as against Mormon polygamy, or the African practice of female genital mutilation, or the handling of snakes in Pentecostal church services. Certain "hate crimes" are illegal, whether in or out of a religious context. On the other side, how far should one push the separation of church from state? Few people, whether atheist or believer, deeply care that our coins and dollars carry "In God We Trust," or that the Pledge of Allegiance contains the phrase "under God". Surely there are better causes for our time, money, and political capital than erasing these traces of religion from public life.

American Fundamentalism and Politics

Many American Christians who immediately recognize the fanaticism of Islamist or Jewish extremists are slower to see the fault in their own fervid fundamentalists. After the World Trade Center and the Pentagon were attacked on September 11, 2001, the popular televangelist Pat Robertson announced that it was because of God's displeasure with secular immorality (Phillips 2006: 219). When the people of Dover, Pennsylvania voted out of office those members of the school board who mandated that intelligent design be taught in science classes, Robertson denounced the voters for rejecting God and warned them not to be surprised if disaster struck their town (*New York Times*, 11/11/05). When Israeli prime minister Ariel Sharon suffered an incapacitating stroke, Robertson declared it divine punishment for withdrawing Jewish settlements from Gaza. "God considers this land to be his," Mr. Robertson told his television audience. "You read the Bible and he says, 'This is my land,' and for any prime minister of Israel who decides he is going to carve it up and give it away, God says, 'No, this is mine'" (*New York Times*, 1/6/06). A few months earlier, Robertson urged that the United States assassinate President Hugo Chavez of Venezuela, apparently for nationalistic rather than religious reasons (*New York Times*, 8/24/05). Robertson, a national figure who once campaigned for the presidency, reaches many people with his ideas. His popular book, *The New World Order* (1991), claims superrich plotters, acting through secret societies like the Illuminati, are attacking Christianity and American civil liberties, and are on the verge of imposing a world government. (For a critique of Robertson's conspiracy theory see Lind and Heilbrun, 1995.) Reverend Robertson says of the relationship of church to state: "There is no way that government can operate successfully unless led by godly men and women under the laws of the God of Jacob" (Phillips 2006: 215).

One such godly man is Rick Santorum, until recently U.S. senator from Pennsylvania, a conservative Catholic and favorite of the religious right. "How is it possible" he asks, "to believe in the existence of God yet refuse to express outrage when his moral code is flouted? To have faith in God, but to reject moral absolutes?" (Sokolove 2005: 59). But what are these moral absolutes, and how do we know them if not from holy writ? And whose interpretation of scripture is correct?

Although there is a widespread perception that the proportion of Americans in fundamentalist Protestant denominations has greatly increased in recent decades, that is not true, as we shall see. There has been a sharp rise in fundamentalists' *visibility* in the mass media, and in their influence and involvement in Washington politics. Pat Robertson garnered considerable support during his campaign for the presidency in 1988. The administration of George W. Bush, unlike that of his father, is permeated by religious fundamentalism, as was the Republican Congress during most of his tenure.

This ultra-religiosity has been a persistent concern of liberals and Democrats, but even the conservative Republican strategist Kevin Phillips complained of it in his book, *American Theocracy*: "The rapture, end-times, and Armageddon hucksters in the United States rank with any Shiite ayatollahs, and the last two presidential elections mark the transition of the GOP into the first religious party in U.S. history" (2006: vii). According to Phillips,

> In Republican politics theological correctness – call it TC – became a policy-shaping force in determining Middle Eastern geopolitics, combating global AIDS, defining the legal rights of fetuses, pretending that oil was not a cause for the invasion of Iraq, and explaining geological controversies in language compatible with the Book of Genesis. As church congregations became GOP auxiliaries and a host of religious right organizations provided essential scorecards of senators and congressmen up for reelection, the nature of constituency pressure changed from share our values to support our doctrine – or else....
>
> By 2001 theology – the yardstick of belief, not judgment – began to displace logic and realpolitik in official Washington.... First and foremost were the issues involving birth, life, death, sex, health, medicine, marriage, and the role of the family...These are areas where perceived immorality most excites stick-to-Scripture advocates and the religious right. Closely related is the commitment by the Bush White House and the religious right to reduce the separation between church and state.... Topics such as natural resources, climate, global warming, resource depletion, environmental regulation, and petroleum geology – all surprising targets for religious attacks – mark out a third important arena. Such debates draw in the energy industry, automobile producers, utilities, industries that pollute, and the environmental movement, as well as the forces battling for so-called intelligent design, creationism, or the literal interpretation of the Book of Genesis. Major business lobbies, all too aware of the GOP's religious blocs, harness their biases where possible and avoid trespassing on matters of theology (Phillips 2006: 236-37).

When Tom DeLay was the powerful House majority leader, he found his answers in the Bible, as did many of his colleagues in Congress. At that time, two-thirds of Republicans in the Republican-controlled House and Senate enjoyed 80 percent or more voting ratings from such groups as the Christian Coalition and the National Right to Life Committee (Phillips 2006: 234). Among the most visible religion-based issues during the presidency of George W. Bush were a ban on gay marriage, opposition to stem cell research except under very limiting conditions, teaching intelligent design in science classes, refusal to fund United Nations population-control or disease-prevention programs that fostered contraception, nominating Supreme Court justices who might overturn Roe v. Wade, and the extraordinary effort to keep a woman named Terri Schiavo on a feeding tube.

Many of these stances strengthened the Bush base but some backfired. The brand of conservative who objects to government intrusion in private lives was more incensed than liberals over the Terri Schiavo episode. In 1990, at age twenty-six, Schiavo had collapsed, suffering irreversible brain damage. She was kept alive by a feeding tube, over the objections of her husband who asserted that artificial life support was contrary to his wife's previously expressed wish. But her parents fought in the courts to keep Terri alive, arguing that she had some level of consciousness. In 2005, after a court decision to remove the tube, the religious right mobilized to keep her on life support. The Schiavo case became front page news, involving Florida Governor Jeb Bush, his brother the president, Congress, the Supreme Court, and the Vatican. Bill Frist, formerly majority leader of the Senate and a physician, epitomized the pandering when he told the press, after viewing a video of Terri Schiavo, that she appeared ''clearly responsive,'' thus contradicting her own physicians, who knew she was vegetative with no chance of recovery, as later proven when an autopsy revealed the extent of brain atrophy.

Other of the administration's Bible-based postures, while less heart rending, are noteworthy for their fundamentalist bias. In 2003 the bookstore at Grand Canyon National Park began selling *The Grand Canyon: A Different View*, by Tom Vail, a creationist interpretation of the canyon's origin in Noah's flood 4,500 years ago. It ranked seventeenth among 800 products sold. National geological organizations cautioned the Park Service against promoting the Genesis picture of a young earth as if it were scientifically credible. Against the recommendation of the Park Service's senior geologist, the book remained on sale (Wilgoren 2005).

In August 2005, President Bush himself joined those advocating that "intelligent design" (ID) be taught in public schools alongside evolution, an endorsement soon joined by Bill Frist. ID was then brewing in many states, the latest attempt by creationists to countermand the Darwinian challenge to Genesis. In 1982 and again in 1987 the Supreme Court prohibited the teaching of "creation science" in public schools because of its religious content. ID, as promoted in 2004 and 2005, was a new version of the same idea, intended to skirt the court's prohibition by removing all references to God. Its nub is that life is too complex to arise by chance and therefore must have had a designer. The great designer is unnamed.

In 2004, fundamentalists on the Dover, Pennsylvania school board, encouraged by national interest groups, required ninth-grade biology teachers to read a statement making students aware of the gaps and problems in evolutionary theory, and to call attention to ID as an alternative explanation for the diversity of life. The objecting parents of eleven Dover students brought a civil suit against the board. The court case in Dover became the focus of national attention, some calling it "the Scopes II trial."

U.S. District Court Judge John E. Jones III, a Republican, heard opposing arguments for six weeks. In December 2005, Judge Jones issued a 139-page ruling that ID is not science and cannot uncouple itself from its creationist, thus religious, antecedents. Therefore it is unconstitutional to teach ID as an alternative to evolution in a public school science class. He further concluded from the testimony of plaintiffs' scientific experts that the theory of evolution is overwhelmingly accepted by the scientific community. He chastised the school board for duplicity in pretending that ID wasn't revised creationism, commenting tartly that several members "who so staunchly and proudly touted their religious convictions in public, would time and again lie to cover their tracks and disguise the real purpose behind the ID policy." The pretense by ID proponents to having wholly secular motives was "ludicrous" and "a sham," according to the judge. In the most quoted phrase of his decision, Jones wrote of the "breathtaking inanity" of the board's decision and its utter waste of monetary and personal resources. Dover taxpayers were liable for the cost of the trial and attorney fees (Jones 2005; Mervis 2006).

I think it unlikely that Judge Jones's no-holds-barred ruling changed any minds that were firmly planted beforehand. But it did kill intelligent design as a news story. By eliminating free publicity in the mass media, the anti-evolution campaign was derailed, at least temporarily.

The Media

The mass media are a powerful engine, although they do not, as once thought, directly mold public opinion. Instead, consumers selectively attend to articles, books, and programming that are consistent with their preexisting views, interpreting news and events to fit their prior positions. Thus the media more often fortify already-held positions than change them. Strident or emotionally inciting commentary on a controversial subject can raise the level of political polarization.

The most solidly demonstrated effect of news media on opinion is agenda-setting, the placing of certain issues or problems foremost in the minds of people, including policymakers, simply by making them salient in news broadcasts and publications. Put succinctly, the news media are not successful in telling us what to think, but they do succeed in telling us what to think about (McCombs and Shaw 1972). Precisely what is said in articles and programs matters relatively little compared to the amount and saliency of exposure. People are affected more by the quantity of coverage, especially the repetition of simple images, than by detailed content, which often is skipped over.

Nearly all news stories of national or international scope, or on specialty subjects like science and environment, are first brought to widespread attention by a small, central group of large news organizations including major newspapers, wire services, and television networks. The *New York Times* is especially important as an agenda setter for other news organs; the *Washington Post* is important for news from the federal government; the *Wall Street Journal* for business news. These national organizations have the resources and personnel to cover wide ranging stories and specialty topics. Every day they produce a pool of news articles from which thousands of local organs select their news of the day, sometimes simply repeating stories and sometimes embellishing them from local sources. Therefore the rise and fall of attention to a particular topic, and consequent public and governmental concern, may be traced back to the rise and fall of journalistic interest by the central news organs and their sources. (Network television "news," between commercials, brings visual imagery to a handful of stories prominent in the national print media, thus amplifying the effect of the newspapers by reaching the television-watching public.)

The *New York Times* brought intelligent design and the Dover school board to national attention with a long critical editorial on January 23, 2005, and again on February 7 with an op-ed rejoinder by an ID proponent, which elicited a spate of letters to the editor. President Bush's endorsement of the creationist position in August was the hook for intensified coverage, including an in-depth series of front-page articles in the *Times*. The Dover trial in the final months of 2005 was heavily reported, but after Judge Jones's decisive rebuke, ID nearly disappeared from the news.

The Schiavo affair had an even sharper attention trajectory, skyrocketing from Florida to national news on January 25, 2005 as the U.S. Supreme Court decided against Governor Jeb Bush's efforts to keep the brain-damaged woman alive. News coverage and controversy peaked in March when the feeding tube was removed, then diminished rapidly after Ms. Schiavo's burial in early April.

Tabloids, television, motion pictures, and trade books—even those coming from respectable publishers and producers—routinely sensationalize and present misinformation. A case in point is the ultra best-seller *The Da Vinci Code* (2003), which promulgates the idea that Jesus and Mary Magdalene were married and had a child whose bloodline continues to this day. Obviously a work of fiction, the novel is prefaced by a page titled "FACT," explaining that the Priory of Sion—a European secret society (that in the story is devoted to the protection of the bloodline) – is a real organization founded in 1099, and among its prominent members were Isaac Newton, Botticelli, Victor Hugo, and Leonardo Da Vinci. It further claims that "All descriptions of artwork, architecture, documents, and secret rituals in this novel are accurate." Actually, author Dan Brown's statements about early Christian documents contain many errors and historically baseless claims (Ehrman 2004). The Priory of Sion, whose existence is undocumented prior to the mid-twentieth century and unsupported by any serious scholarship, is almost certainly a hoax to which Brown may have fallen victim. His venerable publisher, Random House, seems neither to have checked facts nor cared about conflating truth and fiction.

In American journalism, the customary style of reporting controversial issues is to balance opposing views, juxtaposing statements from both sides and letting readers or viewers draw their own conclusions. Thus, a feature about astrology would present both believers and skeptics. This format, ostensibly unbiased, implicitly attributes equal credibility to both positions. Our best journalists and news organizations follow this practice (Mooney and Nisbet 2005). Atop my stack of UFO articles is one from The *New York Times* by respected science writer William Broad (1997). It tells of the Air Force's fiftieth anniversary report on the famous 1947 incident near the desert town of Roswell, NM that is said by flying saucer buffs to have been the crash of a spaceship and the recovery of extraterrestrial bodies, or in some versions of live aliens. In properly balanced fashion, Broad includes a statement by a professional ufologist named

Stanton Friedman: "This is the biggest story of the millennium, a visit to the Earth by extraterrestrial spacecraft and the cover-up of the best evidence, the bodies and the wreckage, for 50 years."

Balanced coverage is fine when the opposing positions have equal credibility, but it should be rejected by journalists when one side is scientifically incredible. It is a sad memorial for Peter Jennings, longtime anchor of ABC News, that one of his last television appearances before his death in 2005 was as narrator of a two-hour primetime special, "The UFO Phenomenon – Seeing is Believing," giving balanced voice to promoters of flying saucers and alien abduction.

Science

By *science* we generally mean a body of knowledge that describes or explains features of the observable world. Scientific explanations are based on simplified theories, which are supposed to be consistent with observations and testable against future observations. Pragmatically, science is what professional scientists do for a living, and "scientific truth" consists of the theories and observations that are consensually held within the scientific community, which change over time.

Even a cursory history of science during the past half millennium shows several intellectual revolutions or "paradigm shifts" associated with such names as Copernicus, Newton, Lavoisier, Darwin, and Einstein. These are periods when the educated understanding of natural phenomena changed radically, rendering core ideas incorrect. Physics experienced such a paradigm shift around the early decades of the twentieth century with the advent of radioactivity, relativity, and quantum theory.

Knowing that scientists (or "natural philosophers") of the past have been spectacularly wrong, many believers in incredible ideas are confident that today's science is equally mistaken. Some future theory of the cosmos will explain how a person's life is affected by the ascension of Saturn rather than Jupiter at the moment of birth, or how spaceships travel between distant stars at speeds far exceeding that of light. Perhaps a physicist of the twenty-second century will disprove the Second Law of Thermodynamics, opening the prospect for a perpetual motion machine, so we cannot wholly discount the possibility that some inventor will successfully produce one is his garage. Perhaps a paleontologist will discover the fossilized skeleton of a *Homo sapiens* thrusting a spear into the ribcage of a *Tyrannosaurus rex*. But the odds are slim.

Since the revolution in modern physics nearly a century ago, we have seen a slowing of paradigm upheaval. Despite enormous increases in

research funding and the number of working scientists, producing remarkable advances in knowledge and the opening of whole new fields
in genetics, cryogenics, nanotechnology, cosmology, human evolution,
and more, it is difficult to find core ideas in natural science that recently
have been turned on their heads. (One instance is geology's flip during
the 1960s from its long-held view of fixed continents to the realization
that they move.) Modern science is a rapidly expanding enterprise, but
it is expanding from a fairly reliable base.

There are continual changes in specific findings, sometimes very
important specifics, and there are always disputes in areas of active research about what is true and what is not. Complete agreement within the
scientific community is like the end of the rainbow: You may approach
it but you will never reach it. There are bona fide scientists today who
insist that the fluoridation of drinking water is a major source of cancer,
that "cold fusion" is a real phenomenon, that AIDS is not caused by HIV
infection, and that Noah's flood was a historic worldwide catastrophe.
Science is not like a slot machine, where in one sublime moment three
cherries come up and everyone knows that's a winner. Scientists have all
the human foibles that create dissenters, including stubbornness, envy,
defensiveness, and simple variation in the kind of evidence one requires
to be convinced of something.

If it is true that sophisticated observers once regarded science as wholly
objective, surely that is no longer the case. Today we often see scientists
who represent opposing interest groups making contradictory factual
claims to bolster their respective sides. We recognize that the products
of science, like all human productions, are to some extent arbitrary social
constructs reflecting personal, structural, and historical influences. Some
sociologists of science argue that science is not fundamentally different
from other methods of knowing, such as philosophy, religion, or astrology. From their position it follows that scientific claims have no special
status as statements of truth.

More numerous are those, including most scientists themselves, who
believe that modern science, despite its subjective elements, does discover
real features of nature (viruses, ions, planets, gravitational attraction,
electromagnetic radiation, supernovas) in a way that other methods of
knowing cannot, and that the special quality of this knowledge is seen in
the power of modern technologies that are based on scientific theory.

For those of us who hold this latter (realist) view, "objectivity" and
"subjectivity" are taken as relative – not absolute – terms, and scientific
knowledge is considered more objective than other systems of belief

about the natural world; thus it deserves special status. We regard the novel claims of an individual scientist as less objective than claims that appear in standard textbooks or are accepted by most informed scientists, though we expect that these novel claimants will occasionally be correct (but usually not). Furthermore, we distinguish established scientific knowledge, wherein scientific claims are trustworthy, from areas of active research where knowledge is uncertain.

In my own view, the power of science lies in three advantages. First, scientists tend to be intelligent, which is a necessary though not sufficient condition for intellectual achievement. Second, scientific reasoning is rational, meaning that theories must be consistent, logical, and mathematically correct, which is a clear improvement over other forms of reasoning still current. Finally, the requirement of modern science that theory be consistent with observation, for all its flexibility in application, is a unique constraint on speculation and has an excellent record of discovery. These features do not guarantee good science, but they greatly help. When established science contradicts one's personal beliefs, it is worthwhile examining the source of one's ideas with an open mind.

The Revision of Faith

In past eras there have been, and presently are, religions and religious leaders who have been a blessing to the people of the earth.[3] They offer solace in times of grief; rituals that celebrate the passages of life and bind a community together; charity for the needy; companionship for the lonely; hope in desperate situations; meaning to life's mysteries; scholarship; the preservation of culture; and sponsorship of glorious works of art, music, and architecture. The twentieth-century nations that suppressed religion failed dismally to produce improved societies or happier people. Possibly religion is an inevitable feature of good societies, or at least contributory. Belief in a god, or gods, or some transcendent spirit, or an afterlife, is not implausible in itself because we have no empirical evidence or decisive logic that strongly favors either existence or non-existence. No reader should leave this book thinking it is a brief against religion.

My argument is against the propagation and acceptance of implausible beliefs, whether from religious or secular sources. Since full and literal adherence to the Bible carries with it a commitment to moral principles that are despicable by modern standards, my corollary argument is that archaic prescriptions for behavior must be continually reevaluated. Modern morality, but not the full Bible, rejects collective guilt, slavery, subordination of women, and mass slaughter.

Passages from the Old and New Testaments are among the most beautiful in the English language, treasures to be enjoyed into the distant future. But they should not dictate our laws, our morality, or what is taught as science in our public schools. Many religious leaders realize this, interpreting the Bible or Koran as metaphor or parable. They draw moral lessons from verses that are consistent with modern sensibilities while ignoring those about stoning and dismemberment, or that are anti-Semitic, or that encourage suicide bombers to seek paradise by sending infidels to hell.

Implausible beliefs in non-religious domains like astrology and UFOs presently offer no comparable threat to public policy. They can, however, play havoc on personal lives. Followers of cults like Heaven's Gate or People's Temple, or those convinced by hypnotists that they were abducted and sexually abused by space aliens, are victims of manipulation. Selling astrological horoscopes or psychic surgery or spirit communication as veridical is fraudulent, taking money from the gullible.

A free society cannot dictate belief, but it can foster critical thinking. It can support a vigorous scientific enterprise and quality education in verified knowledge. A free press, at least its respectable sector, can forego unbridled tolerance for, and propagation of, incredible claims on the grounds of religious tolerance or balanced news coverage or higher sales. This requires that journalists, publishers, and producers understand the difference between sensible and implausible statements, and treat them accordingly. The United States, unlike Canada, has no law against reporting false news; our First Amendment protections are too precious to even hint at media censorship. The quality press guards its own practices, sometimes rigorously. A peculiar instance was the World War II agreement among American journalists to avoid showing President Franklin Roosevelt as crippled. Today the quality press self-enforces bans on language and visuals that violate common standards of decency; on insults to minority groups; and on identification of confidential sources even when such a ban denies accused parties knowledge of their accusers. Journalists exercise admirable responsibility in such matters. Perhaps they could add to that list a ban on reporting extremely implausible claims as if they may be true.

The profit motive will guarantee a supply of sensationally false publications, television programs, and movies (Park 2000). It would help if open-mined consumers could depend on at least some of our news organs, and our scientific and educational institutions, for cogent statements of present-day knowledge.

Analyzing Controversy

There is a relativistic tradition in sociology to study conflicts in an even-handed way, treating each side's claims as legitimate from its own perspective. Analyzing World War II, for example, would require an understanding – an attempt to "get into the heads" – of Nazi and Japanese viewpoints as well as the Allied perspective. At least initially, the analyst does not treat either side as privileged, or presume one stakeholder to be correct or singularly truthful.

This relativist tradition saves an analysis from becoming a polemic. It often demonstrates that the black-and-white perspective of a partisan has unrecognized grays, and that the opposing sides see the world in very different ways. Often it raises new doubts about which side is innocent and which blameworthy, or whose claims are truthful. I usually adopt this approach in my studies of social and scientific controversies (Mazur 1981, 1998, 2007c).

Even-handed analysis becomes problematic as the weight of evidence favoring one side becomes overwhelming. While historians looking back at the sixteenth century would give equal voice to proponents of a geocentric universe versus a heliocentric one, few would remain open to a claim made today that the earth is the center of the solar system. Controversies in science and technology are often settled to nearly every informed person's satisfaction (Mazur 2004). Psychiatrists adequately distinguish delusions from reality. In such cases, where – by reasonable criteria –one side is almost certainly right and the other wrong, relativism loses much of its value. I would be patronizing and insincere in applying an even-handed approach to the beliefs studied here. I make no attempt to do so.

Overview

This book has a threefold agenda. My first goal, in part 1, is to describe criteria for judging beliefs implausible, and to assess the scope of the problem in the United States. Other than by religious faith, scientists and philosophers long ago abandoned the search for absolute truth. It cannot be attained from the inferential logic of empirical research. Generalizations that the sun always rises, that all swans are white, and that there are no unicorns in nature, although sustained by numberless observations (or lack of observations in the case of unicorns), could not exclude the possibility of a contradiction in the future. There are even limits on discerning the truth or falsity of theorems in a closed logical system, because some theorems can be neither proved nor disproved, and there is the fact that logicians sometimes make errors.

The situation is not hopeless as long as we accept a lower standard than absolute truth. Chapter 2 describes and defends commonsense criteria that together make a strong case that certainly views should not be sustained in the face of present-day understanding. Of course, true believers will refute these criteria when they are used to discredit cherished ideas, but I suspect even they would accept them in domains of knowledge that are less sensitive. Chapter 3 concludes part 1 with a statistical portrait of implausible beliefs in the United States, and who tends to accept them.

My second goal is to apply criteria for implausibility to the Bible, astrology, and visitation to earth of intelligent being from other worlds. The Bible has enjoyed more scholarship than any other topic, intimidating non-specialists who enter the field. I reduce the onus slightly by limiting myself to the first five books of the Old Testament, the Torah, and relying heavily on work of scriptural specialists. Everyone knows about the Bible, but few actually read it. We will scroll through the text, seeing point after point that undermines scripture's natural history and moral guidance.

I have gathered all biblical topics together in part 2, for convenience of exposition, while part 3 critiques secular beliefs in astrology and UFOs. One should not infer from the separation of part 2 from 3 that implausible *religious* views are fundamentally different from implausible *secular* views. I do not think they are. This sets me apart from commentators who regard religion as *sui generis*, a uniquely evolved feature of the human mind, where transcendent religious and mystical experiences arise from specific neural processes in the brain, perhaps the result of peculiar "God genes" (e.g., Dennett 2006; Newberg and Waldman 2006; Hammer 2004). To me, there is little difference between believing in Noah's ark and believing in flying saucers. Religion is simply one domain of belief, like other domains. Besides, I do not regard all religious beliefs as implausible. (For a contrary argument see Dawkins [2006].)

My third goal, in part 4, is to explain why we all accept implausibilities – some of us more than others – despite evidence and logic that refutes them. My explanations are mainstream sociology and psychology. Very briefly, we are socialized as children into these or similar beliefs, and as adults we are influenced by spouses and friends. Personality is also a factor, sometimes abetted by stressful or lonely life situations. That is where we are headed, so now we may begin.

Notes

1. Luke, the other source for the doctrine of virgin birth, glosses the line of descent without inserting a female name, writing, "He [Jesus] was the son (as was thought) of Joseph" (3:23). The genealogies in Matthew and Luke are not consistent.
2. While France's revolutionary ethos encouraged religious toleration, that nation did not formally adopt the separation doctrine until 1905, having earlier given state support to Catholicism, Protestantism, and Judaism.
3. Few would argue with Catholic historian Richard McBrien's appraisal of John XXIII (1958-63): "Probably the most beloved, ecumenical, and openhearted pope in history, he touched the worldwide human community in a way no other pope has ever done... Every pope, before and after him, is to be measured against the standard he set" (1997: 432).

2

Implausible Beliefs

Obviously, believers in a claim that I regard as implausible will deny its implausibility. I say, for example, that it is incredible to think that space aliens in flying saucers abduct humans to remove their sperm or eggs, but many non-psychotic people insist that they have suffered this indignity. There is no ironclad way to resolve this difference in judgment, but here I propose criteria for regarding a claim or belief as implausible.

First we must acknowledge that a belief is implausible only from a particular perspective. People believe the traditions in which they are raised, guaranteeing that even the silliest things taught during family socialization are plausible to children and may remain so throughout their lives. Also, we must allow for changes in historical perspective. Anyone can cite beliefs once thought incredible that are today commonplace: the earth is a globe; humans fly around it in hours, or speak instantaneously to someone on the other side of it. From this track record we understand there is necessarily some parochialism in judging certain beliefs more reasonable than others. I use the term "implausible" rather than "impossible" to acknowledge that no judgment is infallible.

I retain philosopher David Hume's (1711-1776) distinction between beliefs about what *is* and what *ought* to be, that is, between facts and values.[1] There can be no empirical truth or falsity to moral assertions such as that slavery is good or bad, right or wrong. These are wholly subjective judgments about what ought to be, about some desired or deplored status. We may disagree with another person's evaluation of slavery, or with their aesthetic judgment of a piece of art, but we cannot call their evaluations "implausible" in any empirical or logical sense. I restrict judgments of implausibility to statements of fact or ostensible fact, to assertions about whether or not something actually occurs, or occurred historically, or could feasibly occur in the future.

One could begin with a definition of *plausibility*, the notion that a factual claim is probably true, valid, feasible, or reasonable. Like writers of dictionaries, we might then back into a definition of *im*plausibility as the negation or opposite of plausibility. I do not like that approach because it suggests to me a false dichotomy, that factual claims are either plausible or implausible, one or the other. I prefer to allow some middle or neutral ground in which to plant certain assertions that seemingly lack cogent reasons either for or against them. The classic stance of this kind is agnosticism, the indecision between atheism and belief in a god (or gods) on the grounds that, apart from tradition, there is a complete lack of tangible evidence one way or the other. One might be similarly agnostic about the existence of an afterlife, or about such mundane matters as whether the next flip of a coin will come up heads or tails. Everyone has beliefs or hunches that can be neither sustained nor refuted with sound argument. My concern is not with these moot beliefs, but with beliefs that are incredible. Therefore I want a stronger sense of "implausibility," one connoting that certain factual claims are almost certainly incorrect. To that end, I list criteria for disbelief. This is not an exhaustive list, and each criterion has escape clauses, but together they provide adequate grounding for the present.

Beliefs that Imply a Logical Contradiction are Implausible

Any claim that violates valid logical or mathematical reasoning should be rejected.[2] The area of a rectangle is necessarily the product of its length and width. The quantity π (the ratio of a circle's circumference to its diameter) necessarily equals 3.14159265....[3] No claim is tenable if on close inspection it contradicts established logical or mathematical truths.

We are told in 1 Kings 7: 23 and 2 Chronicles 4:2 that King Solomon made a round "molten sea" –apparently this refers to a pool of hot water intended for bathing. Its diameter is given as ten cubits ("brim to brim"), and it could be completely encircled by a line of thirty cubits. That implies $\pi = 3$, a value often used in the sixth century BCE but well off the true mark.

A rabbi and mathematician named Nehemiah, living in Palestine around 150 AD, spotted this contradiction between logic and scripture. Using an improved value for π, in decimals about 3.14, Nehemiah knew that a circle of diameter ten cubits must have a circumference of 31.4 cubits, not 30 cubits. To remove this inconsistency the rabbi assumed that ten cubits was the *outside* diameter of the structure (including the thickness of the opposite brims), and the reported circumference was for the *inside* of the brim (Bergmann 1993). If we assign the encircling brim a thickness of 0.22 cubits, then its inside diameter would be 9.56 cubits, and the corresponding circumference would be about 30 cubits. As in this case, it is often possible to escape a logical contradiction by introducing subsidiary assumptions.

In his *A History of Pi*, Petr Beckmann (1993) tells of amateur mathematicians who occasionally "prove" that π has a different value than is conventionally established. One of these frustrated innovators, John A. Parker of Cleveland, found "the Professors as a body, though learned in received theories, to be among the *least competent* to decide on any newly discovered principle" (1993: 179). Beckmann also comments on a widely circulated but apparently false story, which I too have heard, that a state legislature, for religious reasons, once passed a law making $\pi = 3$. He suspects the myth grew out of a documented incident in the Indiana legislature in 1897. A physician named Edwin Goodman claimed, among other implausible mathematical feats, to have proved that $\pi = 3.2$. Acting through his local legislator, Goodman offered this mathematical truth to the state as a contribution to education, to be used freely by Indiana, without paying the royalties that would be required from other users. A bill to confirm this arrangement was passed unanimously by the Indiana House of Representatives, and it passed its first reading in the Senate. Fortunately a professor of mathematics from Purdue, visiting the capitol for unrelated reasons, heard of the bill and persuaded some senators to move it no further toward becoming law.

In purely cognitive terms, logical inconsistency would seem to effectively undermine the credibility of a claim, but in practice it matters little, as shown by the long-term and widespread belief in the literal truth of Genesis. Human thought is not rigorously logical (Tversky and Kahneman 1974; Sutherland 1992; Schick and Vaughn 2002; Sherman 2002). While some thinkers labor to explain away ostensible contradictions, more often we simply ignore them or become sufficiently accustomed to them that they cease to be bothersome. Physicists of the early twentieth century were puzzled that certain experiments showed light behaving like particles, while other experiments showed light acting like waves. This seemed to be a physical inconsistency: light could be particles or waves but not both. By the time I studied physics, physicists accepted that light sometimes acts like particles and sometimes like waves. To me this duality still seems contradictory, rather like the one Christian deity being tripartite, but it has not undermined quantum theory.

Beliefs that Violate Common Experience or Understanding are Implausible

This is the weakest of my criteria because it is most culturally bound and therefore most arbitrary and changeable. Astrology was widely accepted by scholars as recently as the seventeenth century, a time when it was plausible to think that witches flew on brooms but implausible to believe that ordinary people could fly in metal fuselages.

Despite the fallacies and changing currents of common knowledge, it would be foolish to wholly reject popular wisdom as a guide to implausibility. People everywhere have a serviceable understanding of their social and natural surroundings. They know when a strange claim, perhaps of raising the dead or stopping the sun in its course, makes no sense in ordinary terms. The invocation of miracles has always implied recognition by contemporary observers that such reports defy common understanding and are therefore implausible unless caused by a supernatural agent.

David Hume's critique of miraculous claims may not have dissuaded many true believers, but it remains impressive for its commonsense rationality:

> When anyone tells me that he saw a dead man restored to life, I immediately consider...whether it be more probably that this person should deceive or be deceived, or that the fact which he relates should really have happened. I weigh the one miracle against the other; and...I always reject the greater miracle. If the falsehood of his testimony would be more miraculous than the event which he relates, then, and not till then, can he pretend to command my belief (1758: 491).

Like Hume, most of us, most of the time, do not believe reports of witches flying on broomsticks or of dead people returned to life because these assertions do not pass the commonsense test of face validity. It seems more likely that the witness has lied or been deceived.

Today, picturing the earth as flat rather than round, as the center of the universe, and as having a sky surrounded by water above as well as below, is nowhere taken seriously except possibly by adherents to archaic interpretations of scripture. These were once plausible ideas, but now they violate our common understanding. When stories of an epic flood were fashioned in Mesopotamia, the largest local animals were camels and cows, and there was no hint of the enormous variety of fauna that now or once populated the world, so the picture of a few men with simple tools building a wooden boat sufficiently large to hold every kind of animal ever created was not terribly far fetched. In the twenty-first century, one need not be a rocket scientist to see that the story is fabulous.

Beliefs that Violate Established Scientific
Principles are Implausible

In modern times we have the benefit of more valid knowledge than popular understanding. Scientific expertise, within its domain of inquiry, trumps lay knowledge. Consider the numerous and continual claims by inventors of perpetual motion machines. The Second Law of Thermodynamics states unequivocally that in any closed system, it is impossible to have a machine that works forever without any input of energy. In the United States and many other nations, every application for a patent on a perpetual motion machine is rejected outright without examining the particular design. Some nonscientists may regard this as closing one's mind to a potentially revolutionary breakthrough, but the Second Law is so firm a bedrock of physics that the likelihood of its being overridden is nil.

Genesis is simply wrong in describing the history of life. Incredibly, there are still people today, some of them intelligent and educated, who insist Earth is less than 10,000 years old, that the Grand Canyon was carved 4,500 years ago by Noah's flood, and that fossils of "ancient" vegetation and animals were planted by God to deceive paleontologists (Wilgoren 2005). Some theologians, sensitive to the absurdity of a "young earth," accept the great age of the world and interpret the "days" of creation as geological eras, seeing a vague concordance between life's history as described in the Bible and as documented by science. This is not a satisfactory resolution because the two (inconsistent) sequences in which plants and animals are said to have appeared, in Genesis 1 and 2, are both incorrect.

Has earth been visited by space aliens in UFOs? Earth is the only body in our solar system with conditions to support complex life, but our galaxy, the Milky Way, has at least 200 billion stars, some known to have planets. Science does not preclude the existence of life elsewhere. To the contrary, there has for several years been a scientific program, partly federally funded, to search for electromagnetic signals produced by sentient beings living near other stars. Visitors to New York City's American Museum of Natural History can see a show in the magnificent Hayden Planetarium apparently intended to convince them that there *is* intelligent life around other stars. So why do scientists almost universally scoff at the notion that aliens have visited earth?

The problem lies in transportation. Einstein's theory of relativity, now a century old and empirically well established, sets the speed of light as the upper limit at which an object can travel. A starship of nearly any conceivable kind would travel slower if only because the mass of the vehicle and its passengers would approach infinity as their speed approached that of light. (Do not expect relativity or quantum theory to conform to common sense.) The nearest star to Earth, other than the Sun, is Alpha Centauri, 4.4 light years away, which means that a beam of light takes 4.4 years to traverse the distance. Earth is 28,000 light years from the center of our galaxy. Beyond the Milky Way, the nearest large galaxy is Andromeda at 2.9 million light years.

Given the immense interstellar distances, and the upper limit on a starship's speed, the problem of traveling from any home star to Earth is extraordinarily difficult. Even if travelers from another solar system did have the capability of interstellar travel, the likelihood that our world would be their destination seems exceedingly remote. Science cannot say that alien visitation is impossible, but it is exceedingly improbable.

Occam's Razor: Among Competing Explanations for a Phenomenon, the Simplest and Most General One – Based on Validated and Widely Applicable Principles – is Preferred

William of Ockham (or Occam), a medieval Churchman, is credited with this maxim, which I render in modern terms. I don't know why it is called a "razor," perhaps because it cuts through the thicket of obfuscation to reach a core truth. Forged in the era of Scholasticism, when Thomas Aquinas and other Church scholars sought consistency between revealed scripture and Aristotelian logic, the razor retained its cutting edge through the Age of Reason. Philosopher David Hume's critique of miracles, cited above, is essentially an application of Occam's razor.

As another example, consider alternate explanations of Noah's flood: (1) It happened as described in Genesis. (2) It is a fable derived from the Mesopotamian Gilgamesh epic or a common progenitor. Enlightenment skeptics like Hume were loath to accept miracles, supernatural forces, ad hoc explanations, or special pleading as intrinsically simple. They favored general explanations from known principles, as I have stated in the razor. From that modern perspective, the simplest explanation of the flood is the second, that it is a fable.

The irony is that Ockham himself, as a medieval clergyman, probably thought the first explanation preferable. To someone imbued with the faith, each of the Bible's astounding events is most simply explained as a miracle, implying there is a miracle worker, who is God. We have no reason to believe that William's thinking in this regard was unlike that of other scholastics. But times have changed. To post-Enlightenment philosophers, explanations based on special pleading or miraculous interventions, such as God planting fossils to fool paleontologists, or Noah's flood creating the Grand Canyon, seem flaccid and witless.

Unsubstantiated Claims of Extraordinary Expertise or Esoteric Knowledge are Implausible

Comedian Andy Kaufman, who played the sweet-tempered auto mechanic Latka Gravas in the TV sitcom *Taxi*, had in reality a bizarre and not so affable personality. Off the *Taxi* set, Kaufman was repeatedly seen in violent or obnoxious situations. He toured colleges with the well-known intention of screwing attractive coeds on every campus. He presented himself as an inter-gender wrestler, offering $500 to any woman who could pin him. Several women tried but no one succeeded, and often the grappling continued more intimately in Kaufman's dressing room. Matched against a professional male wrestler named Jerry Lawler, Kaufman claimed a serious injury from Lawler's pile driver. When the two ostensibly embittered adversaries met again on the David Letterman Show, Lawler slapped Kaufman out of his chair. Kaufman walked off the program, threatening to sue.

In 1984, when news leaked that Kaufman, at age thirty-five, had inoperable lung cancer, many assumed it was another of Andy's outrageous stunts. After conventional but ineffective therapy in Los Angeles, he traveled to the Philippines for treatment at the clinic of "psychic surgeon" Jun Roxas. Kaufman's longtime producer and co-conspirator, Bob Zmuda, visited his friend there and described the congregation of surgical hopefuls stripped to their underwear, their outer clothes placed in plastic bags to shield them from blood:

> Roxas's hands writhed over and onto the bellies, chests, arms, legs, and heads of his patients, blood flew in every direction. He extracted great gobs of foul, blood-drenched tissue, which he laid in pans that his assistants took away. As I watched the procession and waited for Andy's turn, I counted about twenty-five patients in the room. I calculated that at an average of forty-five seconds per patient, at a charge of $25 each, Roxas would rack up about $625 in twenty or so minutes. Not a bad wage in a third-world country.... Roxas concentrated on Andy's head that day, removing all manner of bloodied items.... At one point I noticed Roxas palming the "sick tissue" – probably chicken guts – before he "removed" them from Andy's head. After what was the most bizarre twenty or so minutes of my life, Andy cleaned up and we got ready to drive back (1999: 277).

Two days later, with Kaufman in convulsions and his left side paralyzed, people at the clinic said these were signs that the healing was working. Roxas pronounced Andy "cured" and sent him home. Kaufman moved on to Colorado where he heard there was a wonder treatment involving crystals. Then he returned to Los Angeles for conventional chemo and radiation but lasted only two weeks more. After his funeral it was rumored that Andy was still alive, waiting to spring the joke.

Magician James Randi, a debunker of paranormal claims, easily replicates psychic surgery by kneading the "patient's" flesh, feigning to reach through skin while spilling blood-like fluid from a hidden vial, and then displaying the "extracted" tumor, actually a palmed animal organ. Psychic surgery is a cruel hoax on people in distress, though there is no denying that it can bring relief as a placebo, and I suppose one can riposte, at least in cases like Kaufman's, that orthodox medicine does no better and is more expensive.

The notion that a psychic can reach painlessly through someone's skin, with his hand or an instrument, and extract diseased tissue without leaving any lesion, is absurd on commonsense or scientific grounds. I raise it here to illustrate a derivative criterion for implausibility: Be skeptical of anyone claiming extraordinary skill or special knowledge that is possessed by no one else, or by few others, unless they offer sound evidence in support.

Astrology is a particularly interesting example because its credibility has changed completely since the seventeenth century, when there was little reason to be chary. Scholars of that time who cast horoscopes for princes were doubtless more skillful than the pitchmen who sold penny fortunes in the market, but astrology itself was an established practice, its efficacy rarely questioned. Today we recognize, at least in scholarly circles, that astrology has no sound theoretical or empirical basis for predicting people's lives. Modern astrologers rely on the symbolic qualities of gods and animals for which the constellations of the zodiac are named. Astrologers still accept the authority of the Hellenistic scholar Ptolemy, who thought the sun revolved around the earth and knew of only five planets. No one can conjure a mechanism, remotely feasible by scientific standards, through which planets affect human lives. Almost certainly there were no attempts in antiquity to test astrological forecasts with statistical data because that kind of research methodology is a modern concept. No extant documentation suggests any testing of predictions except by selective anecdote. Statistical tests that have been conducted in modern times give no support for traditional astrological forecasting.

Astrologers, psychic surgeons, spirit mediums, channelers, clairvoyants, spoon benders, levitators, snake oil salesmen, faith healers, mystics, ghost busters, exorcists, homeopaths, dowsers, and telepaths are all of a kind. They claim extraordinary abilities or esoteric knowledge without credible evidence of their authenticity.

If Personal Testimony Sounds Incredible It Probably Is

My foregoing criteria for implausibility are neither exhaustive nor infallible, but they are sufficient for present purposes. Now it is time to wave a red flag over the kind of evidence often given *in support* of implausible beliefs: personal testimony, whether spoken or written.

The Royal Society's motto, *Nullius in Verba* ("On the words of no one"), signifies the commitment of its seventeenth-century founders to establishing scientific truth through experimentation and direct observation rather than accepting the word of scripture, or of Aristotle, or anyone else. No doubt they were overly zealous. Every student necessarily learns from textbooks and professors, trusting their words as given. After all, no one can personally replicate science's whole body of experimental results. For that reason, modern scholars carry an unusual onus of integrity and honesty. The cardinal sins of academia are falsification and plagiarism, virtually the only non-criminal acts for which a tenured professor can be fired. These sanctions, plus peer review, enhance the credibility of academic books and journals.

Many other media operate with lower standards. The United States has no law against publishing or broadcasting false information as long as a living person is not libeled. Some producers of trade books, magazines, political reports, television programs and movies exaggerate or blatantly fabricate. The nation is awash in misinformation, a confusion of fact and fiction, much of it purposively so.

Even sincere personal testimony, offered without intentional deception, is often misremembered or otherwise mistaken. Once considered the gold standard for evidence in criminal trials, eye-witness testimony is today recognized as unreliable because so many inaccuracies of memory and perception have been documented, or experimentally implanted, by psychologists (Loftus and Doyle 1997; Ofshe and Watters 1996; McNally 2003; Thompson and Madigan 2005; Brainerd and Reyna 2005).

Most public knowledge is passed on as say-so, offered without verification, so we necessarily accept unsubstantiated testimony every day. If a claim is plausible on its face, if it fits consistently with our prior knowledge, if it evokes no surprise or incredulity, if the consequences of error are not too costly, then we have no important reason to doubt it. But claims that are extraordinary, *sui generis*, paranormal, or have the smell of rot from Denmark – these should not be trusted unless corroborated.

Aging adults require no scientific studies to convince them that observation and memory are fallible. I have revisited scenes from my youth – homes, schools, national parks seen on family vacations – and been impressed with discrepancies between my memory of the place and the reality in front of me. Sometimes two places merge into one. Often my remembered picture is correct in the main but wrong in detail.

Seven years ago, when I became interested in my family's genealogy, my older brother recalled for me the deaths of our paternal grandparents, who died one day apart. Though he was only five years old at the time, he remembered the scene vividly. Uncle Dave entered the room, announcing Grandfather's death, the day after Grandmother's passing. When I obtained copies of the death certificates, I saw that they showed exactly the reverse of my brother's recollection: Grandfather died on February 12, Grandmother on February 13. My brother was incredulous, doubting the accuracy of the death certificates.

While writing this chapter, I spoke again with my brother about our grandparents. His memory of the death scene is still detailed: "We were sitting in the flat, on wooden straight-backed chairs around the wall.... Uncle Dave came into this room and said, 'Papa died, he probably couldn't live without Mama.'" Perhaps someone at the records office accidentally reversed the dates on the death certificates, my brother again suggested.[4]

Hypnosis and the Memory Wars

When I was a boy the *Chicago Daily News* carried a much-discussed series of articles about a woman named Bridey Murphy, born in Ireland in the late eighteenth century. Remarkably, Bridey was still alive in the mid-1950s, or rather alive *again*, reincarnated as a housewife named Virginia Tighe who lived in Pueblo, Colorado. This came to light when an amateur hypnotist, Morey Bernstein, put Tighe into a series of trances, directing her to remember scenes from her early life. Reaching her birth date, she continued further back, recovering memories from former lives.

Under Bernstein's hypnosis, Tighe became Bridget Kathleen Murphy (1798-1864), speaking in brogue, singing Irish songs, dancing jigs, and telling stories of her life in County Cork. The *Daily News* was one of several newspapers excerpting Bernstein's book, *The Search for Bridey Murphy* (1956), which became a best-seller and then a movie. Recordings of the hypnotic sessions sold well too.

Someone socialized into Hinduism might accept reincarnation without a blink, but most Chicagoans were raised as Christians so skepticism was rife. The Hearst newspaper chain, with its *Chicago American* a rival of the *Daily News*, set out to debunk the story. A search of records in Cork produced no mention of Bridget Kathleen Murphy. The story was further undermined when Hearst reporters, aided by the pastor of the church in Wisconsin where Tighe went as a girl, found that she had lived across the street from a woman named Bridey Corkell née Murphy, who had grown up in Ireland. As a high school student, Tighe was involved in theatrics, learned to dance Irish jigs and to speak in an Irish brogue. Virginia Tighe was once spanked for scraping paint off a newly painted metal bed, had a baby brother who died, had an "Uncle Plazz," loved the "Londonderry Air" and potato pancakes, and reddened her brown hair with henna. In Bernstein's book, all these details are attributed to Bridey Murphy (James Randi, 2001, http://www.randi.org/jr/08-31-01.html).

I don't know if Tighe or Bernstein intentionally deceived, but the case is more intriguing if at least one of them believed what they were saying. Did Virginia Tighe, under hypnosis, innocently conflate her Wisconsin childhood with a fantasized prior life in Ireland? If so, by what interaction between hypnotist and subject did this conflation emerge?

The exact nature of hypnosis remains elusive. It may have something in common with trance states found in other cultures, but for Europeans and Americans it primarily derives from the practice of an eighteenth-century Viennese, Franz Mesmer, who conveyed the expectation that subjects who surrender their self control to the hypnotist are capable of extraordinary feats (Forrest 1999). Popular culture in the West has since evolved mysterious and powerful images of hypnosis, from the evil Svengali manipulating an unwilling Trilby to *The Manchurian Candidate*, a film starring Frank Sinatra, Laurence Harvey, and Janet Leigh (1962, remade in 2004 starring Denzel Washington) in which Chinese and North Korean communists "brainwash" captured American soldiers, turning them into robot-like assassins.

In the meantime, experimental psychologists have drawn a more restrained though still controversial picture of hypnosis. Some lump it with phlogiston and the ether as a wholly discredited scientific concept. Others still believe that hypnotism produces an altered state of consciousness though not as powerful as popular images would have it. The simplest view of hypnosis is that it involves nothing more than a relaxed and compliant subject who willingly follows directions from a trusted instructor (Kirsch 1985; Barker 1990).

In my classroom I induce hypnosis using a typical technique that takes about two minutes and utilizes the preexisting status difference between professor and students. I instruct those willing to participate—usually everyone is—to intertwine their fingers and raise their arms above their heads, to close their eyes, and to imagine they are at the top of a flight of twenty stairs. I then "walk" them down, one step at a time, continually suggesting that they relax their muscles but keep their arms overhead and their fingers locked. When they reach the bottom stair I say, "Open your eyes and try to unlock your fingers, *but you won't be able to do it*." The students open their eyes and most bring their arms down, but there are always some whose fingers remain intertwined overhead. I have no idea if they are faking or really feel incapable of lowering their arms. Either way, it makes a good class demonstration.

That is essentially how a stage hypnotist operates. Subjects drawn from the audience usually comply with what is asked of them, good naturedly playing along with the act. Nothing extraordinary is going on between the hypnotist and the volunteer subjects. Stunts performed under hypnosis for an audience – people barking like a dog, or lying rigid between two support chairs – can be performed without hypnosis, but they are more theatrical and entertaining when cloaked in hypnotic powers.[5] Leaving aside stage hypnosis, the most impressive evidence that hypnosis does produce a special mental state is its apparent ability to render a subject insensitive to pain, allowing surgery without anesthesia. But this too has been questioned as a special quality because most if not all the pain tolerance is due not to hypnosis per se but the accompanying relaxation, anxiety reduction, distraction, and stoicism, all achieved without hypnosis in various techniques for natural childbirth (Milling et al. 2006).

Some attribute to hypnosis a laser-like ability to probe the mind and replay lost memories with the fidelity of a CD. Others are skeptical. Marilyn Smith of the University of Toronto, after reviewing many studies of this matter, concluded "When proper control subjects are used and they attempt to recall the same material as hypnotized subjects, with relevant variables held constant, performances for the two groups typically do not differ" (Thompson and Madigan 2005: 101). The matter turned very serious during the late 1980s and early 1990s when hypnosis was widely used to retrieve "lost memories" of childhood sexual abuse (Goldstein 1992). The ensuing debate about whether therapists were recovering real memories or creating false ones became so heated that it was named "the memory wars" (Crews 1995). Science writer Martin Gardner regards this episode the greatest mental health scandal in North America:

Thousands of families were cruelly ripped apart. All over the United States and Canada, previously loving adult daughters suddenly accused their fathers or close relatives of sexually molesting them when they were young. A raft of bewildered, stricken fathers were sent to prison, some for life, by poorly informed judges and juries. Their harsh decisions were in response to the tearful testimonies of women, most of them middle-aged, who had become convinced by a psychiatrist or social worker that they were the victims of previously forgotten pedophilia (2006: 28).

We owe to Freud the notion that a child may actively repress very painful memories, particularly of sexual abuse, into subconsciousness, where they fester and later cause mental or physical disturbances. Freudian psychoanalysis presumes it is curative to retrieve these repressed memories, thereby removing the unacknowledged source of manifest distress. Freud initially used and then abandoned hypnosis as a means to this end, but other therapists continue to depend on hypnosis (or related techniques of relaxation and guided imagery) to recover anxiety-ridden memories buried in the subconscious.

There is presently considerable doubt about the reality of Freudian repression. According to memory researcher Richard McNally, "Events that trigger overwhelming terror are memorable, unless they occur in the first year or two of life or the victim suffers brain damage. The notion that the mind protects itself by repressing or dissociating memories of trauma, rendering them inaccessible to awareness, is a piece of psychiatric folklore devoid of convincing empirical support" (2003: 275; also see Crews 1995; Ofshe and Watters 1999; and Geraerts et al. 2007). This issue has not been fully settled, and many therapists continue to operate at least loosely from a psychoanalytic perspective.

During the 1980s, psychoanalytically oriented writers asserted that a large portion of emotional and behavioral problems suffered by women were caused by forgotten childhood sex abuse (Bass and Davis 1988). Therapist E. Sue Blume (1990) thought it not unreasonable that half of all women are survivors of childhood sexual trauma. Mass media played up the theme, as in *People* magazine's 1991 cover story about TV actress Roseanne Barr remembering during therapy that her mother abused her in infancy. These ideas became widely accepted in the helping community, perhaps because of their consonance with contemporary concerns about abuse of women and children, which surely was and remains a real and serious problem.

In 1991 George Franklin, Jr. became apparently the first American tried for murder on the basis of a repressed memory freshly unearthed. The victim, eight-year-old Susie Nason, had been killed twenty years earlier. Franklin's own daughter, Eileen, also eight years old at the time, was the major witness against him. Eileen's memory of her father's heinous actions had come back gradually, starting with a flashback while playing with her own toddler, and then more details filled in the episode. Eileen recalled being with her father and Susie in a van, where her father sexually assaulted her young friend. She remembered the three of them outside the van, her father raising a rock over his head, screaming, and then Susie covered with blood, the silver ring on her finger smashed. Eileen's therapist believed her memory, as did several family members, a district attorney, and the jury that convicted George Franklin of murder.

The conviction was overturned by a California appeals court in 1995 without definitively resolving whether or not Eileen's memory was authentic. Had she really witnessed her father assaulting Susie, then repressed all memory of the event for years, and then recovered it accurately? Or had she constructed a false memory based on details reported in the news, which told where the body was found, that Susie's skull was fractured, and that her silver Indian ring was crushed, apparently during the attack. Eileen's memory changed from one telling to another. For example, in her statement to police in 1989, the van ride was either on the way to school in the morning or on the way back from lunch. During the preliminary hearing, presumably after learning that Susie did not miss school that day, Eileen placed the ride in late afternoon (Loftus 1993).

Such stories echoed through the media, raising similar concerns in other areas. Hundreds of preschool teachers and daycare personnel were accused of sexual depravity, based on the testimony of small children who, under questioning by therapists and social workers, told stories of molestation, some of them utterly fantastic. The child witnesses in these cases were not hypnotized, but interrogators led them through probing inquiries that, like hypnosis, can influence compliant subjects toward implicating responses (Ofshe and Watters 1996). In the highly publicized case of a North Carolina daycare center, one child witness "recalled" seeing one of the center's owners murdering babies (though no babies were missing), while another child claimed this owner routinely shot children into outer space.

About the same time there was a spate of media reports about the proliferation of Satanic cults in the U.S. and Canada. People admitted to their therapists attending rituals where babies were killed and eaten. In 1991 a woman told Geraldo Rivera's television audience that while in a Satanic cult she murdered forty babies but forgot about it until her memories were recovered during psychotherapy (Victor 1993; Gardiner 2006). The FBI has investigated and found no evidence of such cults, rituals, or baby sacrifices. Richard Ofshe and Ethan Watters (1994) regard Satanic cults as the Achilles' heel of the recovered memory movement, clear proof that the therapist-client relationship can produce detailed recollections of abominations that never happened.

This is a delicate issue because no one doubts the reality of childhood abuse and serial murder. Some zealots see any skepticism toward incredible or uncorroborated personal testimony as an attempt to exonerate perpetrators. I certainly don't want to turn a blind eye to real crimes, nor, I think, do the researchers who have cast strong doubt on the Freudian notion of repressed memory, and on the special ability of hypnosis and related techniques to accurately recover lost memories.

Implausibility be Damned!

I visualize this chapter floating on a balloon of rationality, barely anchored to the grounds upon which people actually form their beliefs. Vulcans like Mr. Spock are said to reach their personal views via logic and dispassionate examination of evidence. These are less important desiderata for humans. Our religious and political beliefs are grounded mostly by childhood socialization, as will be described in chapter 12.

Still, the human mind requires some reconciliation between prior belief and contradictory evidence or logic. Otherwise there would be no advance of scientific knowledge, and no poker player would learn the stupidity of drawing to an inside straight. Most of us, most of the time, reach some balance, if only by ignoring the implausibility of some of our own beliefs.

Despite knowing full well that people are not wholly rational, we are sometimes struck by the extremes to which irrationality is taken, asking, "Is this person nuts?" A one-time spiritualist and confessed fraud named M. Lamar Keene, impressed by the gullibility of his victims, put the question this way: "What is it that compels a person, past all reason, to believe the unbelievable? How can an otherwise sane individual become so enamored of a fantasy, an imposture, that even after it's exposed in the bright light of day he still clings to it – indeed, clings to it all the harder?" (1976: 148).

Before pursuing this question further, we examine in the next chapter the extent to which Americans do believe implausible things.

Notes

1.   Modern philosophers and sociologists of science agree that Hume's separation between facts and values is not absolute. Cultural and personal biases do affect to some extent scientific analyses and conclusions.

2. Philosophers and mathematicians note many limitations of logical reasoning. It is possible to construct mathematical systems based on arbitrary postulates, such as non-Euclidian geometries, which have little relationship to our everyday world. Gödel's famous theorem demonstrates the possibility of theorems that can be neither proved nor disproved in a logically consistent system. One can construct sentences that entail logical inconsistencies, such as "This statement is false." (If we assume the statement is true, then it is false; if we assume it is false then it is true.) Furthermore, one can pose seemingly paradoxical but actually nonsensical questions: "Can God make a rock so heavy that he can't lift it?" Such limitations are essentially irrelevant in the present context.

3. π is an irrational number, i.e., one that cannot be written as the ratio of two whole numbers. Expressed as a decimal fraction, π can be calculated to any level of accuracy, and modern computational methods have worked it out to millions of digits. For practical purpose, the approximation 3.14159 is adequate. Archimedes (ca. 289-212 BCE) did not use decimals, but the accuracy to which he calculated π can be expressed in decimal terms as about 3.14. By the end of the 16th century, when decimals came into widespread use in Europe, π was known to thirty decimal places (Beckmann 1993).

4. I easily locate age peers who "remember" the scene in *Casablanca* where Humphrey Bogart says, "Play it again, Sam." This false memory, widespread among older Americans, probably derives from Woody Allen's movie, *Play It Again, Sam*, which makes frequent references to the Bogart film. In fact, Bogart never said the line.

5. In his autobiography, Mark Twain tells of his boyhood experience as the subject of a traveling mesmerist named Professor Simmons, pretending to be sleepy and acting out bizarre suggestions, including making love to imaginary girls and fishing in an imaginary lake, even having pins stuck in his arms. "I didn't wince; I only suffered and shed tears on the inside... Those dear good people...would stick a pin in my arm and bear on it until they drove it a a third of its length in, and then be lost in wonder that by a mere exercise of willpower the professor could turn my arm to iron and make it insensible to pain. Whereas it was not insensible at all; I was suffering agonies of pain" (quoted in Barker 1990: 187).

3

Scientifically Implausible Beliefs in the U.S.

It is a common but nonetheless disquieting observation that many Americans do not believe in evolution. In 1993, 1994, and 2000 the General Social Surveys (GSS), which sample opinions of U.S. adults annually or biennially, asked how true is the statement, "Human beings evolved from earlier species of animals." Of 3,673 respondents offering an opinion, a majority (53 percent) called the statement definitely or probably *not* true. (Davis and Marsden 2001; Mazur 2004)

The modern American movement to stop the teaching of evolution in public schools, or to at least give students equal exposure to creationism, gained momentum in the 1970s and continues vigorously (Nelkin 1982; Eve and Harrold 1991; Pennock 2001). Perhaps for this reason, the currently high level of public disbelief in evolution is often regarded as an erosion of scientific views. However, Gallup polls spanning the period 1982-2007 show barely any change in the percentage of Americans who believe that "God created human beings pretty much in their present form at one time within the last 10,000 years or so," a reflection of belief in Genesis. Asking whether the Bible is to be taken literally or as an ancient book of fables and moral precepts, Gallup shows little change from 1976 to 2007. Probably there was never a time when the majority of Americans believed in evolution, and today's level of acceptance is as high as it has ever been.

Disbelief in evolution is high in the United States compared to other nations. A Eurobarometer (2001) poll reported that only 17 percent of Europeans denied that humans "evolved from older animal species." Nations around the world that participate in the International Social Survey Programme included in 1993 and 2000 the GSS's evolution question. In nations that asked the question both years, responses were similar both times. Figure 3.1 shows (in descending order) the percentage of each nation NOT believing that humans evolved from earlier species.[1]

Perhaps because of our retrograde views on Darwinism, some commentators attribute the wildest irrationalities to Americans, as if we are a nation gone bonkers over paranormal beliefs, superstitions, and pseudoscience. But outside the limited domain of religious literalism, which subsumes the rejection of Darwin, the United States on the whole seem no more irrational than Europe. Minorities of Americans do profess belief in diverse paranormal phenomena including extrasensory perception, haunted houses, and psychic powers. Gallup polls from 1990 to 2005 showed that roughly one-quarter of Americans think astrology, or the position of the stars and planets, can affect people's lives. But Europeans are twice as likely as Americans to believe there is some scientific basis for astrology, or to believe in lucky numbers (National Science Board 2006).

There are other implausibilities beside biblical literalism and creationism that are particularly successful in the United States, for example flying saucers. Although sighted in many nations, UFOs have a special affinity for the U.S. because they originated here, are most often reported here, and are a popular topic in our mass media. But other nations have their own outré specialties. Séances, fortune telling, and diverse forms of mysticism were strong in nineteenth-century Europe before arriving in America. Psychic surgery is especially big in the Philippines and Brazil. Not surprisingly, the Virgin Mary appears most often in devoutly Catholic countries.

Apart from biblical literalism, the extent of Americans' implausible beliefs may be overstated because simplistic forced-choice poll questions, as about UFOs, impel respondents toward a "belief" response. Gallup and other polling organizations avoided this trap in five national samples between 1950 and 1999 by asking respondents to say in their own words what they think flying saucers are. Roughly half of respondents said they don't know. About one-quarter attributed the sightings so some natural phenomenon, or to some earth-made objects such as a weather balloon, an aircraft, or some kind of secret weapon under development. No more than 6 percent said UFOs are space vehicles.

Beliefs at Odds with Science

There are several popular theories about why political opinion is sometimes at odds with modern science. When speaking of disbelievers in evolution, these theories usually infer an active rejection of established fact, but we should hold open the possibility that unscientific beliefs often reflect a misunderstanding rather than an overt disavowal of the science.

Figure 3.1
Percent Who Do NOT Believe Humans Evolved from Earlier
Species of Animals, by Nation

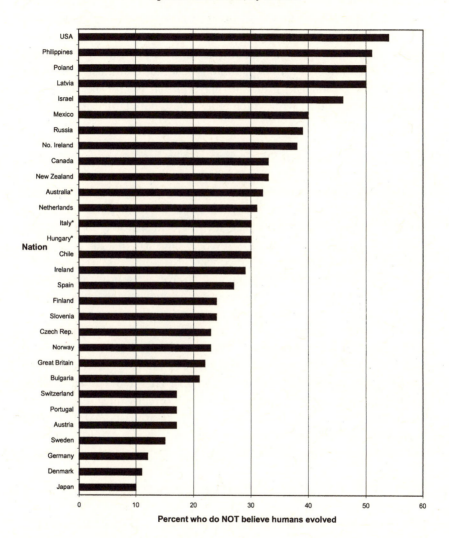

Percent who do NOT believe humans evolved

The simplest theory presumes *ignorance* – that many people with unscientific beliefs do not understand the evidence, either because of a general lack of education, or because they specifically lack "scientific literacy." Women are presumed to be less informed than men about science and technology. Another obvious explanation for disbelieving evolution focuses on *religion,* noting that fundamentalists are committed to the creation stories in Genesis and therefore reject contradictory scientific claims. A third explanation associates antiscientific beliefs with particular *political views*, suggesting that political conservatives are more likely to reject evolution while liberals are more likely to entertain New Age beliefs like astrology. A fourth explanation sites antiscientific disbeliefs in certain regional (Southern), or lifestyle (rural), or minority (black) *subcultures*. A fifth explanation presumes that those who reject scientifically established principles have *closed minds*. The GSS is a reliable source of data with which to test these popular theories.

Ignorance

In 1993 and 1994, the GSS included "test" questions about established scientific knowledge, asking respondents whether or not it is true that all radioactivity is made by humans (not true); that antibiotics kill bacteria, not viruses (true); that astrology has some scientific truth (not true); and that all man-made chemicals can cause cancer if you eat enough of them (not true). Figure 3.2 shows for each question that the percentage of correct answers increases with education.

At first blush, these findings suggest an overall improvement in scientific knowledge with higher education. However, pair-wise Pearson correlations among the test questions are generally low, ranging from r = .01 to r = .26, indicating that respondents who answered any one question correctly were not especially likely to correctly answer the others. Responses to the evolution question have especially low correlations with correct responses to other test items (r < .15). Therefore the tendency of more highly educated respondents to answer correctly must reflect something other than better scientific literacy per se (Losh et al. 2003). Men are slightly more likely than women to answer questions correctly, the greatest gender difference being on astrology (56 percent versus 41 percent).

Religion. The GSS categorizes religious denominations as fundamentalist, moderate (including Catholicism), or liberal. Figure 3.3 shows the percentage of correct responses to the questions about astrology and evolution as a function of denominational fundamentalism. Not surprisingly, fundamentalists are far less likely to believe in evolution than those in moderate or liberal religious denominations.[2] In contrast, religious denomination has little effect on belief in astrology.

Political Views

Figure 3.4 shows the percentage of correct responses to the astrology and evolution questions as a function of self-reported political view,

Figure 3.2
Percent Correct Answers to Five Science Questions, by Education

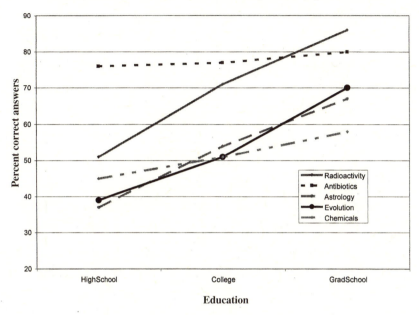

Education

Figure 3.3
Percent Correct Answers to Astrology and Evolution Questions,
by Religious Fundamentalism

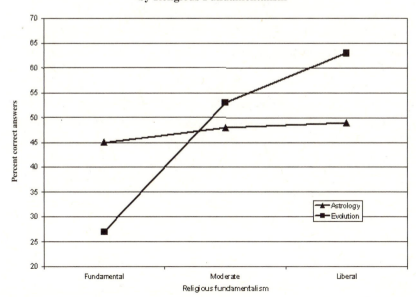

Figure 3.4
Percent Correct Answers to Astrology and Evolution Questions, by Political View

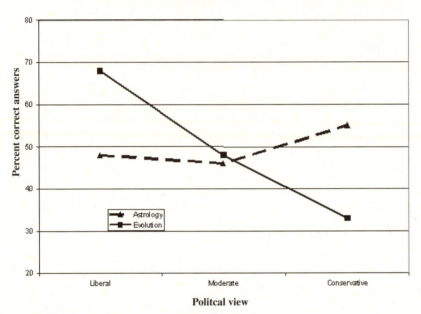

characterized as liberal, moderate, or conservative.[3] Liberals are markedly more likely than conservatives to believe in evolution. In contrast, political view has little effect on belief in astrology.

Subcultures

In Table 3.1, percentages of correct answers on astrology and evolution are compared for respondents in the South versus non-South, as are answers from urban versus rural areas,[4] and among white versus black respondents. Southerners did worse on both items, though the difference for astrology is so slight as to be inconsequential. About 10 percent more urban than rural dwellers gave correct answers to

Table 3.1
Percent Correct Answers to Astrology and Evolution Questions, by Region, Urbanism and Race

QUESTION	REGION		URBANISM		RACE	
	Non-south	South	Urban	Rural	White	Black
	(n = 2,362)	(1,311)	(2,619)	(1,054)	(3,043)	(458)
Astrology	49	46	50	41	**50**	**35**
Evolution	**52**	**40**	**51**	**40**	49	40

Boldface indicates a percentage difference > 10 percent.

both questions, and there is a roughly similar difference favoring whites over blacks.

Closed Minds

Closed mindedness, or *dogmatism,* is usually conceptualized as an unwillingness to consider alternative beliefs to one's own, rejection or rationalization of ostensibly inconsistent evidence, discomfort with ambiguity, and intolerance of deviants. Open minded (non-dogmatic) people, in contrast, are willing to entertain novel ideas, especially in light of new evidence, and are tolerant of views other than their own and of people unlike themselves. The classic treatment of the topic by psychologist Milton Rokeach (1960) has inspired a stream of research as well as continuing criticism. The tendency of researchers to find high levels of dogmatism among political conservatives, and among biblical fundamentalists,[5] invites a rejoinder from creationists that it is the evolutionists who are dogmatic for rejecting "intelligent design" as an alternative theory. Acknowledging possible biases in the measurement of dogmatism, it is nonetheless pertinent to consider it as an explanation for antiscientific disbeliefs.

The GSS contains items on free speech that tap the intolerance aspect of dogmatism, asking if the respondent would be willing to allow certain types of deviants to speak in the community, or teach in a college, or author books on loan in the public library. Some of these "deviations" (homosexuality, opposition to churches and religion) contradict Christian doctrine and therefore cannot fairly measure dogmatism among fundamentalists. To avoid confounding with Biblical injunctions, I select a single item as my dogmatism variable (DOGMAT): "Suppose…[someone] wrote a book advocating doing away with elections and letting the military run the country. Somebody in your community suggests that the book be removed from the public library. Would you favor removing it, or not?"

I presume the 37 percent of respondents who would remove the book are more dogmatic than those who would not. These dogmatists are considerably less likely than the non-dogmatists to believe that humans evolved from other species (35 percent versus 55 percent), and they are more likely than non-dogmatists to believe there is some truth to astrology (63 percent versus 49 percent).

Summary

So far we have found support for the non-surprising surmise that better educated respondents are most likely to believe in evolution, to disbelieve in astrology, and to correctly answer test questions about other scientific information. However beliefs about evolution and astrology do not reflect any general construct of scientific literacy because they do not correlate much with each other or with the other test responses.

We find subcultural differences: Southerners, rural dwellers, and blacks are more likely to hold incorrect views about evolution or astrology than are people outside the South, urbanites, and whites. Dogmatists are more likely than non-dogmatists to be wrong about both evolution and astrology. Beliefs about evolution, far more than beliefs about astrology, are tied to religiosity and political liberalism-conservatism.

Multivariate Analysis

The explanatory variables used in this analysis are not completely independent of one another. Blacks, for example, are slightly over-represented among religious fundamentalists. It is therefore appropriate to test the above findings with multiple regression models, which may take readers who lack statistics beyond where they wish to go. Multivariate analysis produces no important change in the findings about belief in astrology, but it does modify findings about belief in evolution. Very briefly, the analysis verifies that low education, high religiosity, and political conservatism importantly contribute to disbelief in evolution. Once these are taken into account, subcultural variables and dogmatism *do not* independently affect one's view of evolution. Non-statistical readers may skip directly to this chapter's closing discussion.

Table 3.2 presents a correlation matrix of all explanatory variables, allowing us to explore their inter-relationships.[6] There is moderate clustering among the three measures of religiosity (BIBLE, FUND, and ATTEND), their pair-wise correlations ranging in magnitude from r = .28 to .38. Education is inversely related to liberal belief in the Bible as God's word, and to dogmatism. Blacks and Southerners are slightly more fundamentalist than whites and non-Southerners. No correlation in the table exceeds .38, so subsequent analysis is not plagued by multicollinearity. We therefore move to a multivariate analysis, aiming to pinpoint the most essential explainers of belief or disbelief in evolution.

The four-valued test question on evolution (high score = disbelief) was regressed on three models to compare the importance of different explanations. Results for each model are reported in table 3.3 as standardized regression coefficients (betas), which compensate for the differing

Table 3.2
Pearson Correlations among Explanatory Variables

	AGE	RACE	REGION	URBAN	BIBLE	FUND	ATTEND	POLVIEW	DOGMAT
EDUC	**-.26**	-.13	.11	-.16	**-.29**	-.22	.01	-.04	**-31**
AGE		-.05	-.01	.06	.09	.00	.14	.12	.21
RACE			-.14	-.12	.15	.24	.08	-.09	.09
REGION				-.14	-.16	-.22	-.09	-.06	-.12
URBAN					.13	.10	.07	.06	.11
BIBLE						**38**	**.33**	.17	**.26**
FUND							**.28**	.12	.18
ATTEND								.17	.15
POLVIEW									.09

Boldface indicates r > .25.

ranges among the explanatory variables. Significance levels are indicated by boldface, but with so large a sample (n > 2,000), magnitude of the betas is a far more important criterion of importance.

Model #1 may be regarded as a test of the ignorance and subculture theories. It corroborates prior bivariate results with the exception that RACE is now rendered irrelevant as an explanatory variable. Low education remains a potent predictor of disbelief in evolution. To a lesser extent, living in the South and in a rural area predict disbelief.

Model #2 adds to the first model the three measures of religiosity. Doing so considerably enhances explanatory power, raising the explained variance (R^2) from 8 percent (in Model #1) to 25 percent. With religiosity controlled, the differences between Southerners and non-Southerners, and between rural and city dwellers, are reduced to nearly zero, leaving no support for the subculture theory. The explanatory power of education is somewhat reduced. In Model #2, each of the three religiosity variables has a larger beta than education, emphasizing the important contribution of religion to disbelief in evolution. Indeed, since the three religiosity variables overlap (inter-correlate), it is remarkable that each one – in the presence of the others – retains a relatively strong beta in the model.

Table 3.3
Standardized Coefficients (Betas) for Belief in Evolution, for Three Models

Variable:	Model #1	Model #2	Model #3
EDUCATION	**-.19**	**-.13**	**-.11**
AGE	**.11**	**.09**	**.08**
RACE	.04	-.02	-.05
REGION	**-.09**	-.02	-.05
URBAN	**.07**	.02	.01
BIBLE		**.25**	**.30**
FUND		**.16**	**.14**
ATTEND		**.15**	**.09**
POLVIEW			**.10**
DOGMATISM			.00
R^2 =	.08	.25	.26

Boldfaced betas indicate p < .01 (t-test).

Model #3 adds political view (POLVIEW, conservative = high) and dogmatism to the second model. Despite these additional controls, education, age, and religiosity retain their explanatory effects. However dogmatism no longer has any relationship to disbelief in evolution. Political conservatism holds its place as one of the stronger predictors of disbelief.

It is no surprise that religiosity, especially biblical literalism, is associated with disbelief in evolution. More puzzling is the association between political conservatism and disbelief in evolution *after other variables are controlled*. One might conjecture that it is a spurious relationship, explained by the (modest) association between political conservatism and religiosity. (That is, political conservatives tend to be religious conservatives, which may be why they reject evolution.) But Model #3 essentially eliminates this hypothesis by controlling on religiosity. POLVIEW remains nearly as potent as education in predicting evolutionary belief.[7]

Summarizing

Aside from biblical literalism and its corollaries, American beliefs are probably no more irrational than those in other industrialized nations. Astrology, for example, has more credence in Europe than in the United States.

It is our inordinately fundamentalist religiosity that leads Americans to reject evolution in favor of creationism. Religiosity is not the only factor but the most important one. Not surprisingly, highly educated respondent are more likely to correctly answer test questions about evolution, astrology, and other scientific information. However, it is difficult to attribute much of this to improved "scientific literacy" because a correct answer to any one test question barely predicts correct answers to the others. One way to account for these seemingly inconsistent results is to assume that test answers were given more or less randomly and that higher education somewhat improved the odds of a correct guess. In any case, we can say that popular theories attributing America's anti-evolutionary stance to strong religion and poor education are sustained.

While disbelief in evolution or belief in astrology is higher in Southerners than non-Southerners, in rural people compared to urbanites, and in blacks more than whites, these differences partly or completely disappear after controls on education or religiosity or both. Dogmatism, the one personality variable considered here, does not explain disbelief in evolution, after controlling on education and religiosity, but dogmatic people are more accepting of astrology, even after controls.

Many commentators attribute antievolutionary positions to conservative political ideology, pointing to various attempts over the years by ideologues to keep evolution out of public school textbooks, or more recently to give equal voice to creationist theories of "intelligent design." Often, at least implicitly, the commentators presume that these motivations are ultimately rooted in the fundamentalist religiosity or Southern mentality of politically conservative activists. Consistent with this presumption, the correlation between political conservatism and disbelief in evolutionary is diminished by controlling on religiosity. However, to this author's surprise, the relationship is not wholly explained by this, or by additional controls for education, race, age, and region. After holding these potential confounders constant, political liberalism-conservatism remains nearly as powerful as education in predicting evolutionary belief. Even among respondents who have attended graduate school, and who do not belong to a fundamentalist religious denomination, political liberals are more likely than political conservatives to believe that humans evolved from earlier species.

The persistent covariation of political and evolutionary beliefs, despite statistical controls, is illustrated in figure 3.5. Here the percentage

Figure 3.5
Percent Believing Humans Evolved from other Species, by Religious Denomination, Education, and Political View

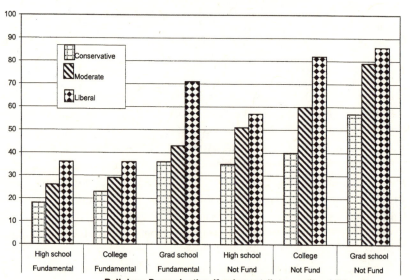

of respondents believing that humans evolved from earlier species is plotted simultaneously against political view (conservative, moderate, liberal), education (high school or less, some college, graduate school), and respondent's religious denomination (fundamentalist or not[8]). Whether respondents belong to fundamentalist denominations or not, and whatever their education level, belief in evolution rises along with political liberalism.

Notes

1. Modules on Environment, I and II, ISSP archive, University of Cologne, Germany. http://www.issp.org/data.htm .
2. Other indicators of religiosity or fundamentalism relate similarly to belief in evolution. Respondents were asked to select which of three statements most closely described their perception of the Bible. The three choices (and percentages selecting each) were: The Bible is the actual word of God and is to be taken literally, word for word (34 percent); the Bible is the inspired word of God but not everything in it should be taken literally (50 percent); the Bible is an ancient book of fables, legends, history, and moral precepts recorded by men (16 percent). With increasing acceptance of a literal Bible, belief in evolution rose from 26 percent to 50 percent to 79 percent.
3. For this figure, a 7-point self-report scale of liberalism-conservatism was collapsed into three categories: liberal or extremely liberal (14 percent); slightly liberal, moderate, and slightly conservative (69 percent); and conservative or extremely conservative (17 percent).
4. The GSS variable XNORCSIZ was dichotomized to distinguish urban areas (codes 1-5; 70 percent of the population) from rural areas (codes 6-10).
5. For a meta-analysis of studies relating dogmatism to political conservatism, see J. Jost, J. Glaser, A. Kruglanski, and F. Sullowell, "Political Conservatism as Motivated Social Cognition," Psychological Bulletin 129 (May 2003): 376:82. B. Altemeyer, in "Dogmatic Behavior among Students," J. Social Psychology 142 (December 2002): 713-21, reports high dogmatism in college students who believe in the literal truth of the Bible, and furthermore that those literalists with the highest dogmatism scores were least likely to see contradictions among varying accounts taken from the four Gospels.
6. Respondents' years of education (denoted EDUC) range from 0 to 20 (where usually "12" means a high school graduate and "16" a college graduate). RACE is coded white (0), black (1). REGION is coded South (0), Non-South (1). The respondent's perception of the BIBLE is coded (from low to high) fable, inspired, or God's word. FUND is the GSS categorization of religious denominations, coded (from low to high) liberal, moderate, or fundamentalist. ATTEND is a 9-point ordinal measure of the respondent's frequency of attending religious services, ranging from never to several times a week. POLVIEW is retained as a 7-point scale for this analysis, with higher score more conservative. DOGMAT is coded high for respondents who would remove a militarist's book from the public library (dogmatic), and low for those who would not.
7. The correlation between the evolution test question and POLVIEW is r = .25, which is equivalent to beta when POLVIEW is the sole independent variable in a regression model. In Model #3, POLVIEW's beta is reduced to .10, indicating

that part of its bivariate association with evolution is explained by the covariance with religiosity.

8.   For this graph the GSS categories for religious denominations were dichotomized into fundamentalist versus not fundamentalist (i.e., moderate plus liberal).

Part 2

Is the Bible Interrant?

Introduction to Part 2

Part 1 spoke of implausible belief in general. Now it is time to become specific. The venue for implausibility that is most central to American life, setting the United States apart from other industrialized nations, and that most affects our politics and public policy, is religious fundamentalism, the belief that the Bible is true in fact and infallible in moral prescription. My intent in Part II is to show the depth of credulity required of literalist believers. Here most lay readers will encounter problems with the Bible of which they were unaware, but my discussion will be familiar to biblical scholars. None of it is controversial except to biblical literalists. To the contrary, much of this section is taught in basic Religious Studies courses.

First a note on translation: Authorship of the first five books of the Bible – Genesis, Exodus, Leviticus, Numbers, and Deuteronomy – is traditionally attributed to Moses. The five books together are called by Jews the *Torah* (meaning Instruction in Hebrew) or the Five Books of Moses, and by Christians the Pentateuch (derived from Greek). According to ancient rabbinic interpretation, Moses's successor Joshua had the Torah engraved on the stones of the Israelite altar, not only in the original Hebrew but in all human languages so that anyone might learn it. In fact, since few Jews read English before their great migration to America, an authoritative Jewish translation into English did not become available until the early twentieth century, and the translators of that work expressed deep gratitude to non-Jewish predecessors who had rendered the Hebrew into "admirable diction, which can never be surpassed" (Jewish Publication Society of America 1917: viii).

They were referring to the King James Version (KJV) of the Bible, published in England in 1611. It is perhaps the only product created by a committee that is superior to what could have been done by a single talented worker. Though long recognized to contain errors and to reflect contemporary biases of the translators, it has some of the most beautiful prose ever written. Subsequent revisers, seeking more accuracy, incorporating newer scholarship, and reflecting the biases of their own times, often try to preserve phrases from the KJV.

Here I depend on the New Revised Standard Version (NRSV) of the Bible produced by the Division of Christian Education of the National Council of the Churches of Christ in the U.S.A. and published by Oxford University Press in 1989. If we count the KJV as the first "authorized version" of the Bible in English, in the sense of being widely accepted by religious institutions, then the NRSV is the fourth generation, not counting numerous "unauthorized" translations. The NRSV is officially acceptable for use in all major Christian churches: Protestant, Anglican, Roman Catholic, and Eastern Orthodox. Its rendering of the Old Testament is similar to Jewish translations. The NRSV is notable for removing unnecessarily sexist language, an editorial judgment inducing some congregations to retain earlier versions.

I make slight adjustments to the translation. In the creation story, the NRSV uses "the man" as an alternate translation to Adam, but I revert to the KJV use of Adam. Like most English translations, the NRSV conventionally prints "LORD" (*Adonai* in Hebrew) when the personal name of the Israelite deity is intended. God's personal name is not known with certainty because Jews traditionally regarded it too holy to utter. It was written in Hebrew consonants that are transliterated into English as YHWH. Since the scribal Hebrew that is used in the Torah lacks vowels, the pronunciation cannot be discerned from the text. Modern scholars assume the missing vowels are *a* and *e*, producing the name YaHWeH, pronounced YAH-way. Whenever LORD (or the LORD God) appears in NRSV passages, I replace it with Yahweh.[1]

4

Creation

The opening pages of Genesis contain two different and inconsistent versions of creation. One tells the events of seven days; the other is a tale about Adam and Eve.

Seven Days

In the beginning when God created the heavens and the earth, the earth was a formless void and darkness covered the face of the deep, while a wind from God swept over the face of the waters. And God said, "Let there be light"; and there was light. And God saw that the light was good; and God separated the light from the darkness. God called the light Day, and the darkness he called Night. And there was evening and there was morning, the first day.

And God said, "Let there be a dome in the midst of the waters, and let it separate the waters from the waters." So God made the dome and separated the waters which were under the dome from the waters which were above the dome. And it was so. And God called the dome Sky. And there was evening and there was morning, the second day.

And God said, "Let the waters under the sky be gathered together into one place, and let the dry land appear." And it was so. God called the dry land Earth, and the waters that were gathered together he called Seas. And God saw that it was good. Then God said, "Let the earth put forth vegetation: plants yielding seed, and fruit trees of every kind on earth that bear fruit with the seed in it." And it was so. The earth brought forth vegetation: plants yielding seed of every kind, and trees of every kind bearing fruit with the seed in it. And God saw that it was good. And there was evening and there was morning, the third day.

And God said, "Let there be lights in the dome of the sky to separate the day from the night; and let them be for signs and for seasons and for days and years, and let them be lights in the dome of the sky to give light upon the earth." And it was so. God made the two great lights—the greater light to rule the day and the lesser light to rule the night—and the stars. And God set them in the dome of the sky to give light upon the earth, to rule over the day and over the night, and to separate the light from the darkness. And God saw that it was good. And there was evening and there was morning, the fourth day.

And God said, "Let the waters bring forth swarms of living creatures, and let birds fly above the earth across the dome of the sky." So God created the great sea monsters and every living creature that moves, of every kind, with which the waters swarm, and every winged bird of every kind. And God saw that it was good. God blessed them, saying, "Be fruitful and multiply and fill the waters in the seas, and let birds multiply on the earth." And there was evening and there was morning, the fifth day.

And God said, "Let the earth bring forth living creatures of every kind: cattle and creeping things and wild animals of the earth of every kind." And it was so. God made the wild animals of the earth of every kind, and the cattle of every kind, and everything that creeps upon the ground of every kind. And God saw that it was good.

Then God said, "Let us make humankind in our image, according to our likeness; and let them have dominion over the fish of the sea, and over the birds of the air, and over the cattle, and over all the wild animals of the earth, and over every creeping thing that creeps upon the earth." So God created humankind in his image, in the image of God he created them; male and female he created them. And God blessed them, and God said to them, "Be fruitful and multiply, and fill the earth and subdue it; and have dominion over the fish of the sea and over the birds of the air and over every living thing that moves upon the earth."

God said, "See, I have given you every plant yielding seed that is upon the face of all the earth, and every tree with seed in its fruit; you shall have them for food. And to every beast of the earth, and to every bird of the air, and to everything that creeps on the earth, everything that has the breath of life, I have given every green plant for food." And it was so. And God saw everything that he had made, and indeed, it was very good. And there was evening and there was morning, the sixth day.

Thus the heavens and the earth were finished, and all their multitude. And on the seventh day God finished his work that he had done, and he rested on the seventh day from all his work that he had done. So God blessed the seventh day and hallowed it, because on it God rested from all his work which he had done in creation (1:1 to 2:3).[2]

Aspects of the story may seem peculiar. Evenings and mornings alternate for three days before there is a sun, and for the same reason plants and fruit trees initially grow without photosynthesis. The dome of the sky has water above it (different from clouds within it) as well as below. Perhaps to the ancient mind an invisible sea above the sky was the source of rainfall.

Bible scholars note the affinity of the opening passage of Genesis to *Enuma Elish*, a Mesopotamian creation myth dated to about 1100 BCE (Freedman 1992: 526-28). This poem, written in cuneiform on seven tablets and named for its first words, was discovered in the ruins of the library of Ashurbanipal in Nineveh (www.crystalinks.com/babylonian-creation.html). The story, now known in different renditions, opens when there is no heaven or earth. Only the male god Apsu (fresh water) and the female god Tiamat (sea water) exist. Their mingling of waters produces other gods and silt in the waters. Then a horizon separates clouds from silt, forming heaven and earth. Much of the narrative is concerned with discord and battle among the gods from which Marduk emerges as dominant. Along the way, celestial lights are placed in heaven, and

Tiamat produces fearful animals to aid her struggle against other gods. Marduk heaps up mountains and opens springs to create the Tigris and Euphrates. He creates temples and the city of Babylon, and then makes man. The work of creation is finished within the first six tablets. The seventh tablet exalts the creation and greatness of Marduk's work.

Adam and Eve

The second creation story in Genesis, concerning Adam and Eve, immediately follows the account of seven days and is printed here in boldface:

> **In the day that Yahweh made the earth and the heavens, when no plant of the field was yet in the earth and no herb of the field had yet sprung up—for Yahweh had not caused it to rain upon the earth, and there was no one to till the ground; but a stream would rise up from the earth and water the whole face of the ground—then Yahweh formed man from the dust of the ground, and breathed into his nostrils the breath of life; and man became a living being. And Yahweh planted a garden in Eden, in the east; and there he put the man whom he had formed. Out of the ground Yahweh made to grow every tree that is pleasant to the sight and good for food, the tree of life also in the midst of the garden, and the tree of the knowledge of good and evil.**
>
> **A river flowed out of Eden to water the garden, and there it divides and becomes four branches. The name of the first is Pishon; it is the one which flows around the whole land of Havilah, where there is gold; and the gold of that land is good; bdellium and onyx stone are there. The name of the second river is Gihon; it is the one that flows around the whole land of Cush. And the name of the third river is Tigris, which flows east of Assyria. And the fourth river is the Euphrates.**
>
> **Yahweh took the man and put him in the Garden of Eden to till it and keep it. And Yahweh commanded the man, "You may freely eat of every tree of the garden; but of the tree of the knowledge of good and evil you shall not eat, for in the day that you eat of it you shall die."**
>
> **Then Yahweh said, "It is not good that the man should be alone; I will make him a helper as his partner." So out of the ground Yahweh formed every animal of the field and every bird of the air, and brought them to Adam to see what he would call them; and whatever Adam called every living creature, that was its name. Adam gave names to all cattle, and to the birds of the air, and to every animal of the field; but for Adam there was not found a helper as his partner. So Yahweh caused a deep sleep to fall upon Adam, and while he slept took one of his ribs and closed up its place with flesh. And the rib that Yahweh had taken from the man he made into a woman and brought her to the man. Then Adam said, "This at last is bone of my bones and flesh of my flesh; she shall be called Woman, because she was taken out of Man." Therefore a man leaves his father and his mother and cleaves to his wife, and they become one flesh. And the man and his wife were both naked, and were not ashamed (2:4-2:25).**

As in *Enuma Elish,* the Tigris and Euphrates situate us in the Middle East. The rivers are said to branch from an outflow of the Garden of Eden.

Since the headwaters of these two great rivers are in Turkey, that nation is the closest we can come to locating the biblical origin of humankind. Anomalously, the Mormons, following a revelation to founder Joseph Smith, locate the Garden of Eden in western Missouri (Brodie 1971).

We read of Eden as being "in the East," indicating the author's own location as west of the Tigris and Euphrates, plausibly in or near ancient Israel. We have no modern identification of the Pishon and Gihon Rivers, said to branch from the same source as the Tigris and Euphrates. These names may be fictitious, reflecting the "western" author's imperfect knowledge of Mesopotamia, or they may have been real rivers now lost through geological change.

Small details of text have come to have deep cultural meaning. Forming Adam "from the dust of the ground" evokes each person's life course: "ashes to ashes, dust to dust." Forming Eve from Adam's rib suggests to some readers that women are or should be subordinate to men.

Of Genesis's two accounts of creation, I prefer the story of Adam and Eve. It has characters with whom to empathize, and we can follow the family saga through subsequent passages. It has puzzles to ponder. Why did God so misunderstand his creation Adam as to offer an animal or bird as a suitable partner? Eve's creation seems to be a second attempt at partnering, after it became clear to Yahweh that no animal or bird would do. If the first attempt had worked, would there have been a Cain or Abel? Why was Eve made from one of Adam's bones instead of his hair or muscle or blood? Perhaps the reason is that skeletons are the most enduring remains of a body, and ribs are among the few redundant bones that, if taken away, would not leave Adam crippled, but a tooth might have done as well. One can speculate endlessly. There is no way to reach a correct answer except by faith or fiat.

Some traditionalists see the Bible's two stories of creation as a telescopic narrative, with the opening account giving the "big picture" while the story of Eden narrows the focus. Adam and Eve's tale is so engagingly different from the impersonal catalog of seven days that casual readers may not notice their contradictions. In the seven days story, all vegetation including seed plants and fruit trees is made on the third day. All sea creatures and flying birds are made on the fifth day. All land animals from cattle to creeping things are made on the sixth day, and afterward God makes humans – male and female – to rule over these fish, birds, and animals, and to use the plants for food.

In the second story, Adam comes first "when no plant of the field was yet on the earth." Then plants are created in Eden. Then "out of the ground Yahweh formed every animal of the field and every bird of the air." Finally Eve is made from Adam's rib.

Early readers within both Hellenistic and rabbinic Judaism recognized these inconsistencies and considered how they might be reconciled. Some assumed the first-created human – "male and female" – was an androgyne, later split into Adam and Eve. The Alexandrian Jewish philosopher Philo thought the primal androgyne was without a body, and that humans with bodies described in Genesis 2 represented a separate act of creation (Boyarin 1993: 17, 38).[3]

Was the first man created before plants and animals and birds, or afterward? Did birds appear before land animals or at the same time? The sequences agree on only two points: (1) vegetation preceded animals and birds, and (2) the first woman was created at the end of the process. There is little correspondence between either of the biblical sequences and our modern understanding of life's history. Water animals such as trilobites are the earliest known fossils of complex organisms, appearing long before land plants. Plant and animal life was abundant on land before many kinds of fish appeared; and marine mammals including whales are quite recent. Land plants did precede land animals that fed on them, but seed plants and fruit trees (angiosperms) appeared after dinosaurs and small mammals had long roamed the earth. Birds followed dinosaurs. Humans—of both sexes—are the newest of the major kinds mentioned in Genesis (Fortey 1998).

The Yahwist (J) and Priestly (P) Documents

Literary scholars of the nineteenth century developed methods of text analysis focused on such questions as whether a single author did indeed write all of the works attributed to Shakespeare. Their method, very briefly, is to compare themes and writing styles of the different works, on the assumption that particular authors may be recognized by their unique and consistent forms of expression, grammar, choice of words, and punctuation. In Germany, scholars applied the same method to the Bible, not to undermine belief but to gain a better understanding of this holy text.

As illustration, compare the two versions of creation. We have already seen that they contradict one another in sequencing the appearance of life forms on earth. They also differ in overall style, one a log of seven days, perhaps derived from *Enuma Elish*, the other a tale that a bard might tell about specific people, Adam and Eve. There is in addition an important difference in referring to the deity. The seven days version speaks impersonally of "God" (in Hebrew *Elohim*). In the Adam and Eve tale, God is called by his personal name, Yahweh. In the seven days account, the words used for creation are derivatives of one Hebrew root; in the Adam and Eve account they are derived from a different root (Rofé 1999). There is a strong case that the two passages were written by different authors.

After nearly two centuries of research, many biblical scholars agree that Genesis is a composite, a merger of previously separate documents. The Adam and Eve tale that speaks of Yahweh is the opening portion of what is called the "Yahwist" or J document (for Jahwist, as German scholars spell it). Whenever I quote a lengthy passage consensually identified as part of the J document, I will print it in boldface.[4] The seven days version of creation begins what is called the "Priestly" or P document, because of its exceptional interest in priestly issues. I print P passages in italic. Though each document may be consistent in itself, when juxtaposed they produce inconsistencies or explicit contradictions.

Notes

1.   Spelled *Jahwe* in German (Metzger and Coogan 1993). The medieval English name for God, Jehovah, was partly derived from a mispronunciation of the German J.

2.   *The Holy Bible, New Revised Standard Version* (Oxford University Press, 1989), unless otherwise stated.

3.   See http://www.answersingenesis.org/home/area/faq/genesis.asp for examples of modern commentary that explain away inconsistencies between Genesis 1 and 2 by introducing novel English-to-Hebrew translations, ad hoc interpretation of words or phrases, or ignoring details in the text.

4.   There is controversy over another source, the Elohist or E document (see Chapter 5), which may have been merged with J at an early stage. I do not distinguish J from E, printing both in boldface.

5

Eden to Babel

The Yahwist author continues his (or her) tale of the Garden of Eden, telling of a crafty serpent tempting Eve with fruit from the tree of knowledge of good and evil. (There is no apple.) Eve recalls Yahweh's warning that eating the fruit will bring immediate death, but she eats it anyway, survives, and then gives some to Adam who also survives. Afterward they see their nakedness as unacceptable and sew together fig leaves to clothe themselves (3:1-3:7). I continue the passage in boldface to mark it as part of the Yawhist document:

They heard the sound of Yahweh walking in the garden at the time of the evening breeze, and Adam and his wife hid themselves from the presence of Yahweh among the trees of the garden. But Yahweh called to Adam and said to him, "Where are you?" Adam said, "I heard the sound of you in the garden, and I was afraid, because I was naked; and I hid myself." He said, "Who told you that you were naked? Have you eaten from the tree of which I commanded you not to eat?" Adam said, "The woman whom you gave to be with me, she gave me fruit from the tree, and I ate." Then Yahweh said to the woman, "What is this that you have done?" The woman said, "The serpent tricked me, and I ate." (3:8-3:12)

This accusatory argument seems like a common spat among three people, even though one participant is God. Is Yahweh being coy, knowing all along what Adam and Eve did, or are his questions a genuine attempt to learn what happened? It appears that Yahweh is truly upset by the humans' unanticipated wrongdoing, by their learning good and evil, because he punishes the miscreants. The serpent, who apparently did not heretofore crawl on his belly, is now told to do so, and Yahweh further says "I will put enmity between you and the woman, and between your offspring and hers," seemingly causing women thereafter to dislike snakes. To Eve, Yahweh says "I will greatly increase your pangs in childbearing,… and your desire shall be for your husband, and he shall rule over you." These latter chastisements do not seem disadvantageous to the husband, but Yahweh punishes Adam too "because you have listened to the voice of your wife" and eaten forbidden fruit. Driving Adam from the Garden of Eden, Yahweh requires him to toil and sweat for his food until—in a reference back to the Yahwist creation story—"you return to the ground, for out of it you were taken; you are dust, and to dust you shall return." (3:15-3:19)

There are morality lessons here, as in most of the Bible. The passage infers that those who know good and evil recognize nakedness as shameful, to be hidden or covered by clothing. Few Americans challenge this stricture, but many would recognize its subjectivity, knowing of other cultures (ancient Greeks, peoples of the tropics) without shame in nudity.

Millennia after the presumed event, Augustine, Luther, and other theologians drew the weightier inference that all of Adam's descendants were or would be born with original sin.[1] This is a difficult concept with diverse interpretations, but the nub is that every newborn, before having a chance to do anything wrong, carries a moral flaw inherited because of Adam's fall from grace. It is a theological example of collective guilt, placing the onus of one person's sin on all his relatives. Original sin is a Christian concept not shared by Jews. Still, the Israelites' Yahweh upholds the underlying principle of collective guilt, forcing all of Eve's female descendants into painful childbirth, though they personally have committed no offense. The modern Western notion of individual responsibility, of presumed innocence until proven guilty, opposes collective guilt, one of many biblical moralities that clash with contemporary values.

Once Adam and Eve knew good and evil, they became sexual partners and had children. Perhaps that was intended all along. First came Cain, the farmer, then Abel, the shepherd.

> **In the course of time Cain brought to Yahweh an offering of the fruit of the ground, and Abel for his part brought of the firstlings of his flock, their fat portions. And Yahweh had regard for Abel and his offering, but for Cain and his offering he had no regard.**

We are given no explanation for Yahweh favoring Abel, but Cain reacts angrily, taking Abel into the field and killing him. I depart from the NRSV to render the ensuing scene as dialogue:

Yahweh: Where is your brother Abel?

Cain: I do not know, am I my brother's keeper?

Yahweh: What have you done? Listen; your brother's blood is crying out to me from the ground!... When you till the ground, it will no longer yield to you its strength; you will be a fugitive and a wanderer on the earth.

Cain: My punishment is greater than I can bear!... I shall be a fugitive and a wanderer on the earth, and anyone who meets me may kill me.

Yahweh: Not so! Whoever kills Cain will suffer a sevenfold vengeance.

And Yahweh put a mark on Cain, so that no one who came upon him would kill him. Then Cain went away from the presence of Yahweh, and settled in Nod, east of Eden. (Gen 4)

Unlike the questioning of Adam and Eve, here it is clear that Yahweh knows Cain's guilt, but the scene is problematic for other reasons. There must be more people than the original family because Cain and Yahweh both speak of others who might kill Cain. There must be someone in the land of Nod because Cain soon settles there and marries. Where did these people come from? After Abel's death, Eve bore a third son, Seth. Adam had other sons and daughters, presumably by Eve. Cain and Seth also fathered children. Did they marry their sisters? These are unsolved puzzles. Why is Nod, to the east of Eden, said to be "away from the presence of Yahweh"? Is God's domain limited to the region of Eden?

Calculations

At this point in the text there is a distinct break from folktale to recitation of the generations from Adam to Noah (5:1-27). These are the "begats" of the King James Version, rendered in the NRSV as "became the father of." The passage refers to God but not by his personal name, Yahweh, so no one includes it in the Yahwist document. Some scholars identify it with the Priestly document (e.g., Campbell and O'Brien 1993); others attribute it to a different source altogether (e.g., Friedman 2003), reflecting uncertainties and controversies that remain in parsing the text. As a non-specialist, I avoid taking sides and print the passage in regular font:

> When Adam had lived 130 years, he became the father of a son in his likeness, according to his image, and named him Seth...
>
> When Seth had lived 105 years, he became the father of Enosh...
>
> When Enosh had lived 90 years, he became the father of Kenan...
>
> When Kenan had lived 70 years, he became the father of Mahalalel...
>
> When Mahalelal had lived 65 years, he became the father of Jared...
>
> When Jared had lived 162 years, he became the father of Enoch...

When Enoch had lived 65 years, he became the father of Methuselah...

When Methuselah had lived 187 years, he became the father of Lamech...

When Lamech had lived 182 years, he became the father of a son; he named hi
   Noah...

The enumeration gives sufficient information to tally the elapsed time from Adam's first breath to the birth of Noah, a total of 1,056 years. By such means, and some subsidiary assumptions, Archbishop James Ussher (1580-1656) famously calculated that creation began in 4004 BCE. It follows that the earth was 5,863 years old in 1859, the year Darwin published *Origin of Species*. Ussher's dating, now widely ridiculed, was not unusual or out of line with other estimates based on similar assumptions. The Judaic calendar, still in use for ritual purposes, equates the secular year 2007 with the Jewish year 5767, counting from the beginning.

Noah was 600 years old when water flooded the planet (7:6). That dates the great deluge at 1,656 years after creation, or 2348 BCE according to Ussher's method. By then Noah had, at the age of 500, fathered Shem, Ham, and Japheth (5:32), so the sons were centenarians when they entered the ark.

The longevity of the progenitors is striking. Adam lived to the age of 930, Seth to 912, Enosh to 905, Kenan to 910, Mahalalel to 895, Jared to 962, Enoch to 365, Methuselah to 969, Lamech to 777, and Noah lived 950 years. Only 126 years separate the death of Adam from the birth of Noah. Indeed, all progenitors prior to Noah were alive simultaneously during the fifty-six-year span from Lamech's birth (874 years after Creation) to Adam's death. Living in proximity, they could have spent the weekly rest day together, an unexcelled opportunity to initiate and transmit oral traditions.

By the time of the flood, all Noah's direct male antecedents were dead, possibly excepting Methuselah, who by my calculation died three years afterward. The reason mortal men lived so long in those days is

that the sons of God saw they [i.e., humans] were fair; and they took wives for themselves of all that they chose. Then Yahweh said, "My spirit shall not abide in mortals forever, for they are flesh; their days shall be 120 years." The Nephilim were on the earth in those days – and also afterward – when the sons of God went in to the daughters of humans, who bore children to them. These were the heroes that were of old, warriors of renown (6:1-4).

The Nephilim, heroic warriors produced from the mating of God's sons with human women, appear again in Numbers 13:33 where they are described as giant inhabitants of Canaan, living at the time of Moses. It is not clear how they survived the flood to settle Canaan. This may be another of the contradictions arising from the merger of separate documents (Metzger and Coogan 1993: 556). In any case, here God limits the human life span to 120 years. But the Bible reports later men living far longer: Shem to 500 years, his son Arpachshad to 438 years, Arpachshad's son Shelah to 433 years, etc. (11:10-23, 32).

The Flood

We have reached the flood story, which is recognizable as a variant of earlier myth from Mesopotamia. In the Gilgamesh Epic, dated about 1900 BCE , a man named Utnapishtim is told by a god to build a great covered boat, and to bring into it all kinds of animals. After seven days and seven nights of flooding, the earth is covered with water. The boat comes to rest on a mountaintop. Utnapishtim sends birds from the boat, which return, until finally one does not, indicating the water has receded.

The Bible tells of Noah and his sons building from cypress wood a covered boat that by rough calculation approached in size the ocean liner Queen Elizabeth II.[2] The ark had to be huge to carry a pair of every kind of animal plus provisions. Cattle and horses were the largest creatures then found in the Middle East, but there must have been accommodation for elephants too. Storing food and disposing of wastes from dinosaurs as large as an eighty-ton Brachiosaurus was an accomplishment of barely believable enormity (Farlow and Brett-Surman 1997).

Noah's story contains repetitious and seemingly contradictory statements, indicating an intermingling of the Yahwist and Priestly documents, and perhaps other sources. Quoted below are couplets of redundant passages, one conventionally identified with the Yahwist author (in boldface), and the other with the Priestly source (italic). First we see repeated statements in which the deity tells Noah that humanity is wicked and will be eliminated:

Yahweh saw that the wickedness of humankind was great in the earth, and that every inclination of the thoughts of their hearts was only evil continually. And Yahweh was sorry that he had made humankind on the earth, and it grieved him to his heart. So Yahweh said, "I will blot out from the earth the human beings I have created – people together with animals and creeping things and birds of the air, for I am sorry that I have made them" (6:5-7).

Now the earth was corrupt in God's sight, and the earth was filled with violence. And God saw that the earth was corrupt; for all flesh had corrupted its ways upon the earth. And God said to Noah, "I have determined to make an end of all flesh, for the earth is filled with violence because of them; now I am going to destroy them along with the earth (6:11-13).

Both sources show an infallible deity whose creation has gone awry. In neither is there compunction about destroying blameless animals, nor infants – another application of collective guilt. But the versions differ in characterizing the deity. The Yahwist document describes God in anthropomorphic terms: Yahweh is grieved, blaming himself for creating wicked people. The Priestly writer presents God as an unemotional judge: people are corrupt so they will be terminated. These passages are followed by another redundant pair of narrations in which Noah is told to bring specimens of all kinds of animal into the ark because a flood is coming. Here the Priestly version comes first:

> *I am going to bring a flood of waters on the earth, to destroy from under heaven all flesh in which is the breath of life; everything that is on the earth shall die. But I will establish my covenant with you; and you shall come into the ark, you, your sons, your wife, and your sons' wives with you. And of every living thing, of all flesh, you shall bring two of every kind into the ark, to keep them alive with you; they shall be male and female. Of the birds according to their kinds, and of the animals according to their kinds, of every creeping thing of the ground according to its kind, two of every kind shall come in to you, to keep them alive. Also take with you every kind of food that is eaten, and store it up, and it shall serve as food for you and for them"* Noah did this; he did all that God commanded him (6:17-22).

> **Yahweh said to Noah, "Go into the ark, you and all your household, for I have seen that you alone are righteous before me in this generation. Take with you seven pairs of all clean animals, the male and its mate; and a pair of the animals that are not clean, the male and its mate; and seven pairs of the birds of the air also, male and female, to keep their kind alive on the face of all the earth. For in seven days I will send rain on the earth for forty days and forty nights; and every living thing that I have made I will blot out from the face of the ground." And Noah did all that Yahweh commanded him (7:1-5).**

Both sources cover the same major points, indicating common roots, but they differ in detail, indicating separate development. The Yahwist says to bring into the ark seven pairs of all clean animals and birds; the Priestly writer is content with a single pair of each kind.

The story continues with every kind of animal and bird entering the ark "two by two, male and female," with no further mention of seven pairs. Still, there are repetitions and inconsistencies. The Yawist times the flood at forty days and nights (7:4, 12, 17). Elsewhere "the waters swelled on the earth for 150 days" (7:24). A different passage tells of the ark coming to rest on the mountains of Ararat five months after the onset; Noah and his family and the animals emerge after a year of confinement (7:11, 8:4, 14-16).[3]

> Then Noah built an altar to Yahweh, and took of every clean animal and of every clean bird, and offered burnt offerings on the altar. And when Yahweh smelled the

pleasing odor, Yahweh said in his heart, "I will never again curse the ground because of humankind, for the inclination of the human heart is evil from youth; nor will I ever again destroy every living creature as I have done (8:20-21).

From this Yahwist passage we infer that Noah had more than one pair of every clean animal and bird on board – earlier the Yahwist said seven pair. Otherwise there would be no pair left for procreation after the sacrifice. Furthermore, God tells Noah that henceforth no violence by one human against another shall go unpunished: "Whoever sheds the blood of a human, by a human shall that person's blood be shed (9:6)." From this, one might think that the remainder of the Bible would be free of divinely inspired killing, but it is not.

Where was there water in sufficient quantity to submerge the entire earth, covering mountains to a depth of fifteen cubits (7:20)? The answer is in the Priestly account of the Second Day, when God made a dome (the sky), separating waters under the dome from waters above it. Both divisions, the sea below and the reservoir of water above the sky, contributed to the flooding: "all the fountains of the great deep burst forth, and the windows of the heavens were opened" (7:11).

After the flood, Noah and his family repopulated the earth, speaking to one another in a common tongue. People set about building a city and within it a tower reaching to heaven. Seeing this, Yahweh thought it best if everyone did not speak the same language, thus limiting the cooperative capability of humans. He declared, though it is not clear to whom, "Come, let us go down, and confuse their language there, so that they will not understand one another's speech" (11:7). Yahweh scattered the people over the face of the earth, and they left off building the city. Thereafter the city was called Babel (Babylon?) "because there Yahweh confused the language of all the earth." Ever since, the peoples of the world have spoken different and mutually incomprehensible languages.

Notes

1. In the NRSV, King David claims in Psalm 51:5, "I was born guilty, a sinner when my mother conceived me," seemingly acknowledging his original sin, though not blaming it on Adam and Eve. The KJV translates the same line, "I was shapen in iniquity; and in sin did my mother conceive me," making ambiguous whether "sin" refers to the zygote or to the mother's copulation. The Jewish Publication Society's English translation is also ambiguous, reading, "I was brought forth in iniquity, And in sin did my mother conceive me" (51:7).

2. The ark's dimensions are given as 300 cubits long, 50 cubits wide, and 30 cubits high (Gen 11:15). The NRSV (p. xvii) equates a Hebrew cubit to 17.49 inches but notes that the cubit described in Ezekiel (40.5; 43.13) equals seven handbreadths, or about 20 inches. The Queen Elizabeth II is 887 feet in length and 105 feet in width (http://www.ocean-liners.com/ships/qetwo.asp).

3.   According to the Priestly writer, Noah tests for the presence of dry land by send-
      ing out a raven. In the Yahwist document, he sends out a dove. In the Gilgamesh
      epic, the hero of the flood sends out a raven, a dove, and a swallow (Friedman
      2003:45).

6

Patriarchs

The term "Abrahamic religions" is increasingly used to encompass Judaism, Christianity, and Islam. This usage stresses that the three often hostile traditions have a common root. As Sheikh Ahmad Kuftaro, Grand Mufti of Syria, put it in a 1992 speech to the United Nations Earth Summit:

> Though there were prophets before Abraham, it was the will of Allah [God] that the later generation of prophets be his offspring... The great succession of these prophets after Abraham called for the message of Allah, each paving the way for the next one...
>
> Prophet Muhammad explained his mission in the following words: "The comparison between me and the preceding prophets is similar to a group of people who took part in building a house and completed it but for an empty space for one block or brick. Onlookers admired it and said in astonishment: 'What a beautiful mansion, if it were not for the place of the missing brick.' I have been this brick, and I am the last or the seal of prophets..." In this analogy the Prophet does not refer to himself as the whole house but as a part of this structure of prophethood. Thus, he...[shows] his nation and the followers of previous prophets that the true glory of the people of faith is only through cooperation and integration...
>
> Islam demands belief in the great caravan of prophets of which Abraham is the vanguard. His offspring includes Isaac, Ishmael, Jacob, Joseph, David, Solomon, Moses, Jesus, and Muhammad (peace be upon them all).... [T]o deny or reject any of the prophets would be the abandonment of faith.[1]

Abraham

The Bible gives no reason why God selected Abraham for special treatment. He is described as a descendent of Noah's son Shem, born 292 years after the flood (11:10-26). Like Adam, Eve, and Noah, Abraham spoke to Yahweh (Allah) as if the deity were a person. In one incident, as Abraham sits at the entrance of his tent in the heat of the day, he sees three men nearby. Recognizing one as Yahweh – the other two are angels – he runs to meet them, bows to the ground, and exclaims,

Yahweh, if I find favor with you, do not pass by your servant. Let a little water be brought, and wash your feet, and rest yourselves under the tree. Let me

bring a little bread, that you may refresh yourselves, and after that you may
pass.... So they said, "Do as you have said." And Abraham hastened into the tent
to [his wife] Sarah, and said, "Make ready quickly three measures of choice
flour, knead it, and make cakes." Abraham ran to the herd, and took a calf,
tender and good, and gave it to the servant, who hastened to prepare it. Then he
took curds and milk and the calf that he had prepared, and set it before them;
and he stood by them under the tree while they ate (18:3-8).

Mixing milk and meat at meal shows that either Yahweh or the author
has not yet adopted kosher dietary rules. More interesting is the person-
to-person nature of the interaction. Abraham and Sarah are elderly and
childless; she is postmenopausal. When Yahweh says they will have a
son, Sarah belittles his prediction and his ability to see it through.

The three travelers are seeking Sodom so Yahweh can confirm or deny
reports coming to him about the city's sinfulness. While showing God
the route to the city, Abraham asks,

"Will you indeed sweep away the righteous with the wicked? Suppose there are
fifty righteous within the city; will you then sweep away the place and not forgive it for the fifty righteous who are in it? Far be it from you to do such a thing,
to slay the righteous with the wicked.... Shall not the Judge of all the earth do
what is just?" And Yahweh said, "If I find at Sodom fifty righteous in the city,
I will forgive the whole place for their sake." Abraham answered..., "Suppose
five of the fifty righteous are lacking? Will you destroy the whole city for lack of
five?" And he said, "I will not destroy it if I find forty-five there" (18:23-29).

Continuing his haggling, Abraham gets Yahweh down to forty for a
reprieve, then thirty, then twenty, then ten.

On reaching Sodom the two angels – God is no longer with them—
meet Abraham's nephew Lot, who offers food and lodging. Sodom's
angry men surround the house, demanding that Lot turn over his guests. To
appease the mob, Lot offers his two virgin daughters. "Do to them as you
please," he says, "only do nothing to these men [angels]." Thus shown to
be righteous, Lot is urged by the angels to escape the city with his family.
They leave just in time. Yahweh rains sulfur and fire on Sodom, killing
all remaining inhabitants, another example of collective guilt. Contrary
to the angels' instructions, Lot's wife looks back to her burning city and
for doing so becomes a pillar of salt. Lot begins repopulating the area
by incestuous union with his two daughters. The passage assures us that
Lot is not culpable because the girls put him into a drunken stupor on
each of two successive nights of insemination (Gen 19).

In the meantime Sarah, because of her inability to have a child, gives
her Egyptian slave girl Hagar to Abraham as his second wife. Easily
impregnated, Hagar becomes contemptuous of her barren mistress. Sarah
responds harshly so Hagar runs away, but Yahweh's angel finds Hagar

and commands her, "Return to your mistress, and submit to her" (16:9). Four hundred years hence Yahweh will free the Israelites from slavery in Egypt, but apparently he has no objection to slavery in principle, or to polygamy. Hagar returns to bear her son Ishmael, from whom the Prophet Muhammad will one day claim descent.

The narrative of Abraham contains many redundant passages, some apparently the result of combining sources; others may have come when a single author used repetition for emphasis or poetic effect ("A rose is a rose is a rose.") The Bible often repeats God's promises that Abraham will have multitudinous offspring who will inherit a particular region of land. Descendants will be as numerous as the heavenly stars, or "so that if one can count the dust of the earth, your offspring also can be counted" (13:16, 15:5). The Promised Land is described sometimes as Canaan, to the west of the Jordan River, but also more expansively as "from the river of Egypt to the great river, the river Euphrates" (15:17). These promises are embedded in an agreement, or covenant, that God proposes in the Priestly document:

"I will make you exceedingly fruitful; and I will make nations of you, and kings shall come from you. I will establish my covenant between me and you, and your offspring after you throughout their generations.... And I will give you, and to your offspring after you, the land where you are now an alien, all the land of Canaan, for a perpetual holding; and I will be their God."

God said to Abraham, "As for you, you shall keep my covenant, you and your offspring.... You shall circumcise the flesh of your foreskins, and it shall be a sign of the covenant between me and you.... Both the slave born in your house and the one bought with your money must be circumcised (17: 6-13).

This passage's reference to kings hints that the Priestly author lived during or after the time when Israel was a kingdom.

Isaac

At that point in the text, Abraham's line of descent runs solely through Hagar's son Ishmael. But Yahweh dealt with Sarah as he said he would, and in her old age she bore Abraham's son, Isaac, who was circumcised when he was eight days old, as God had commanded.

The child grew, and was weaned.... But Sarah saw the son of Hagar the Egyptian... playing with her son Isaac. So she said to Abraham, "Cast out this slave woman with her son; for the son of this slave woman shall not inherit along with my son Isaac." The matter was very distressing to Abraham on account of his son. But God said to Abraham, "Do not be distressed because of the boy and because of your slave woman; whatever Sarah says to you, do as she tells you, for it is through Isaac that offspring shall be named for you. As for the son of the slave woman, I will make a nation of him also, because he is your offspring." So Abraham rose early in the morning, and took bread and a skin of water, and gave it to Hagar, putting it on her shoulder, along with the child, and sent her away (21: 8-14).[2]

Isaac's childhood was not carefree, for God used him to test his father's faith, telling Abraham:

"Take your son, your only son Isaac, whom you love, and go to the land of Moriah, and offer him there as a burnt offering on one of the mountains that I shall show you." So Abraham...cut the wood for the burnt offering, and set out and went to the place...that God had shown him.... Isaac said to his father Abraham,... "The fire and the wood are here, but where is the lamb for a burnt offering?" Abraham said, "God himself will provide the lamb for the burnt of-fering, my son." So the two of them walked on together.

When they came to the place that God had shown him, Abraham built an altar there and laid the wood in order. He bound his son Isaac, and laid him on the altar, on top of the wood. Then Abraham reached out his hand and took the knife to kill his son. But the angel of Yahweh called to him from heaven, and said, "Abraham, Abraham! ...Do not lay your hand on the boy or do anything to him; for now I know that you fear God, since you have not withheld your son, your only son, from me." And Abraham looked up and saw a ram, caught in a thicket by its horns. Abraham went and took the ram and offered it up as a burnt offering instead of his son (22: 2-13).

Thus Isaac survived to wed the beautiful and generous Rebekah. He inherited Abraham's flocks and herds, silver and gold, male and female slaves, camels and donkeys. Rebekah bore twins. Esau, the firstborn, "came out red, all his body like a hairy mantle." Jacob came out "with his hand gripping Esau's heel."

When the boys grew up, Esau was a skillful hunter, a man of the field, while Jacob was a quiet man, living in tents. Isaac loved Esau, because he was fond of game; but Rebekah loved Jacob.

Once when Jacob was cooking a stew, Esau came in from the field, and he was famished. Esau said to Jacob, "Let me eat some of that red stuff, for I am famished!"... Jacob said, "First sell me your birthright." Esau said, "I am about to die; of what use is a birthright to me?" Jacob said, "Swear to me first." So he swore to him, and sold his birthright to Jacob. Then Jacob gave Esau bread and lentil stew, and he ate and drank, and rose and went his way (25:27-34).

Yahweh appeared to Isaac and renewed the covenant he had made with Abraham, telling Isaac that his offspring, as numerous as the stars of heaven, would inherit the Promised Land. At this point the main line of descent is again uncertain because Esau, though Isaac's eldest and favorite son, has sold his birthright to Jacob for some lentil stew. The issue is resolved when Isaac, blind and near death, tells Esau to hunt game for him and prepare it as savory food. Then, Isaac says, "I will bless you before I die."

Having overheard the conversation, Rebekah tells *her* favorite, Jacob, to fetch from the flock two choice kids so *she* can prepare savory food for his father.

> "You shall take it to your father to eat, so that he may bless you before he dies." But Jacob said to his mother Rebekah, "Look, my brother Esau is a hairy man, and I am a man of smooth skin. Perhaps my father will feel me, and I shall seem to be mocking him, and bring a curse on myself and not a blessing." His mother said to him, "Let your curse be on me, my son." ...[S]he put the skins of the kids on his hands and on the smooth part of his neck. Then she handed the savory food, and the bread that she has prepared, to her son Jacob.
>
> So he went in to his father and said,... "I am Esau your firstborn. I have done as you told me; now sit up and eat of my game, so that you may bless me." But Isaac said to his son, "How is it that you have found it so quickly, my son?" He answered, "Because Yahweh granted me success." Then Isaac said to Jacob, "Come near, that I may feel you, my son, to know whether you are really my son Esau or not." So Jacob went up to his father Isaac, who felt him and said, "The voice is Jacob's voice, but the hands are the hands of Esau" (27:10-22).

Despite his suspicions, and being a herdsman all his life, Isaac cannot distinguish a lamb's pelt from Esau's hairy skin so the conspiracy between Rebekah and Jacob is successful. Isaac blesses Jacob, placing him above Esau: "Be lord over your brothers, and may your mother's sons bow down to you." Jacob's coup completed, Esau returns:

> Let my father sit up and eat of his son's game, so that you may bless me." His father Isaac said to him, "Who are you?" He answered, "I am your firstborn son, Esau." Then Isaac trembled violently, and said, "Who was it then that hunted game and brought it to me, and I ate it all before you came, and I have blessed him? ...[Esau] cried out with an exceedingly great and bitter cry, and said to his father, "Bless me, me also, father!" But he said, "Your brother came deceitfully and he has taken away your blessing...." "Have you not reserved a blessing for me?" Isaac answered Esau, "I have already made him your lord..." Esau said to his father, "Have you only one blessing, father?" And Esau lifted up his voice and wept...
>
> Now Esau hated Jacob because of the blessing with which his father had blessed him, and Esau said to himself, "The days of mourning for my father are approaching; then I will kill my brother Jacob." But the words of her elder son Esau were told to Rebekah; so she sent and called her younger son Jacob and said to him, "Your brother Esau is consoling himself by planning to kill you. Now therefore, my son, obey my voice; flee at once to my brother Laban in Haran, and stay with him a while, until your brother's fury turns away...and he forgets what you have done to him" (27:31-44).

Jacob Becomes Israel

One night during Jacob's flight from Canaan to Haran, Yahweh appeared to him in a dream and renewed the covenant he had made with Abraham and Isaac. Reaching Haran, Jacob met his cousin, the lovely Rachel, and fell in love. Jacob and Uncle Laban struck a deal: Jacob would work for Laban for seven years, and at the end of that time would receive Rachel as his wife. So Jacob worked seven years, and at the end of that time Laban prepared a wedding feast. But that night Laban brought his older daughter Leah to Jacob, and Jacob went in to her to consummate the marriage. No more discriminating than his father, Jacob did not recognize the switched brides until the next morning when he saw it was Leah! The parallel between Laban's fraud and Jacob's fraud is unmistakable.

> And Jacob said to Laban, "What is this you have done to me? Did I not serve with you for Rachel? Why then have you deceived me?" Laban said, "This is not done in our country – giving the younger before the firstborn. Complete the week of this one, and we will give you the other also in return for serving me another seven years." Jacob did so; ...then Laban give him his daughter Rachel as a wife.... So Jacob went in to Rachel also, and he loved Rachel more than Leah... When Yahweh saw that Leah was unloved, he opened her womb; but Rachel was barren (29:25-31).

During his second period of servitude to Laban, Jacob produced many sons and a daughter through four women: by Leah (sons Reuben, Simeon, Levi, Judah, Issachar, Zebulun, and a daughter, Dinah), by Rachel's maid Bilhah (Dan and Naphtali), eventually by Rachel herself (Joseph and later Benjamin), and by Leah's maid Zilpah (Gad and Asher). When finally it was time to return to Canaan, Jacob left with his two wives, their maids, their children, plus animals and slaves.

One night along the way, Jacob participates in the following strange incident:

> Jacob was alone; and a man wrestled with him until daybreak. When the man saw that he did not prevail against Jacob, he struck him on the hip socket; and Jacob's hip was put out of joint as he wrestled with him. Then he said, "Let me go, for day is breaking." But Jacob said, "I will not let you go unless you bless me." So he said to him, "What is your name?" And he said, "Jacob." Then the man said, "You shall no longer be called Jacob, but Israel, for you have striven with God and with humans, and have prevailed." Then Jacob asked him, "Please tell me your name?" But he said, "Why is it that you ask my name?" And there he blessed him. So Jacob called the place Peniel, saying, "For I have seen God face to face, and yet my life is preserved" (32: 24-30).

This is one of the Bible's most remarkable passages. Jacob wrestles with God and wins! Henceforth Jacob will be called "Israel" because he has prevailed—not over humans but over God. How can this be unless God has thrown the match? The scene is more fitting to Greek mythology than the Supreme Ruler of the Universe. "Israel" is henceforth the name of the people God has chosen to multiply like the stars in heaven and to inherit the Promised Land. Jacob's twelve sons are the progenitors of the Twelve Tribes of Israel.

Joseph

Israel née Jacob loved Joseph best of all his sons, so the others were jealous. One day when all the brothers were out in the field attending flocks, they threw Joseph in a pit. Then, by one account, the brothers sold Joseph to some Ishmaelites traveling by camel caravan to Egypt (37:25). By another account, Midianite traders drew Joseph from the pit and sold him to the Ishmaelites (37:28). Either way, Joseph was removed to Egypt. The brothers dipped his long robe in animal blood, bringing it to their gullible father as evidence that Joseph was killed by an animal. Israel mourned deeply.

In Egypt, Joseph was purchased by one Potiphar, a captain of the pharaoh's guard. But Yahweh watched over Joseph, and he became a successful and trusted manager of Potiphar's estate. Potiphar's wife was impressed with the young and handsome overseer and tried continually to seduce him. Joseph resisted, unwilling to betray his master. The scorned woman cried rape. "See, my husband has brought among us a Hebrew to insult us! He came in to me to lie with me, and I cried out with a loud voice." Potiphar believed her, and Joseph was imprisoned. But Yahweh stayed with him. Joseph befriended the jailer and did well even in prison, and there he made his reputation as an interpreter of dreams (Gen 39).

Now the pharaoh had a dream that he was standing by the Nile, and there came out of the river seven fat cows, and they grazed in the reeds. Then seven thin and ugly cows came out of the Nile and ate the fat cows. In the morning the pharaoh sent for all the wise men of Egypt, but no one could interpret his dream. Hearing of Joseph, the pharaoh brought him out of jail and told him the dream. Joseph saw that the seven fat cows were seven years with good harvest, and the seven lean cows were years of famine. Joseph told the pharaoh to store crops during the good years, making a reserve so that Egypt would not perish during the famine. This pleased the pharaoh and he appointed Joseph to oversee the store houses, making him a lord of Egypt with authority above everyone but the pharaoh. During the seven plentiful years Joseph directed the storage of food, and during the seven famine years he distributed the food (Gen 41).

The famine affected Canaan too. When Israel learned there was grain in Egypt, he sent his sons to buy food. They did not recognize their brother Joseph, now lord of Egypt, but he recognized them. After much dealing, Joseph announced, "I am Joseph. Is my father still alive?" His stunned brothers could not answer him. But Joseph meant them no harm. He kissed all his brothers and wept upon them, telling them to bring Israel and settle in Egypt where there was food. The pharaoh heard this and was pleased, offering Israel and his sons land in Egypt. The brothers returned to Canaan and told their father all that had happened. At first Israel did not believe them but then cried, "Enough! My son Joseph is still alive. I must go and see him before I die." And so Israel and his sons and their wives and children, seventy people in all, settled in Egypt.

Joseph is one of the best loved characters in the Old Testament, his story the basis of an Andrew Lloyd Webber musical. Good natured, loyal, and forgiving, he meets one adversity after another, always triumphant. His is the ultimate success story. Joseph is less recognized as one of the Bible's consummate exploiters of oppressed people:

> **Joseph collected all the money to be found in the land of Egypt and in the land of Canaan, in exchange for the grain that they bought; and Joseph brought the money into Pharaoh's house. When the money from the land of Egypt and from the land of Canaan was spent, all the Egyptians came to Joseph and said, "Give us food! Why should we die before your eyes? For our money is gone." And Joseph answered, "Give me your livestock, and I will give you food in exchange for your livestock, if your money is gone." So they brought their livestock to Joseph; and Joseph gave them food in exchange for the horses, the flocks, the herds, and the donkeys.... They came to him the following year, and said to him, "We cannot hide from my lord that our money is all spent; and the herds of cattle are my lord's. There is nothing left in the sight of my lord but our bodies and our lands. Shall we die before your eyes, both we and our land? Buy us and our land in exchange for food. We with our land will become slaves to Pharaoh; just give us seed, so that we may live and not die, and that the land may not become desolate."**
>
> **So Joseph bought all the land of Egypt for Pharaoh. All the Egyptians sold their fields, because the famine was severe upon them; and the land became Pharaoh's. As for the people, he made slaves of them, from one end of Egypt to the other (47:13-21).**

The book of Genesis ends with Joseph and his father's household living prosperously and peacefully in Egypt. In the final verse Joseph, now aged, tells his brothers, "I am about to die; but God will surely come to you and bring you up out of this land to the land that he swore to Abraham, to Isaac, and to Jacob." Thus the stage is smoothly set for the Torah's major story.

Notes

1.   www.kuftaro.org/English/wot/The_Abrahamic_Religions.htm.
2.   This passage and the next are sometimes regarded as coming from a third source, the Elohist or E document. Probably J and E were merged at an early stage; their hypothetical combination is referred to as the JE document. Usually I will not distinguish between J and E, marking both with boldface.

7

Exodus

Here we enter the central drama of the Torah/Pentateuch—of God transforming his chosen people from slaves in Egypt to the conquerors of Canaan. It is the story of Moses, reluctant servant of Yahweh, freeing the Israelites from bondage, receiving God's law at Sinai, and leading his people to the Promised Land but never himself entering it.

Like Genesis, the book of Exodus is a composite document with inconsistencies and contradiction. One biblical scholar concisely notes:

> In some passages the sacred mountain is called Horeb, in others Sinai... In Exodus 2:18, Moses's future father-in-law is named Reuel, and in 18:1-27 the same man is called Jethro. Moreover, the narratives differ on the respective roles of Moses and his brother Aaron. According to one view, Moses is the principal figure: God calls him to go before the pharaoh and, when Moses protests that he is a poor speaker, Aaron is delegated to help him persuade the Israelites (4:14-17). Both men are to go to the pharaoh, but Moses is to make the request of him and to work wonders with his rod (4:21). Elsewhere, however, Aaron is the spokesman and with his rod performs wonders (6:28-7:13). And to take just one more example, the Pentateuch has two versions of the Ten Commandments, one in Exodus 20 and the other in Deuteronomy 5 (Anderson 1966: 16).

Moses

In the generations after Joseph's death the Israelites multiplied and grew strong, so that the Egyptians became fearful of them and enslaved them. "They built supply cities, Pithom and Rameses, for Pharaoh" (Ex 1:11). But the more they were oppressed, the more they multiplied. Finally the reigning pharaoh ordered that every newborn Hebrew boy be killed.

A couple from the tribe of Levi saved their infant by putting him in a papyrus basket among the reeds on the river bank. One of the pharaoh's daughters found the boy and recognized (perhaps by his circumcision) that he was a Hebrew. The boy's sister, watching from nearby, said she could fetch a Hebrew woman to nurse the baby, and so the infant's real mother was hired to care for him. When the boy was grown, his mother brought him to the pharaoh's daughter who took him as her own son, calling him Moses.

One day Moses killed an Egyptian who was beating a Hebrew. To avoid punishment, Moses fled to the land of Midian, and there he married Zipporah, the daughter of a Midian priest (sometimes named Reuel, sometimes Jethro). One day, while tending his father-in-law's flock, Moses saw a bush that was burning but not being consumed by the fire, and from the bush God called to him:

> "I have observed the misery of my people who are in Egypt; I have heard their cry.... I have come down to deliver them from the Egyptians, and to bring them out of that land to a good and broad land, a land flowing with milk and honey.... So come, I will send you to Pharaoh to bring my people, the Israelites, out of Egypt."
>
> ...Then Moses answered, "But suppose they do not believe me or listen to me, but say, 'Yahweh did not appear to you.'" Yahweh said to him, "What is that in your hand?" He said, "A staff." And he said, "Throw it on the ground." So he threw the staff on the ground, and it became a snake; and Moses drew back from it. Then Yahweh said to Moses, "Reach out your hand, and seize it by the tail" – so he reached out his hand and grasped it, and it became a staff in his hand – "so that they may believe that Yahweh, the God of their ancestors,... has appeared to you..."
>
> But Moses said to Yahweh, "O my Lord, I have never been eloquent,... I am slow of speech and slow of tongue." Then Yahweh said to him, "Who gives speech to mortals? Who makes them mute or deaf, seeing or blind? Is it not I, Yahweh? Now go, and I will be with your mouth and teach you what you are to speak." But he said, "O my Lord, please send someone else." Then the anger of Yahweh was kindled against Moses and he said, "What of your brother Aaron the Levite? I know that he can speak fluently; even now he is coming out to meet you, and when he sees you his heart will be glad. You shall speak to him and put the words in his mouth; and I will be with your mouth and with his mouth, and will teach you what you shall do. He indeed shall speak for you to the people; he shall serve as a mouth for you, and you shall serve as God for him" (Ex 3, 4).[1]

By this negotiated arrangement, Aaron speaks for Moses, and Moses speaks for God. Here are more puzzles. If Yahweh has the power to give speech, why doesn't he give it to Moses? Indeed, why doesn't Yahweh himself instruct the pharaoh to free the Israelites? Instead he does the opposite, *hardening* Pharaoh's heart, making him more resistant to Moses (4:22). Since Yahweh can harden the pharaoh's heart, could he soften it as well – if he wanted too? Why is God escalating the confrontation between the pharaoh and Moses when that course leads to the frightful slaughter of Egyptian firstborns? Why does Yahweh try to kill Moses, an act averted only by Zipporah cutting off her son's foreskin and touching it to Moses's feet (4:24)?

Confronting Pharaoh

Moses and Aaron went to the pharaoh, telling him, "Yahweh, God of Israel, says, 'Let my people go.'" The pharaoh is unimpressed, responding, "Who is Yahweh, that I should heed him and let Israel go?" Rather than freeing the slaves, the pharaoh makes their work harder, and the Israelites blame Moses and Aaron for their added burden.

> *Yahweh said to Moses and Aaron, "When Pharaoh says to you, 'Perform a wonder,' then you shall say to Aaron, 'Take your staff and throw it down before Pharaoh, and it will become a snake.'" So Moses and Aaron went to Pharaoh and did as Yahweh had commanded; Aaron threw down his staff before Pharaoh and his officials, and it became a snake. Then Pharaoh summoned the wise men and the sorcerers; and they also, the magicians of Egypt, did the same by their secret arts. Each one threw down his staff, and they because snakes; but Aaron's staff swallowed up theirs. Still Pharaoh's heart was hardened, and he would not listen to them....*

How could the sorcerers turn their staffs to snakes as easily as Aaron? Little wonder that the pharaoh is unmoved, and besides, Yahweh has hardened his heart. So Yahweh escalates, turning the Nile to blood, a plague described in two versions:

> **Then Yahweh said to Moses..., "Go to Pharaoh in the morning, as he is going out to the water; stand by at the river bank to meet him.... Say to him..., 'See, with the staff that is in my hand I will strike the water that is in the Nile, and it shall be turned to blood. The fish in the river shall die, the river itself shall stink, and the Egyptians shall be unable to drink water from the Nile.'" (Ex 7:14-18)**

> *Yahweh said to Moses, "Say to Aaron, 'Take your staff and stretch out your hand over the waters of Egypt – over its rivers, its canals, and its ponds, and all its pools of water – so that they may become blood; and there shall be blood throughout the whole land of Egypt, even in vessels of wood and in vessels of stone.'" Moses and Aaron did just as Yahweh commanded (Ex 7:19-20).*

The first version does not mention Aaron. The second account of the same speech gives Aaron an active role, reflecting the Aaronid bias typical of the Priestly document. Either way, Yahweh's messengers could not impress the pharaoh because his sorcerers also could turn blood to water by their secret arts (7:22), and they could replicate the next plague, swarming frogs.

But more plagues—gnats, swarms of flies, a pestilence among Egypt's livestock, festering boils on both humans and animals, hail, locusts, and darkness – are beyond the sorcerers' capabilities, convincing them that "the finger of God" is acting. Pharaoh himself remains intransigent so the severity of punishment is continually elevated. This is Yahweh's deliberate strategy, as he explains repeatedly to Moses: "I have hardened his heart...in order that I may show these signs [plagues] of mine among them, and that you may tell your children and grandchildren how I have made fools of the Egyptians...so that you may know that I am Yahweh" (10:2); "Pharaoh will not listen to you, in order that my wonders may be multiplied in the land of Egypt" (11:9).

Finally Moses plays God's trump card, warning the pharaoh that if he does not let the Israelites go, "Every firstborn in the land of Egypt shall die, from the firstborn of the Pharaoh who sits on his throne to the firstborn of the female slave who is behind the handmill, and all the firstborn of the livestock." Only the Israelites would be excluded.[2] Apparently this mass killing of firstborns -- including infants, slaves, prisoners, Egyptians who had no hand in the Israelites' captivity, even livestock—was intended all along as the culminating demonstration of Yahweh's power.

It worked. "There was a loud cry in Egypt, for there was not a house without someone dead." Pharaoh summoned Moses and Aaron in the night, telling them to go, take the Israelites, finally pleading that they worship Yahweh "and bring a blessing on me too!" (12:32). Thus, after 430 years residing in Egypt, the Israelites depart hastily, taking their dough before it was leavened; hence the matzo as a symbol of Passover. As they leave they plunder the Egyptians of silver and golden jewelry and clothing.

The Israelites then numbered "about six hundred thousand men on foot, besides children" (12:37), an enormous though not impossible increase from the seventy people who came to Egypt with Jacob/Israel. If we assume every man had a wife, and each couple had four children who survived to bear their own children, that could cause a doubling of population every twenty-five to thirty years (for 430 years), producing the required growth. The total departing population – men, women, and four children per couple – would have been about 3.6 million people. The logistic problems of moving and sustaining so many in the wilderness must have been enormous.

Yahweh went in front of the Israelites in a pillar of cloud by day and a pillar of fire by night, leading them toward a sea, translated as either the Red Sea or the Sea of Reeds. There God told Moses, "I will harden Pharaoh's heart, and he will pursue them, so that I will gain glory for myself over Pharaoh and all his army; and the Egyptians shall know that I am Yahweh" (14:4). As planned, the pharaoh and his charioteers and horsemen caught up to the Israelites as they were camped by the sea. The fearful campers complained to Moses,

> **"Was it because there were no graves in Egypt that you have taken us away to die in the wilderness? What have you done to us, bringing us out of Egypt? Is**

this not the very thing we told you in Egypt, 'Let us alone and let us serve the Egyptians'? For it would have been better for us to serve the Egyptians than to die in the wilderness." But Moses said to the people, "Do not be afraid, stand firm, and see the deliverance that Yahweh will accomplish for you today; for the Egyptians whom you see today you shall never see again" (14:11-13).

Following Yahweh's instructions, Moses lifted his staff over the sea and divided it, allowing the Israelites to pass through on dry ground. The pillar of cloud took a position between the escaping horde and the Egyptian army. Then Moses stretched his hand over the sea and the waters returned to normal depth. In the Yahwist version the returning water covers the pharaoh's entire army (14:28); in the Priestly version, God "tossed the Egyptians into the sea" (14:27). Either way, the Egyptian army was dead.

The Covenant at Sinai/Horeb

The now free Israelites wander through the wilderness of Sinai for forty years before reaching Canaan. Despite miraculous provisioning by bread (manna) raining from heaven, they often complain about Moses and Aaron, wishing they were back in the relative safety of Egyptian slavery.

The text tells us little about most of the decades of wandering but focuses on events at a mountain that thunders, smokes, and erupts like a volcano, sometimes calling it Mount Sinai and other times Horeb. There God offers to the Israelites a renewed covenant. He agrees to lead his chosen people to the Promised Land of milk and honey, making them conquerors over its present occupants so that it will be their own land. In return, they agree to follow his commandments, foremost that "you shall have no other gods before me" (20:3). This clearly affirms Yahweh as the prime deity for Israel but does not imply monotheism with the exactitude of the Koran's, "There is no god but Allah." Indeed, nothing in Exodus precludes the existence of other gods for other peoples, or of subsidiary gods below Yahweh for Israel.

After the elders of Israel pledge obedience to Yahweh, Moses goes up on the fiery mountain for forty days and nights, and there God writes with his finger the covenant's commandments on two tablets of stone. Also God gives lengthy instructions for the Israelites to build a large portable tabernacle in which Yahweh will dwell among them, and a holy ark of acacia wood and gold that will hold the stone tables and reside in the tabernacle.[3] Yahweh designates Aaron and his sons to serve as a hereditary priesthood (kohanim), administering the tabernacle and the Ark of the Covenant, and making ritual offerings, animal and vegetable.

Moses stays so long on the mountain that the Israelites left below lose faith. They gather around Aaron, urging, "Come, make gods for us; as for this Moses, the man who brought us up out of the land of Egypt, we do not know what has become of him." Aaron complies, gathering gold from the people and molding from it a calf. Building an altar before it, Aaron offers burnt offerings while the Israelites worship the calf and revel in paganism (Ex 32).

Yahweh is angered by the people's perversity and intends to destroy them until Moses dissuades him. But when Moses descends the mountain and sees the calf, he breaks the tablets in his rage, burns the calf, grinds it into power, mixes it with water, and makes the Israelites drink it. Aaron offers the lamest of excuses—They asked me for a god, so I made them one – which does not assuage his brother.

> Moses stood in the gate of the camp, and said, "Who is on Yahweh's side? Come to me!" And all the sons of Levi [Moses's tribe] gathered around him. He said to them, "Thus says Yahweh, the God of Israel, 'Put your sword on your side, each of you! Go back and forth from gate to gate throughout the camp, and each of you kill your brother, your friend, and your neighbor.'" The sons of Levi did as Moses commanded, and about three thousand of the people fell on that day. Moses said, "Today you have ordained yourselves for the service of Yahweh, each one at the cost of a son or a brother, and so have brought a blessing on yourself this day" (Ex 32).[4]

Yahweh sent a plague on the people who made the calf but survived the massacre. It is not stated if Aaron was stricken, but if so he survived. Moses returned to the mountain and obtained duplicate tablets. The ark and tabernacle were constructed. Yahweh came to dwell in the tabernacle, among the Israelites, and they continued their wandering.

Across Jordan

The Torah ends with Moses's death at the age of 120, his sight unimpaired and his vigor unabated. But his job was finished. He had led the squabbling Israelites from slavery through a forty-year transformation into a powerful and disciplined nation of nomadic warriors. Yahweh too had evolved into "the Lord of Hosts," the god of armies. This conversion was essential because the land of milk and honey promised to the patriarchs was already settled. There were Canaanites, Amorites, Hittites, Perizzites, Hivites, and Jebusites. As worshipers of idols and lesser gods, they had no property rights. Yahweh instructed Moses,

> Speak to the Israelites, and say to them: When you cross over the Jordan into the land of Canaan, you shall drive out all the inhabitants of the land from before you, destroy all their figured stones, destroy all their cast images, and demolish all their

high places. You shall take possession of the land and settle in it, for I have given you the land to possess.... But if you do not drive out the inhabitants of the land from before you, then those whom you let remain shall be as barbs in your eyes and thorns in your sides; they shall trouble you in the land where you are settling (Num 33:51-55).

On the eve of invasion, Moses went up from the plains of Moab to Mount Nebo, across the Jordan River from Jericho, where he could look over the Promised Land. "I have let you see it with your eyes," said Yahweh, "but you shall not cross over there." Then, at God's command, Moses died. "He was buried in a valley in the land of Moab, opposite Bewth-poer, but no one knows his burial place to this day" (Deut 34). The Israelites wept and mourned him for thirty days. Then Joshua, whom Moses had laid his hands on as successor, crossed the Jordan with his army.

Notes

1. Friedman (2003) attributes some of this passage to E rather than J. The distinction is unimportant here.
2. The Israelites are told to mark their doorposts with the blood of a lamb. When Yahweh goes through Egypt to strike down every firstborn, he will pass over the houses marked with blood. Hence the name Passover for the Jewish holiday celebrating the exodus.
3. According to Steven Spielberg's *Raiders of the Lost Ark*, the ark still survives, now packed in an unmarked wooden crate and stored in a huge government warehouse.
4. The story of the golden calf, unflattering to Aaron and his priestly descendants, does not appear in the P document. The P version emphasizes the loyalty of the Levites and, to readers not appalled by the slaughter, enhances their status (see Chapter 5).

8

Who Wrote the Torah?

Moses is traditionally regarded the sole author of all five books of the Torah/Pentateuch. To the objection that Moses would not have known of events before the existence of humans, or that he could not have described his own burial, one may respond that he was divinely informed. If so, it is difficult to account for contradictions in the text and the inclusion of older polytheistic myths.

Excepting fundamentalist Christians and some Orthodox Jews, there is broad agreement that the writings traditionally attributed to Moses comprise multiple contributions by different authors (Blenkinsopp 1992; Nicholson 1998). Moses, if he actually existed, may not have contributed anything to the corpus. On the other hand, he could have been a real person and the source of traditions that were eventually incorporated into the Scriptures. If so, the question remains, who wrote the Torah, or more specifically, who wrote the different source documents?

In *The Book of J*, Professor Harold Bloom, an eminent and provocative humanist at Yale University, imagines that J, the Yawist, was a great lady of post-Solomonic court circles, herself a descendant of King David, who began her writing in the late years of King Solomon's reign, around 930 BCE , in close rapport with her good friend the Court Historian, who wrote most of what we now call 2 Samuel (Bloom and Rosenberg 1990: 19). Bloom admits that his details are fiction, but he makes a plausible case. Other scholars, without stepping so far off the edge, have complied sufficient clues to draw a more believable if less detailed picture of Torah authorship.

The Documentary Hypothesis

The notion that the Torah is a compilation of texts by different authors is called the Documentary Hypothesis and has been debated and developed by biblical scholars for two centuries. I depend heavily on the recent treatment by Richard Friedman (2003), who has cogently assembled the largest collection of evidence in one place. Friedman's picture is widely accepted in its broad lines, if not in all details (also see Friedman 1992).

Some source documents, incorporating earlier traditions and myths, may have been written and edited as early as the tenth century BCE when the Israelites lived in a united kingdom under the biblical monarchs Saul, David, and Solomon. King David made Jerusalem his capital, and it was there, according to the Bible, that his son Solomon built the great Temple. Jerusalem eventually developed a court of sufficient literacy for the compilation of history, the codification of law, and the composition of poetry.

After Solomon's death, the realm split in two, its northern portion becoming the Kingdom of Israel. The southern portion, including Jerusalem and the Temple, became the Kingdom of Judah. The two kingdoms coexisted from the tenth to eighth centuries, their relations often antagonistic.

Friedman, like Bloom and many other scholars, places authorship of the Yahwist or J document in the southern kingdom of Judah. J tells the stories of Adam and Eve, Noah, the tower of Babel (Babylon), of Abraham, Isaac, Jacob and Joseph, and of Moses, the exodus from Egypt, the Ten Commandments at Mount Sinai, and wandering through the wilderness toward the Promised Land.

There is less agreement about another source, the Elohist or E text, regarded by Friedman and others to have been written about the same time but in the northern kingdom of Israel. It refers to God by the generic term *Elohim* until the stories of Moses and then begins to use Yahweh. This is because, according to E, the personal name Yahweh was not known until God revealed it to Moses. The E document does not tell of the creation or the flood, perhaps because its early part is missing. It begins with Abraham and continues through Moses, the plagues, the exodus, the revelation at the mountain, and traveling through the wilderness. J and E are often parallel, indicating that they derive from a common oral tradition or possibly an earlier written document. However, there are clear differences in terminology and content. The story of Sodom and Gomorrah appears in J but not in E. The near sacrifice of Isaac and the story of the golden calf are in E but not in J. Apparently both texts coexisted in the southern kingdom and were there merged into a document called JE. I have not distinguished J from E in prior chapters, printing both in boldface.

In about 720 BCE the Assyrian empire destroyed the northern kingdom of Israel, and we hear no more of its residents. Folklore refers to these dispersed people as the Ten Lost Tribes of Israel. Subsequent history is of the residents of Judah, so the remaining Israelites are called Jews. JE shows no awareness of the Assyrian catastrophe or of the dispersion of the northern tribes, an indication that it was completed prior to that time.

The Priestly document or P postdates JE and was produced by the Jerusalem priesthood as a version more favorable than JE to Aaron's priestly lineage. (For instance, JE identifies Aaron as the maker of the golden calf; P does not.) P describes the exacting methods whereby the Aaronid priests made ritual sacrifices of animals and crops to God. It is a clear reminder that ancient Judaism, with its focus on burnt offerings to Yahweh, made by a hereditary priesthood, was far different from "modern" Judaism of the past two thousand years, which is institutionally based on non-hereditary rabbis (teachers), Torah and Talmudic instruction, and daily prayer at a synagogue by a *minyan* of at least ten men.[1]

P's stories parallel those in JE in both content and order, including the creation, the flood, etc. It gives far more attention than JE to laws, genealogies, numbers (ages, dates, measurements) and priestly duties. Some of P's instructions for religious practice are meaningless outside the local setting—for example, stating prices in shekels. P occupies half the books of Exodus and Numbers and nearly all of Leviticus. Unlike JE, much of P is intensely boring.

The final major source is called D because it largely coincides with the book of Deuteronomy, a name derived from the Greek term *deuteros* ("second" or "copy") and *nomos* ("law"). It comprises law, Moses's farewell speech, and his last acts, including his death and burial. D reprises portions from the other sources.

> It is of decisive importance to recognize that in the book of Deuteronomy we have the voice of a tradition that is completely contrasted to the Priestly voice by which we have thus far been addressed in the Pentateuch. Consequently the...Torah is constituted in two distinct literary units: Genesis-Numbers as the *voice of the Priestly tradition* and Deuteronomy as the *voice of the Deuteronomic tradition*. These two quite distinct literary units reflect two quite different interpretive voices in Israel that articulate quite contrasting theological intentionalities (Brueggemann 2003: 86).

Deuteronomy uses terminology that is distinctively different from P or JE. Theologically, it most expressly condemns the worship of other gods and gives a new view of Yahweh as completely transcendent. Whereas earlier sources encouraged or at least tolerated sacrifices in diverse places, Deuteronomy absolutely forbids sacrificial worship anywhere but the Temple in Jerusalem. Scholars have long recognized Deuteronomy's disconnect from the first four books, and its intimate connection to the books that immediately follow the Torah: Joshua, Judges, 1 and 2 Samuel, and 1 and 2 Kings. These latter books are so close to Deuteronomy linguistically and theologically that they are called, collectively, the "Deuteronomistic History" and regarded as a second great literary work, apart from Genesis-to-Numbers. The Deuteronomistic History describes the people, events, and laws of Israel from the beginning of the conquest of Canaan, through the establishment of monarchies, to the destruction of Jerusalem and the Temple by Babylonia in 586 BCE .

The major sources, JE, P and D, were combined with minor sources by an editor or editors (called the Redactor). Perhaps the Torah that Ezra is reported to have read in the 5th century BCE was complete, and Ezra himself, or someone near him, was the final redactor. It is fairly certain that the Torah existed in essentially its present form before the 3rd century BCE though no copy close to that age is extant. This is inferred from the similarity of the Samaritan Pentateuch and the Hellenistic Septuagint to the Jewish Torah, indicating their derivation from a common pre-existing document.[2]

Parsing Documents

The primary evidence for multiple authorship and for identifying component documents consists first of the Torah's large number of doublets; there are over thirty instances where two variations of the same story appear. Second, there are extensive terminological differences in different passages (e.g., the deity is called Yahweh in some passages, God in others). More importantly, the terminological differences fall consistently into one or another group of doublets. Lining up the corresponding doublets– i.e., the Yahweh version of creation with the Yahweh version of the flood, the God version of creation with the God version of the flood, etc. – produces a sensible narrative flow, though sometimes containing gaps. Nearly all of the many contradictions within the Torah fall along the same lines identified by doublets and terminology. For example, in J the deity limits the human life span to 120 years (Gen 6:3), but in P many later people are reported to have lived longer (Gen 9:29; 11:10-23). Each source document, as it has been reconstructed, is consistent within itself. Contradictions are produced by juxtaposing different sources.

Professor Bloom regards J as one of the masters of world literature and believes her passages can be identified from her superior writing style. Even casual readers will appreciate the bard-like story telling quality of the J document, once it stands alone (see *The Book of J* [Rosenberg and Bloom 1990]), especially when compared to some of the numbing passages in the Priestly document. Professor Friedman (1992, 2003) eschews such subjective stylistic differences, preferring straightforward tabulations of easily countable markers to distinguish one document from another. D uses terminology that is blatantly different from the other sources.

Of course there are ambiguities and controversial aspects of any parsing, especially for brief or transitional passages without overt clues. Furthermore, the editing of the Redactor(s) may have blurred what once were clearer boundaries between documents. Friedman's (2003) fully parsed Torah with supporting evidence gives a good picture of current scholarship and allows readers to judge for themselves the adequacy of deconstruction.

Written Hebrew evolved during the first millennium BCE . Friedman suggests that the writing of JE comes from the earliest stage of biblical Hebrew, while P and D use later language. This linguistic differentiation is controversial, but from other clues there is wide agreement that JE is older than P or D.

The kingdom of Judah remained in existence for more than a century after the Assyrian empire crushed the northern kingdom. By then Babylon had wrested control from the Assyrians. In 586 BCE the Babylonians sacked Jerusalem and destroyed the Temple. King Nebuchadnezzar brought some of the city's most prominent citizens back to Babylon, commencing a fifty or sixty year exile. The Old Testament book of Ezekiel, written during the Babylonian exile, uses Hebrew that Friedman claims is more recent than any of the Torah's source documents. This suggests that all the source documents, if not the final editing, were available at the time of the exile. Other scholars believe that D or parts of P were written during the exile.

When the source documents are read separately, each contains hints of its provenance. For example, many associations exist between J and the Court History of David, which occupies nearly all of 2 Samuel. Possibly these documents were written by the same author or, as Professor Bloom imagines, "J was in close rapport with her good friend the Court Historian." In any case, J seems closely connected to the court in Jerusalem, the capital of Judah, suggesting this was the site of authorship. Jacob's son Judah – eponymous progenitor of the southern kingdom of Judah– is a significant (and positive) figure in J and only in J.

I have already noted the reason that a priest or priests from Aaron's lineage is thought to have authored P. It justifies in many ways Aaron's male descendants as the only legitimate priesthood and the sole access to the deity.

> In all the stories in P, there are no mentions of dreams, of angels, or talking animals, though these things occur in J, E, and D. As for human leaders: the words "prophet" and "prophesy" occur thirteen times in E and D, but not in P (or J). The single exceptional occurrence of the word "prophet" in P (Exod 7:1) uses the word figuratively, and it refers to the High Priest Aaron himself! Judges, too, are never mentioned in P (as opposed to D, which says: go to the priests *and the judges* in matters of law). In P, only the Aaronid priests have access to the Urim and Tummim [i.e., sacred devices]. In P, all other, non-Aaronid Levites are not priests. [In D, all male Levites are priests, not just Aaron's line.] In P, atonement for sin is to be achieved only by means of sacrifices that are brought to the Aaronid priests. It is not achieved by mere repentance or through divine mercy (Friedman 2003: 12).

My brief discussion of source documents barely touches the evidence used to parse the Torah and to suggest authorship. I emphasize the hypothetical nature of sources J, E, P and D. There is no extant version of any of these putative texts. If one is ever discovered, it would be an archeological find far more spectacular than the Dead Sea Scrolls.

The Character of God

Different passages of the Old Testament portray the actions, speeches, and appearance of the Israelite deity in dissimilar ways. Sometimes he interacts with humans as if he were a man, even appearing physically as a man. Yahweh makes mistakes, he grieves, he barters, he gets jealous and angry, and he pampers his favorites. At other times God is an impersonal transcendent force, building the universe, creating day and night, breathing life into humankind. Sometimes he is merciful, gracious, and patient, sometimes vengeful and lusting for blood.

J in particular portrays Yahweh as a manlike deity, someone who can be talked to and argued with, who makes errors, changes his mind, acts rashly and later regrets his actions – hardly a picture of infallibility. Later sources, P and D, present a more impervious, less emotional, less anthropomorphic deity. We can hardly escape the conclusion that different authors conceived of the deity differently, and that the god concept evolved during the centuries that the Torah and its parts were composed.

While some of God's moral principles seem paradigmatically just and humane, others are parochial and difficult to reconcile with modern sensibilities. One that today seems especially unfair is Yahweh's continual application of collective guilt, beginning in the Garden of Eden where all humans still unborn are punished for Adam and Eve's disobedience. At Sodom and in the flood, all infants are destroyed with those who were overtly wicked. All the firstborns of Egypt die because of the pharaoh's intransigence (which itself was due to God's hardening of Pharaoh's heart).

Torah law is repeatedly premised on collective guilt, punishing people who personally committed no offense but are related to someone who did:

> I Yahweh am a jealous God, punishing children for the iniquity of parents, to the third and fourth generation of those who reject me (Ex 20:5).

> Those born of an illicit union shall not be admitted to the assembly of Yahweh. Even to the tenth generation, none of their descendants shall be admitted....

> No Ammonite or Moabite shall be admitted to the assembly of Yahweh. Even to the tenth generation, none of their descendants shall be admitted (Deut 23).

If scoundrels in a town are leading inhabitants to worship other gods, "you shall put the inhabitants of that town to the sword, utterly destroying it and everything in it – even putting its livestock to the sword. All of its spoil you shall gather into its public square; then burn the town and all its spoil with fire, as a whole burnt offering to Yahweh" (Deut 13).[3]

In waging war, Yahweh makes little distinction between combatants and noncombatants. When King Sihon was unwilling to let the Israelites pass through his land (because Yahweh had "hardened his spirit and made his heart defiant"), the invaders "captured all his towns, and in each town we utterly destroyed men, women, and children. We left not a single survivor. Only the livestock we kept as spoil for ourselves, as well as the plunder of the towns that we had captured... Yahweh gave everything to us." Next, at God's behest, the Israelites slaughtered all the people of Bashan (Deut 2-3).

To execute Yahweh's vengeance, Moses sent his army of twelve thousand men against the Midianites, his wife Ziporah's people, killing every male.

> The Israelites took the women of Midian and their little ones captive; and they took all their cattle, their flocks, and all their goods as booty, both people and animals....

> Moses, Eleazar the priest, and all the leaders of the congregation went to meet them outside the camp. Moses became angry with the officers of the army... "Have you allowed all the women to live? These women here, on Balaam's advice, made the Israelites act treacherously against Yahweh.... Now therefore, kill every male among the little ones, and kill every woman who has known a man by sleeping with him. But all the young girls who have not known a man by sleeping with him, keep alive for yourselves (Num 31).

Regarding sexual inequality, Yahweh appraises males as more valu-
able than females, in one passage assigning a worth of fifty shekels of
silver to men of ages twenty to sixty years, while women of the same age
are worth thirty shekels. From age five to twenty, boys are appraised at
twenty shekels, girls at ten (Lev 27). Here are Yahweh's guidelines for
the treatment of females captured in war:

> Suppose you see among the captives a beautiful woman whom you desire and want
> to marry, and so you bring her home to your house: she shall shave her head, pare
> her nails, discard her captive's garb, and shall remain in your house a full month,
> mourning for her father and mother; after that you may go in to her and be her hus-
> band, and she shall be your wife. But if you are not satisfied with her, you shall let
> her go free and not sell her for money. You must not treat her as a slave, since you
> have dishonored her (Deut 21).

If a man marries, then learns that his wife is not a virgin and hates
her for the deception, the men of her town shall stone her to death at the
entrance to her father's house (Deut 22). If a widow has no son, her brother-
in-law has the right and obligation to inseminate her (Deut 25). If brothers
are fighting, and one's wife, in coming to her husband's aid, touches her
brother-in-law's genitals, her hand shall be cut off (Deut 25:11).

In some instances there is equality of treatment. Both participants in
an act of adultery shall be put to death (Deut 22:22). If a betrothed virgin
copulates with another man, both shall be stoned to death (D22:24). If a
man has sex with a wife and her mother, all three shall be burned to death
(L20:14). If a man or woman has intercourse with an animal, both the
human and the animal are put to death (Lev 20:15-16). Both men engaged
in homosexual copulation shall be put to death (Lev 20: 13).

Yahweh is a jealous god, highly intolerant of other religions. "You
must demolish completely all the places where the nations whom you
are about to dispossess served their gods, on the mountain heights, on
the hills, and under every leafy tree. Break down their altars, smash their
pillars, burn their sacred poles with fire, and hew down the idols of their
gods, and thus blot out their name from their places" (Deut 12:2-3). Not
only must all idols be destroyed, but all idolaters and anyone tempting
the worship of other gods, as well as the entire town from which they
come (Deut 13, 20:16).

Yahweh is particularly concerned with the purity of his priests, the
male descendants of Aaron, and of their close relatives. The daughter
of a priest who becomes desecrated, who whores, should be burned to
death. The senior priest should "take" only a woman in her virginity, not
a widow, a divorcee, or a prostitute. Yahweh, valuing perfection in those
who serve him, is biased against those disabled and diseased: a priest

who is injured, blind, crippled, deformed, or a leper cannot make burnt offerings (Lev 21).

Some of the punishments prescribed in the Torah seem by today's standards excessive, cruel, or unusual. Anyone striking or cursing their parent shall be put to death (Ex 21:15, 17). Anyone who profanes Yahweh's name shall be put to death (Lev 24:16). Those who repeatedly disobey God's commandments and violate his laws are to eat the flesh of their children (Lev 26:29). A woman believed to be a sorceress shall not be permitted to live (Ex 22:17).

Other important examples of outdated morality are the advocacy or at least permissibility of monarchy by divine right, of polygamy and concubinage, of taking by conquest other people's land, and of slavery.[4] Could anyone run for the U.S. presidency on this platform?

The Torah prior to Deuteronomy is inferentially monotheistic, picturing God as the sole creator of the universe and of all life, then the destroyer of virtually all land life with a worldwide flood, and the differentiation of humankind into diverse language groups. God picks Abraham's line (through Jacob/Israel) as his chosen people. No reason is given for this choice, and the Torah makes amply clear that the Israelites do not always deserve the honor. Nonetheless God, in a series of covenants, reaffirms this special relationship, most importantly at Mount Sinai (or Horeb) where the Israelites are commanded to worship no other god. But that is not the same as saying there *are* no other gods for other people. Virtually all of the Torah makes sense on the supposition that one particularly powerful deity has a special relationship with the Israelites, while lesser gods have relations with other groups.

Certainly God has influence over non-Israelites, as in his ability to harden the pharaoh's heart, but the Israelites are also subject to counter-influences, as in the golden calf story and the many times they are tempted to follow other gods. The pharaoh's magicians have wondrous power from some unstated source to replicate the first plagues. One might infer from God's harsh treatment of the Israelites' enemies and their idols that dominance contests are being settled between gods as well as between peoples.

The story in which "sons of God" mate with women (Gen 6) seems to contradict monotheism. Another apparent contradiction is Yahweh's declaration to Moses that when passing in the night through Egypt to strike down all the firstborn, then too, "on all the gods of Egypt I will execute judgments" (Ex 12:12). What meaning does this have if there are no other gods?

Not until Deuteronomy are there unambiguous statements that Yahweh is not only the most powerful of gods but the only god. In this final book of the Torah, Moses says in his farewell speech, "Yahweh is God; there is no other besides him." A few sentences later is a similar statement: "Yahweh is God in heaven above and on earth beneath; there is no other" (Deut 4:35, 39). Two verses later is the primary vow of Judaism, the *Shema*: "Hear, O Israel: Yahweh is our God, Yahweh is one" (Deut 6:4).

Yet even in Deuteronomy we find other statements that confuse the issue. In 3:23 Moses entreats Yahweh, "What god in heaven or on earth can perform deeds and mighty acts like yours!" In 10:17 Moses tells his people, "Yahweh your God is God of gods and Lord of lords, the great God, mighty and awesome..." In 29:17 Moses wonders if there is among the Israelites someone "whose heart is already turning away from Yahweh our God to serve the gods of those [other] nations."

It is unclear when the singular deity became an established notion among the Israelite elite, but it was not there at the outset. According to 1 and 2 Kings, when Solomon built his Temple to Yahweh in Jerusalem, he also consecrated shrines to Yahweh's subordinates, Ashtoret, Milkom, and Chemosh. The prophet Hosea, writing in the eighth century BCE , contrasts Israel's Yahweh with subordinate deities (Metzger and Coogan 1993: 526)

The idea that Yahweh alone ruled everyone, not just the Israelites, seems to have become firmly established by the time of the Babylonian exile. In the book of Isaiah, the Assyrians and Babylonians are God's instruments for punishing the wayward Israelites; while Cyrus of Persia, who conquered Babylon in 539 BCE and let the Jewish exiles return to Jerusalem, is Yahweh's instrument of redemption (Anderson 1966: 413; Brueggemann 2003: 159-175). Thus, by the sixth century if not earlier, all peoples are controlled by the one and only deity. The text in Isaiah is unequivocal: "Thus says Yahweh, the King of Israel and his Redeemer, the LORD of hosts: I am the first and I am the last; besides me there is no god" (44:6).

Christians would carry this singular God into their own religion, though with the paradoxical twist that the One is really three, a concept that is undecipherable to non-Christians. Centuries later, Muslims reverted to the singular formulation with the vow, "There is no god but Allah," replacing Moses with Muhammad as the central prophet.

Conclusion

One need not accept all or any of the Documentary Hypothesis to see that parts of the Torah/Pentateuch are implausible on their face. The text is rife with factual contradictions, logical inconsistencies, and preposterous claims. Its morality, derived from the ancient Middle East, is not fully acceptable in the contemporary West.

Today in the United States we see creationism juxtaposed against evolution in a culture war to determine what will be taught in the science classes of our schools. The opposition of science to religion is gratuitous. We require no knowledge of evolution to see the falsity of the Bible's picture of creation; the evidence is in the Bible itself. Either birds were created before the first human, as in Genesis 1, or birds were created after the first human, as in Genesis 2. It cannot be both ways.[5]

I have presented nothing that renders implausible the belief in a god or gods as the ultimate creator of life. Nothing here undermines the broadest precepts of the Abrahamic religions. What is implausible is the literal truth of the entire Bible as written. Of course religious faith is an individual matter, but when it becomes the criterion for public policy, then it demands broader attention and evaluation.

There is no point throwing out the baby with the biblical bath water. What we require is some reasonable discrimination, consistent with modern knowledge and public taste, between moral principles in the Pentateuch that are still worthy and those that should be rejected as archaic and inhumane. Collective guilt, slavery, sexual inequality, monarchy, polygamy and concubinage—all upheld in the Bible—are no longer tolerable in the West.

We must also discriminate among ostensibly factual claims. Which biblical events are likely true and which are false or unverifiable? There has been no worldwide flood in the past 6,000 years. But was there an Israelite exodus from Egypt?

Notes

1. Biblical scholars have long recognized that practices in Hebrew antiquity did not even correspond with Mosaic law, implying that the law was formulated after the period of monarchy (Nicholson 1998). For example, one of Deuteronomy's main demands is the centralization of sacrificial worship, but Samuel, Saul, David, and Solomon knew nothing of this, judging from their practices. Samuel's reluctance to allow a monarchy is incomprehensible in the face of Deuteronomy's law of kingship (17:14-20).

2. The Samaritans, an offshoot of Judaism, are mentioned in the Bible and still exist. The Samaritan Pentateuch is the entire canon of the Samaritan community (Waltke 1992). Septuagint is the traditional term for translations of the Hebrew Bible into Greek, a practice usually dated to the 3rd century BCE (Metzger and Coogan 1993).

3. The 6th-seventhth century BCE prophet Jeremiah seems to refute the principle of collective guilt in the metaphorical passage 31:29-30.

4.   Exodus 21 has guidelines for selling one's daughter as a slave.
5.   I write this fully aware that intransigent minds can always find a loophole: Perhaps birds were destroyed after Genesis 1 and then created anew in the presence of Adam.

9

Archaeological Evidence

The *Weekly World News* reported in 2000 that Adam and Eve's skeletons had been discovered in Syria. A rib, missing from the male skeleton, was found grafted to the female's spine. Twenty-five yards away were petrified fragments of an apple tree (February 22: 46-47). A similar story ran in the supermarket tabloid four years later. This time the "perfectly preserved" couple was discovered in the Iraqi desert. A photograph shows mummy-like corpses with full heads of hair nestled together as if in slumber (October 17, 2004:1).

I envision the writers for the *Weekly World News* fashioning their stories late at night over pizza and beer. Occasionally they report the discovery of Noah's ark, most recently in North Korea:

> According to archaeologist Martin Bemis, reports reaching the West reveal that the 5,000-year-old Ark, resting on a barren mountainside, is largely intact, though roofless.... When word of the Ark's appearance on the Korean peninsula reached Bemis, the archaeologist rushed to Pyongyang..., only to be told that [dictator Kim Jong Il] had placed the Ark under around-the-clock armored guard. Bemis was then given 24 hours to get out of the country. Reports already reaching Washington warn that Kim Jong Il, desperate and deranged, is threatening to blow up the Ark unless his demands [for trade concessions and financial aid from the United States] are met (June 15, 2005).

Some consumers of the *WWN* believe its hilarious nonsense (Lehnert and Perpich 1982). The most impressive evidence of reader gullibility is the tabloid's advertisements on astrology, pyramid power, biorhythms, diverse religious charms that bring instant luck, and $3 watches. These ads, not inexpensive, must be worthwhile because they appear issue after issue.

A more credible source, BBC News, reported in 2004 that American and Turkish explorers were hoping to discover traces of Noah's Ark on the slopes of Mount Ararat in eastern Turkey. Project leader Daniel McGivern, a businessman and Christian activist who—unlike Martin

Bemis—really exists, announced at a press conference that satellite pictures taken the prior summer reveal the ark's final resting place, now exposed by melting snow (April 27). *National Geographic* magazine quotes McGivern's assurance: "In one [satellite] image we saw the beams, saw the wood. I'm convinced that the excavation of the object and the results of tests run on any collected samples will prove that it is Noah's ark" (April 27, 2004).[1]

Despite its newsworthiness, there is little point in evaluating the veracity of biblical events until we reach the patriarchs. As Richard Friedman comments,

> For the book of Genesis, the primeval history is barely capable of being considered from the point of view of historicity, given its conception of a finite universe surrounded by water, a talking snake, "sons of God(s)" having relations with human women, a box [ark] containing the whole of animal life, and simultaneous creation of languages (2002: 620).

Unearthing the Bible

In the nineteenth-century scholars first looked to the landscape of ancient Israel for verification of events described in the Bible. They were encouraged by the presence of sites mentioned in the Old Testament. Beside places still occupied like Jerusalem, Hebron, Jaffa, Jericho and Gaza, they identified specific ruins with Gibeon, Bethel, Shiloh, and other biblical locales. Eventually archaeologists made marvelous excavations at Megiddo, Hazor, and elsewhere.

More important than specific sites was a growing understanding of the broader biblical arena during the first and second millennia BCE . Canaan, because of its placement between the Mediterranean and the desert, was part of a natural corridor between Egypt and Mesopotamia, two of the greatest and most literate of ancient civilizations. When the Frenchman Jean-François Champollion deciphered Egyptian hieroglyphics in the 1820s, using the Rosetta Stone as his key, he opened a wealth of documentation about the pharaohs and their affairs. A victory stele erected for Pharaoh Merneptah in 1207 BCE told of a triumph over a people named Israel. A triumphal inscription commissioned for the temple at Karnak by a later pharaoh, Sheshonq I (reigning 945 to 924 BCE), tells of his razing about 150 Canaanite towns. This pharaoh is identified with the Shishak who demanded tribute from Solomon's son in 1 Kings (14:25-26), a passage that is the earliest known correspondence between biblical text and external historical records (Finkelstein and Silberman 2001: 161).

In Mesopotamia archaeologists uncovered the cities and cuneiform archives of Assyria and Babylonia, where ancient scribes mentioned monarchs of the kingdoms of Israel and Judah. Most importantly, the long and detailed records of Mesopotamia and Egypt provided an accurate chronology for the entire Near East, allowing a correlation of events and kings recorded in different regions.

"Not since ancient times has the world of the Bible been so accessible and so thoroughly explored...We now know what crops the Israelites and their neighbors grew, what they ate, how they built their cities, and with whom they traded...Modern excavation methods and a wide range of laboratory tests have been used to date and analyze the civilizations of the ancient Israelites and their neighbors the Philistines, Phoenicians, Arameans, Ammonites, Moabites, and Edomites" (Finkelstein and Silberman 2001: 5).[2] By the beginning of the twenty-first century, archaeologists had shown enough correspondences with the Bible to conclude that its narrative was not wholly fanciful. But there were too many contradictions to suggest that the history was precise.

Patriarchs

Abraham is said to have lived some 4,000 years ago in the city of Ur in southern Mesopotamia. He resettled in Haran on a tributary of the Euphrates, and then wandered into Canaan with his flocks, moving among Shechem, Bethel, and Hebron. He lived in the vicinity of Sodom and Gomorrah at the time of their destruction. His son Isaac lived near Beersheba in the Negev desert. Isaac's son Jacob lived in some of the same Canaanite locations before moving to Egypt. Most of these are known sites and can be placed on the map (though not Sodom and Gomorrah). The pastoral lifestyle of the patriarchs seemed consistent with bedouin habits.

But the peoples, places, and dates do not fit together. The Philistines whom Isaac encountered (Gen 26:1) did not establish settlements along the coastal plane of Canaan until after 1200 BCE . The Arameans who are important in the stories of Jacob's marriages to Leah and Rachel are not recognizable as an ethnic group before 1100 BCE . Edom is also too late for its biblical setting. Genesis shows familiarity with the Assyrian and Babylonian empires, which long postdate the patriarchal period.

Stories of the patriarchs frequently mention camels as herd property or beasts of burden, but historical and archaeological evidence shows that camels were not widely used in the Near East before 1000 BCE (Köhler-Rollefson 1996: 287). The camel caravan said to have brought Joseph to

Egypt carried "gum, balm, and myrrh," all major products of the Arabian caravan trade that flourished under the Assyrians in the eighth to seventh centuries BCE (Finkelstein and Silberman 2002). These anachronisms reflect the time the stories were written, not a thousand years earlier when the events were said to have occurred.

Exodus from Egypt

Archaeologists trace Egyptian society back seven millennia (Rice 2003), placing its origins a thousand years before the biblical creation of the universe. Hieroglyphs were in use by 3100 BCE . In another century separate societies along the upper and lower Nile were unified under a single pharaoh.

Egypt's long-following dynastic history is divided into the Old, Middle, and New kingdoms, each a centuries-long period during which the nation was unified and strong. The kingdoms are separated by intermediate periods when the polity was again divided or under foreign rule. The great pyramids were built during the Old Kingdom, lasting from the twenty-sixth to the twenty-second century. This was a golden age, setting patterns in religion, government, and art that lasted until ancient Egypt's final decline in the first millennium BCE . Noah's flood occurred midway through the Old Kingdom but caused no apparent disruption.

We need not dwell on the Middle Kingdom except to say that it ended in the 18th century when invaders from Canaan, called the Hyksos, conquered Egypt with a new military technology, the horse-drawn chariot. The Hyksos occupied the Nile Delta (biblical Goshen) and ruled for about two centuries before being overthrown. Scholars once identified the Hyksos as the Israelites, and their expulsion with the biblical exodus. Today this notion is generally dismissed. First, the Hyksos were rulers, not slaves. The timing of their entry into Egypt and the duration of their presence do not conform to biblical chronology. Also, there is no archeological evidence of subsequent Hyksos migration to Canaan (Finkelstein and Silberman 2001).

The Israelites' entry into Egypt, their enslavement, the plagues, and finally the exodus – all these events are usually placed in the New Kingdom (sixteenth to eleventh century BCE). Although "the Pharaoh" of Exodus is not named, he is often identified with the powerful Rameses II because Exodus 1:11 states that the Israelites "built supply cities, Pithom and Rameses, for Pharaoh." Egyptian sources attribute the city of Pi-Rameses (House of Rameses) to Rameses II, who ruled 1279-1213 BCE .

This nomination is consistent with the earliest mention of Israel outside the Bible, on the stele mentioned previously, which describes a victory by Pharaoh Merneptah, the son of Rameses II. The inscription, dated 1207 BCE, says that Merneptah destroyed a people named Israel in Canaan (Frerichs and Lesko 1997). By placing Israelites in the Promised Land at that time, the stele fortifies a thirteenth-century date for the exodus.

Unfortunately the Bible is inconsistent on this dating. According to 1 Kings 6:1, the construction of the Temple began in the fourth year of Solomon's reign, 480 years after the exodus. Correlating the dates of Israelite kings with Egyptian and Assyrian sources places the exodus around 1440 BCE, still too late for the Hyksos but too early for Rameses II (or for Rameses I who ruled for a year or two near the beginning of the thirteenth century). Despite 1 Kings, Rameses II is usually favored as the adversary of Moses.

Whichever date is preferred, we come to the major archaeological problem with the exodus. There is no sign of it in Egyptian sources or anywhere else outside the Bible (Dever 1997). One cannot shrug this off, as we can the lack of any mention of the patriarchs. Egyptian sources are abundant from the New Kingdom. How could they totally ignore a million or more slaves fleeing Egypt, the killing of all firstborn in the land, and the destruction of the Egyptian army at the Red Sea? Yet these spectacular events caused no ripple in Egyptian writings.

The Israelites wandered in the wilderness of Sinai for forty years, living on manna and moving between oases. But repeated archaeological surveys of the Sinai reveal no trace of a large group of people in the thirteenth century. They camped for about a year near a mountain with volcanic manifestations, sometimes called Sinai, sometimes Horeb, where Moses twice received from Yahweh the Ten Commandments, but its location is unknown.[3] For thirty-eight years the encampment was at Kadesh-barnea, identified by archaeologists with the large and well-watered oasis of Ein el-Qudeirat in eastern Sinai. Excavations and surveys there show no human remnants from that time, "not even a single shred left by a tiny fleeing band of frightened refugees" (Finkelstein and Silberman 2001: 63).

During their wanderings, the Israelites are said to have encountered peoples or cities in the Negev. Archaeologists have found remains of habitations from earlier and later times, but the Negev was uninhabited during the thirteenth century. The same is true east of the Jordan River where the Israelites are said to have battled Amorites at the city of Heshbon. There was not even a small village at Heshbon in the thirteenth century, nor was there an Edom at that time. William Ward succinctly commented about the exodus, "there is not a word in a text or an archaeological artifact that lends credence to the biblical narrative as it now stands" (1997: 105).

That does not mean that the story must be totally rejected. Some evidence indirectly supports the biblical account (Hoffmier 1997). The Nile's annual flooding is a more reliable source of irrigation than rainfall in Canaan, beckoning hungry migrants during times of famine or drought. There is ample evidence that people moved between Canaan and the Nile Delta, consistent with the migration of Jacob's family to Egypt. Some foreigners attained high positions in Egyptian government, consistent with Joseph's assent. Canaanites sometimes worked in the delta as slaves. Possibly a Moses led some Israelites out of slavery in Egypt, but if so it was on a far smaller scale than is recounted in the Bible.

Conquest of Canaan

Many scholars believe that the book of Joshua, which follows Deuteronomy, was composed by Deuteronomist writers of the seventh century BCE . The strongest clue to that provenance is the list of towns in the territory of the tribe of Judah (Joshua 15:21-62), which precisely corresponds to known sites within the borders of the kingdom of Judah under King Josiah (reigning 639-609 BCE). Some of these sites were occupied only in the final decades of the seventh century (Finkelstein and Silberman 2002: 92).

According to the narrative, Joshua ordered the Israelite army of 40,000 across the Jordan River to conquer the Promised Land. Priests carrying the Ark of the Covenant were the vanguard; as soon as their feet entered the river, Yahweh stopped its flow so the people could cross on dry land. Then Yahweh commanded Joshua to have men circle the walled city of Jericho for seven days and blow their trumpets. On the seventh day the walls fell flat, allowing the Israelites to enter the city and slay its men and women, young and old, oxen, sheep, and donkeys. After removing all precious metals for their treasury, the Israelites burned down the city and everything in it. Finally Joshua placed Yahweh's curse on anyone who tried to rebuild Jericho.

Present-day Jericho is located on an oasis close to the eastern border of Israel. Nearby, archeologists have uncovered the ruins of biblical Jericho, one of the earliest known "cities" with one of the longest records of habitation. Its lowest level, dated at 10,000 years ago, is a hunting and gathering site with flint tools and remnants of a small building. At a little higher (and later) level, from 9,000 years ago, are the remains of one of the first settlements based on irrigation farming of grain and legumes. At that time the town was composed of round houses constructed from mud brick. It covered an area equivalent to one square city block, partly enclosed by a wall of stone, six feet thick, to which was attached a stone tower, thirty feet high and twenty-eight feet in diameter with an inner staircase leading to the top of the wall.

Following the destruction of this town, a new one was built on its ruins about 8,500 years ago and again enclosed by a stone wall. The houses were now rectangular with polished plaster floors colored red or yellow. Several structures may have served as public buildings or temples. Over subsequent millennia the city walls were destroyed and repaired many times. Jericho was sometimes prosperous, sometimes poor, and sometimes deserted, its character changing repeatedly (Avigad 1974). In the fourteenth century BCE Jericho was small, poor, and unfortified. The following century it was uninhabited. There is no sign of tumbled down walls or destruction that can be associated with Joshua's attack (Finkelstein and Silberman 2002: 82).

The Bible says that after Jericho, the Israelites attacked Ai, a city small enough that Joshua thought 3,000 men a sufficient force, but the defenses held. Joshua returned with an army of 30,000 and killed all Ai's people, 12,000 men and women, hanging the king from a tree (8:25-29). Here again, the story is about a real place. Archaeologists identify Khirbet et-Tell, just east of Bethel, as biblical Ai. At this site was a relatively large city between four and five thousand years ago, but like Jericho, there was no settlement at the time of the supposed conquest.

The Bible recounts Joshua devastating one group of Canaanites after another with the help of God. At one point, facing a coalition of opposing city-states and with time passing too quickly, Joshua asks Yahweh to make the sun stand still. "The sun stopped in midheaven, and did not hurry to set for about a whole day" (10:13), a miracle unnoted in Egyptian or other sources. The added daylight provided time to finish the slaughter. But excavations at several of the sites—including Gibeon, Chephirah, Beeroth and Kiriath-jearim -- indicate that like Jericho and Ai, these sites were not occupied at the time (Finkelstein and Silberman 2002).

Apart from findings at individual digs, it is important to consider the broader political arena around the thirteenth century BCE . Many Egyptian and Canaanite documents attest that Canaan was an Egyptian province, closely controlled by Egyptian administrators. The Canaanite kings were vassals of the pharaohs, sending tribute or requesting help for their defense. There were Egyptians forts across Sinai on the Mediterranean coast, protecting access to Canaan. Egyptian garrisons were stationed near modern Tel Aviv and south of the Sea of Galilee. Overseen by Egypt, Canaanite cities of that period were generally small and without walls, housing only a local king and his family and bureaucrats.

> Canaan was a mere shadow of the prosperous society that it had been several centuries before.... Many cities were abandoned and others shrank in size, and the total settled population could not have greatly exceeded one hundred thousand. One demonstration of the small scale of this society is the request in one of the...letters sent by the king of Jerusalem to the pharaoh that he supply fifty men "to protect the land." The miniscule scale of the forces of the period is confirmed by anther letter, sent by the king of Megiddo, who asks the pharaoh to send a hundred soldiers to guard the city from an attack by his aggressive neighbor, the king of Shechem (Finkelstein and Silberman 2002: 78).

While the most detailed evidence comes from the fourteenth century, all indications are that the pharaohs still held Canaan in a tight grip at the presumed time of the Israelite invasion. It seems unlikely that Egyptian forces would have stood aside while Israelites decimated the province. Even if they did, perhaps for fear of Yahweh,

> it is inconceivable that the destruction of so many loyal vassal cities by the invaders would have left absolutely no trace in the extensive records of the Egyptian empire. The only independent mention of the name Israel in this period – the victory stele of Merneptah – announces only that this otherwise obscure people, living in Canaan, had suffered a crushing defeat. Something clearly doesn't add up when the biblical account, the archaeological evidence, and the Egyptian records are placed side by side (Finkelstein and Silberman 2002: 79).

On the other side of the argument, there were inhabited Canaanite cites destroyed and burned in the thirteenth century, most notably Bethel, Lachish, and Hazor. These have been taken as corroboration for a violent Israelite conquest. Finkelstein and Silberman rejoin that the destroyers were probably not Israelites. New powers were rising on the periphery, including the early Greeks and Trojans portrayed in the *Iliad* and the *Odyssey*. The thirteenth and twelfth centuries were a period of great flux in the eastern Mediterranean. At its end Egypt was diminished in power, having lost most of its foreign territory. This collapse is largely unexplained, but violent groups called by Egyptians the "Sea People" are involved.[4] These raiders attacked mostly along the eastern Mediterranean coast, perhaps also ravaging inland cities. "In any case, the archaeological evidence indicates that the destruction of Canaanite society was a relatively long and gradual process...over a span of more than a century. The possible causes include invasion, social breakdown, and civil strife. No single military force did it, and certainly not in one military campaign" (Finkelstein and Silberman 2002: 90).

If there was no biblical invasion of Canaan, then from where did the Israelites come? There is evidence from recent surveys of archeological sites in modern Israel that the ancient Israelites were indigenous Canaanites who formed a distinctive culture in the hilly interior of the country between the thirteenth and twelfth centuries BCE. I refer interested readers to the fascinating treatment by Finkelstein and Silberman (2001).

Biblical History versus Archaeology

Until recently the following points of biblical history were generally accepted: (1) The Israelites derived from Mesopotamian herders sometime during the second or third millennium BCE. (2) After migrating to Egypt, they increased greatly in number and finally departed en masse, probably during the reign of Rameses II. (3) Within decades of the exodus, Israel conquered Canaan, destroying many of its cities. (4) Settling in Canaan, the Israelites initially governed themselves as separate tribes but eventually accepted a unified monarchy under Saul, David, and Solomon. (5) In opulent Jerusalem, Solomon built the Great Temple and ruled over a rich and extensive realm. (6) After Solomon's death, the realm split into the northern kingdom of Israel, its original capital at Shechem, later Samaria, and the southern kingdom of Judah, its capital at Jerusalem. (7) Assyria destroyed the Kingdom of Israel in the eighth century BCE, scattering its people. (8) Babylonia conquered Judah in the sixth century BCE, destroyed Solomon's Temple, and carried many of Jerusalem's citizens to Babylon. (9) Persia conquered Babylon in the fifth century BCE, allowing the exiles to return to Jerusalem and rebuild the Temple.

The absence of archeological traces of either the exodus or the violent conquest of Canaan raises considerable doubt about the historicity of points 2 and 3, at least on the massive scale portrayed in the Bible. Among archeologists working in the Near East, the exodus-and-conquest model has been largely abandoned (Dever 1997: 81). Other elements of biblical history also seem doubtful but before traveling further down this contentious road, I think it best to mention the firmest points. Not surprisingly, these are some of the most recent events.

It was in Canaan's hilly interior that the divided kingdoms, Israel in the north and Judah in the south, coexisted from the tenth to eighth century BCE. Archeologists have uncovered ruins of both kingdoms from this period. Mesopotamian archives mention biblical kings of both

Israel and Judah. An inscription by the Moabite king Mesha refers to his victory over the armies of Israel, a testament to the war between Israel and Moab that is reported in 2 Kings 3:4-27 (Finkelstein and Silberman 2001: 19).

Around 720 BCE Assyria destroyed Israel's cities, scattered its people, and repopulated the land with outsiders. That disaster did not come out of the blue. The northern kingdom had been a vassal state of the Assyrian empire. When a new Assyrian king, Tiglath-pileser III (known in the Bible by his Babylonian name, Pul), came to power, Israel and some other vassal states used the opportunity to break free. This was a miscalculation, bringing a punitive expedition, destruction, and annexation of the territory to Assyria.

The major corrective to the biblical account of this period is the relative status of Israel and Judah. In 1 and 2 Kings, Judah is presented as the superior of the two kingdoms in all things. But the ruins show that Israel was more prosperous and larger than Judah, and had more widespread trading routes and more sophisticated architecture. Compared to the northern cities of Gezer, Megiddo and Hazor, Jerusalem was a backwater. Probably Assyria never bothered Judah because it was not worth the effort.

The relative poverty of Judah, compared to Israel, reflects a geographical divide that pre-existed the divided kingdoms. Canaan's interior highlands are naturally separated into a rugged, isolated, and arid southern region, including Jerusalem, and a more fertile northern region with broad valleys and easier routes to coastal and interior lowlands. Archaeologists have uncovered three waves of settlement in interior Canaan, the first in the Early Bronze Age (3500-2200 BCE), the second in the Middle Bronze Age (2000-1550 BCE), and the third being Israelite settlement beginning in the twelfth century BCE . Each wave of highland settlement comprised two distinct societies, northern and southern, occupying the areas of the later kingdoms of Judah and Israel. Northern habitations were always denser, possessing a complex hierarchy of large, medium, and small sites, all dependent on settled agriculture. Southern habitations were always meager with few permanent buildings and probably more dependent on migratory herders. Each region was dominated by a single center, apparently of political and economic importance. By the Middle Bronze Age, the southern center was at Jerusalem, and the northern center was at Shechem. Thus, the economic and demographic differences between Judah and Israel reflect long established patterns in the highlands (Finkelstein and Silberman 2001: 153-155).

After the Assyrians destroyed Israel, Jerusalem enjoyed an unprecedented fluorescence. Its temple became the unrivaled site for sacrifice, and Judah was incorporated into Assyria's economic sphere. Jerusalem's population exploded, its residential areas and hinterland expanded, and it built defensive walls. By the seventh century, Jerusalem's court achieved a level of affluence and literacy suitable for Torah composition. This apogee lasted little more than a century, ending when Babylon conquered the city and destroyed the Temple, forcing some citizens into exile. These events and dates are verified by facts on the ground and texts outside the Bible.

Between the no-longer credible exodus and conquest, and the confirmed kingdoms of Israel and Judah, lies the unified monarchy in nebulous uncertainty. Biblical referents date the unification from 1025 to 930 BCE. Were David and Solomon real kings, ruling over a united realm? While there is no strong reason to doubt that something akin to this polity existed, there is little external verification of it. In 1993 an inscription referring to the "House of David" was discovered at the biblical city of Dan in northern Israel, apparently dating from 835 BCE (Finkelstein and Silberman 2001: 177-78). This is good corroboration of a Davidic royal line but says nothing about David's own reign more than a century earlier.

If there was a unified kingdom, it did not have the opulence that the Bible attributes to Solomon's court, where silver was as common as stone and the king's harem contained a thousand wives and concubines (1 Kings 10:27, 11:3). To the contrary, Jerusalem was a minor place in the tenth century BCE, as it had always been and continued to be during the coexistence of Judah and Israel. Despite their ostensibly grandiose stature, neither David nor Solomon is mentioned in any known Egyptian or Mesopotamian text. Archeological evidence in Jerusalem for Solomon's elaborate building projects is nonexistent. Considerable twentieth century excavation around the City of David in Jerusalem revealed no trace of Solomon's Temple or of his famous palace or even of a major city during his time (Finkelstein and Silberman 2001: 128).[5]

Conclusion

Archaeology is a crude instrument with which to measure the accuracy of the Bible. Its discoveries are fragmentary, leaving ample room for diverse interpretations. Until the last third of the twentieth century, archeological finds then in hand were usually seen as supporting biblical history, but newer research has caused a turn of professional opinion. Evidence on the ground does not square with literal accounts of a massive exodus from Egypt, or a sudden bloody conquest of Canaan, or an opulent Jerusalem in the time of David and Solomon.

At the same time it must be acknowledged that "evidence" is often a *lack* of evidence – the absence of expected remnants from spectacular biblical events. Leaving aside miracles and such anachronisms as domesticated camels in the Near East of the 2nd millennium BCE, there is no irrefutable reason to surrender belief in the basic narrative that begins with the patriarchs and continues with a sojourn in the Nile Delta, departure under the leadership of a prince of Egypt, and eventual re-entry into Canaan. Certainly these events must be scaled down from their biblical rendering, but we cannot be sure they did not occur at all.

Biblical history is more credible for the first millennium BCE , though we must diminish the biblical grandeur of David and Solomon's kingdom. During the period of divided kingdoms, northern Israel, whatever its moral and religious failings, was materially superior to Judah. Not until Israel's destruction by Assyria did Judah emerge as a full-blown state with Jerusalem an affluent and literate capital. Seventh-century Jerusalem may well have been the provenance of much of the Torah.

Notes

1.   For the BBC story see http://news.bbc.co.uk/2/hi/europe/3664093.stm; for the *National Geographic* story see http://news.nationalgeographic.com/ news/2004/04/0427_040427_noahsark.html . In a follow-up article dated September 20, 2004, *National Geographic* reported that the Turkish government refused to grant the explorers permission to climb Mount Arafat, which is in a military zone, and the expedition was on hold. The magazine also asked, "How credible was the expedition in the first place?" The expedition's field leader, a Turkish academic who claimed to have climbed the mountain 50 times, was involved in a 1993 documentary aired on CBS television that claimed to have found the ark. In the CBS documentary a man named George Jammal displays a piece of wood from the ark. But Jammal is an Israeli actor who later said the wood was from railroad tracks near Long Beach, CA and that he had never been in Turkey. See http://news.nationalgeographic.com/news/2004/09/0920_040920_noahs_ ark.html .

2.   Much of this chapter derives from *The Bible Unearthed* (2001), a professionally competent and up-to-date treatment by archaeologists Israel Finkelstein and Neil Silberman.

3.   Christian monastics of the 4th-6th centuries CE placed the location of Mount Sinai in the mountains of southern Sinai, building there the Saint Catherine Monastery which still operates and receives tourists. Physicist Colin Humphreys of Cambridge University proposes that the wanderings of the Israelites were not confined to Sinai, and that Mount Sinai is really the volcanic Mount Bedr in Arabia (2003).

4.   Among the Sea Peoples were the Philistines, who gave their name to Palestine.

5.   The famous Western Wall in Jerusalem is a remnant of the "Second Temple" built by Herod when the Roman's controlled Palestine.

Part 3

Secular Implausibilities

Introduction to Part 3

Part 2 was concerned with literal belief in an inerrant Bible. Now I broaden the inquiry, turning to secular implausibilities. Chapter 11 focuses on UFOs and the apparently sincere belief of many Americans that they have been abducted by space aliens for fertility experimentation. Chapter 12 turns to astrology—long regarded as orthodox knowledge but now recognized by orthodox scholars as invalid, despite today's immense popularity of horoscopes.

Many books criticize pseudoscience and paranormal beliefs. Many others point out problems with the Bible. But none, so far as I know, treat both topics. My intention in placing them one after the other is to emphasize common features across these religious and secular domains, particularly the suspension of critical inquiry that is required to accept them at face value. In the final section we consider likely reasons that people accept implausible ideas, independently of whether they are secular or religious beliefs.

10

UFOs and Alien Abduction

I retrieved from the web a long remembered episode of *The Twilight Zone,* televised in 1961. Producer Rod Serling opened the story:

> This is one of the out-of-the-way places, the unvisited places, bleak, wasted, dying. This is a farmhouse, handmade, crude, a house without electricity or gas, a house untouched by progress. This is the woman who lives in the house, a woman who's been alone for many years, a strong, simple woman whose only problem up until this moment has been that of acquiring enough food to eat, a woman about to face terror which is even now coming at her from... the Twilight Zone."

In synopsis, the woman goes up to her roof to investigate a noise and finds a tiny flying saucer with two creatures emerging from it. The creatures torment the woman, until finally she grabs and batters one to death. With an ax she destroys the saucer. Before the final creature is killed he sends a message to his home planet not to send any more ships. The lettering on the side of the saucer reads "U.S. Air Force."[1]

Serling's story was televised during the Cold War when Americans were enrapt by fears of foreign attack, but it had decades of antecedents in science fiction. H. G. Wells used the term "extra-terrestrial" in *War of the Worlds* (1898) nearly a century before it was famously abbreviated to ET. Only three years before that, astronomer Percival Lowell published his nonfiction book, *Mars* (1895), announcing that lines he observed telescopically on the surface of Mars were irrigation canals intelligently designed—an intelligence we now know was on Lowell's side of the telescope. There was in 1896 and 1897 a spate of "mysterious airship" sightings, and a few people described alien visitors (Peebles 1995).

H. G. Wells embellished the idea, transporting the Martians to earth in metallic cylinders. These aliens were ugly grayish rounded hulks, the size of a bear, glistening like wet leather, with tentacles, two large dark-colored eyes, and lipless mouths drooling saliva. And they were hostile, traveling across our landscape in walking metal tripods, firing death rays. Earth would have been scoured of humans had the invaders not succumbed to our lowly bacteria. The story was immediately pirated by the American yellow press and widely read in the United States (Hughes 1966).

Interplanetary traffic became two-way in 1911 when Edgar Rice Burroughs published the first of his eleven books about a Confederate soldier, John Carter, mysteriously teleported to Mars, where he finds an advanced but decaying civilization and diverse inhabitants, some monstrous and mean, others lovely and willing. During the 1930s and 40s Buck Rogers and Flash Gordon flew rocket ships to other planets, again finding sexy extraterrestrials, a tradition continued by the *Star Trek* voyagers who boldly go where no human has gone before.

On Halloween Eve of 1938, twenty-three-year-old Orson Welles gave his adaptation of *War of the Worlds* on network radio. He used realistic-sounding news bulletins, ostensibly interrupting a program of music to tell of Martian cylinders landing in New Jersey, their use of death rays against American troops, and their tripods marching on New York City. Despite the program's compression of days-long events into a one-hour time slot, and repeated announcements that it was fiction, an estimated million Americans were frightened by the broadcast (Cantril 1940). The next morning's front page of the *New York Times* and my own city's *Syracuse Post-Standard* verify the widespread panic. Here was the first instance of people hysterically transforming a space fantasy into a real event. Alarmed callers flooded switchboards; the *Times* was overwhelmed by 875 inquiries. Many people gathered their family members and sought escape, others milled in the streets, not knowing what to do. Several required emergency medical treatment for shock. Afterward there were calls for radio censorship.[2]

Why did so many people swallow this incredible Halloween prank? The context was an important contributor. Radio had grown rapidly, from three million U.S. sets in 1924 to forty million in 1938. During the Depression, the living room radio was a center of family activity, bringing news, entertainment, and the president's fireside chats. It seemed a trustworthy medium. In the Munich Crisis of the month before, when Hitler threatened Czechoslovakia, listeners became accustomed to regular programming interrupted by news bulletins (Brown 1998).

Based on interviews with 920 people who heard the broadcast, psychologist Hadley Cantril (1940) noted that those who tuned in late were most likely to believe they were getting real news. Alarmed listeners often did not think to verify the invasion with another source. Some who did take the trouble found confirmation. As one man told a *Times* reporter,

I came home at 9:15 P.M. just in time to receive a telephone call from my nephew who was frantic with fear. He told me the city was about to be bombed from the air and advised me to get out of the building at once. I turned on the radio and heard the broadcast which corroborated what my nephew had said, grabbed my hat and coat and a few personal belongings and ran to the elevator. When I got to the street there were hundreds of people milling around in panic. Most of us ran toward Broadway and it was not until we stopped taxi drivers who had heard the entire broadcast on their radios that we knew what it was all about. It was the most asinine stunt I ever heard of.

Cantrill found that well educated listeners were more likely to success-fully check the validity of the broadcast, and less likely to be frightened, than those poorly educated. Once convinced of the invasion, people interpreted normal sights as evidence of attack. One man saw smoke from his rooftop and concluded it was from bombs. Others thought the glow of Manhattan's neon signs was the city on fire.

Saucers from Space

World War II diverted attention from extraterrestrials, but with peace restored, imaginations were free to soar. "Flying saucer" entered the language in the summer of 1947. On June 24 of that year a civilian pilot named Kenneth Arnold, flying a private plane in the vicinity of Mt. Rainier, Washington, reported seeing nine peculiar-looking aircraft moving at high speed. Arnold described their fight to a journalist as being "like a saucer would if you skipped it across the water," a simile leading to reports in newspapers of "flying saucers" (Condon 1968). The story flashed via the Associated Press wire through the news media. By July there were sightings across the nation of flying disks, many of them jokes but others sincere. A Gallup Poll released in August 1947 said 90 per-cent of Americans had heard of flying saucers. Perhaps the saucer craze was fueled by a combination of summer fun, Cold War fear, and belief that the Air Force was secretly developing new technology. Whatever its cause, this first UFO wave ebbed by August, but it started a belief in UFOs that continues today.[3]

In analyzing any social movement one must distinguish *activist*s who devote much time and energy, from *passive sympathizers* who attribute less importance to the issue and contribute few resources (Mazur 1981). The activists, relatively few in number, may have pecuniary interests as writers, lecturers, organizational directors, or analysts, but more often they are unpaid and motivated by enthusiasm, ideology, or peer support. Central activists know one another personally and through publications or web postings. They form organizations, attend meetings and conferences, maintain newsletters or internet sites, and weave a web of communications. Highly knowledgeable and committed, the activists are often well educated and sufficiently free of career, family, or other pressing obligations to commit time to the movement.[4]

Passive sympathizers may register their support on an opinion poll or by subscribing to a UFO organization, but they contribute little else. They do not move in the same circles as activists and often lack deep knowledge of the issue. National opinion surveys are useful in describing the characteristics of these numerous sympathizers, as in Chapter 3, but national samples tell us nothing about the activists because they constitute a tiny portion of the public.

One of the first UFO activists was pilot Kenneth Arnold, who published two articles on his sighting in FATE, a then-new magazine devoted to "true reports of the strange and unknown." Here, and later in books, Arnold pressed the possibility that UFOs were secret military aircraft (1948a; 1948b; Arnold and Palmer 1952). About the same time, the editor of the men's magazine *True*, suspecting a military cover-up, assigned Donald Keyhoe, a retired marine major with Pentagon contacts, to write an article on UFOs. Keyhoe's widely read piece in the January 1950 issue argued that saucers were spaceships from another planet. Publishing more on this theme, Keyhoe became director of a UFO investigating organization and remained highly influential into the 1960s.

The Air Force became interested in UFOs soon after the first reports, concerned that the Soviets might be involved. That possibility was quickly discounted but replaced with concern that a flurry of citizen reports of UFOs might clog emergency warning channels. In 1952 the Air Force, with covert CIA cooperation, established Project Blue Book with a small staff to record and debunk saucer sightings.

Many of Blue Book's results have been unclassified since 1953 but were difficult to access. Other aspects of the project, pertaining to military aircraft and CIA involvement, remained hidden for decades. In 1997 a CIA historian asserted that half of all UFO reports from the late 1950s through the 1960s were of its U-2 and SR-71 spyplanes flying over the United States (Haines 1997). Whether or not this is literally true, such inordinate secrecy, illustrating "military intelligence" as oxymoronic, contributed to widespread belief that the government was hiding information about alien visitation.[5]

One of those who eventually became suspicious was J. Allen Hynek, a professor of astronomy at Ohio State University, later at Northwestern, hired as a consultant to help the Air Force recognize astronomical explanations for UFO sightings. Apparently not privy to the CIA's spy plane flights, Hynek was impressed by certain sightings that were not amenable to banal explanation.[6] In his 1974 book, *The UFO Experience: A Scientific Study,* Hynek described several strange sightings that seemed to him credibly reported, entertaining the possibility of alien visitation. He introduced the phrase "close encounters," distinguishing among those of the first kind (seeing a UFO at close range), the second kind (seeing a close-by UFO with physical effects on the land and on animate and inanimate objects), and the third kind (seeing occupants of a UFO). In 1973, Hynek started the Center for UFO Studies and served as its scientific director until his death in 1986.

Almost from the outset, UFO activists divided into opposing camps: the ufologists versus the saucerians. The saucerians included many of a mystical or psychic bent, claiming personal contact with ETs and developing a theology for the age of flying saucers. The ufologists, following the lead of Keyhoe and later Hynek, were more cautious, often debunking UFO hoaxes and usually rejecting claims of humanlike ETs and beautiful space angels. "Contactees and saucerians infuriated ufologists, already struggling to overcome the derision of the very concept of UFOs" (Clark 2000: 135). Hynek regarded contactees as kooks:

The contactee cases are characterized by a "favored" human intermediary...who somehow has the special attribute of being able to see UFOs and to communicate with their crew almost at will (often by mental telepathy). Such persons not only frequently turn out to be pseudoreligious fanatics but also invariable have a low credibility value, bringing us regular messages from the "space men" with singularly little content. The messages are usually addressed to all of humanity to "be good, stop fighting, live in love and brotherhood, ban the bomb, stop polluting the atmosphere" and other worthy platitudes. The contactee often regards himself as messianically charged to deliver the message on a broad basis; hence several flying saucer cults have from time to time sprung up. He regards himself definitely as having been "chosen" and utterly disregards...the statistical improbability that one person, on a random basis, should be able to have many repeated UFO experiences... while the majority of humanity lives out a lifetime without having even one UFO experience. The "repeater" aspect of some UFO reporters is sufficient cause, in my opinion, to exclude their reports from further consideration" (1974: 29-30).

Thus the sightings of 1947 quickly spawned major actors, organizations, and schisms that would dominate the UFO movement for decades. By the early 1950s, there was an embedded – and partially correct – belief that the government was not telling all it knew. As the controversy polarized, claims became more outlandish, and opinions more derisive.

Physical scientists soon regarded flying saucers as an obsession of the lunatic fringe—despite their own presumption that intelligent life may exist elsewhere in the universe. The late Carl Sagan, a famous and respected astronomer at Cornell University, was at the same time the foremost proponent of SETI, the search for electromagnetic signals revealing extraterrestrial intelligence, and the best known debunker of UFOs. These positions seem contradictory to many laypeople but not to scientists, who know that excepting earth, no body in our solar system has physical conditions to support intelligent life. If there are ETs, they must live in other solar systems, which are light-years distant. There is no conceivable way – consistent with scientific understanding – to travel from there to here. (The physics of relativity dictates that no spaceship can travel faster than the speed of light, and if it could approach that speed its mass would approach infinity.) Notions that intergalactic travelers might pass through "wormholes" or "time warps" are the stuff of science fiction, not of science. Even if intergalactic travel were possible, what is the likelihood that a creature from one of the billions of galaxies would chose earth as its destination? More incredulous are claims that aliens, once arrived, abduct humans for experiments in hybridization. Skeptic Susan Clancy (2005) makes the point concisely: "It's one thing to believe that life might exist on other planets, and quite another to believe that it is secretly examining your private parts."

Especially high public concern about UFO sightings in 1966 pressed the Air Force into funding an external evaluation of Project Blue Book. This work, directed by Edward Condon, an eminent physicist at the University of Colorado, was completed in 1968 and concluded that there was no evidence supporting a belief in alien visitation, and that UFO phenomena do not offer a fruitful field for scientific discoveries. The National Academy of Sciences reviewed Condon's report and concurred with his conclusions. Project Blue Book was terminated in 1969.

Statistical History of UFOs

Of more than 12,000 sightings eventually registered by Blue Book, over 90 percent were plausibly attributed to misidentifications of celestial objects such as Venus, of manmade objects like weather balloons or artificial satellites, or to hoaxes (Condon 1968: 11). Surely there are errors in attribution, but activists and skeptics agree that the vast majority of UFO reports indicate nothing extraordinary.

While valueless for physical scientists or engineers, these sightings are useful for sociologists, showing the context in which ET claims occur. For example, UFOs are usually seen after dark but before midnight, and more often in warm months than winter. This reflects the times when people are outside looking at the night sky. Many nations report UFOs, but the United States is the center of activity. Within the U.S. the geographical distribution of sightings correlates roughly with density of non-urban population. Few reports come from urban areas, probably because city lights obscure the night sky.

The Air Force count of UFO sightings ceased with Blue Book's demise. That loss was remedied by ufologists, one of whom, Larry Hatch, has for twenty years tabulated sightings worldwide and posted them in graphical format on the internet (http://www.larryhatch.net/). Mr. Hatch generously provided me with his raw yearly counts of North American sightings for the years 1947 through 2004. Like Blue Book, Hatch's unit of analysis is the UFO event, that is, the sighting of one or more extraordinary objects in the sky, or if on the ground thought capable of flight, at a particular time and place by one or more observers. Sources for his compilation include Blue Book; journals, newsletters, and encyclopedias from UFO organizations; news media; and private catalogs. These pass through his personal filter, weeding out obvious hoaxes, double entries, and misidentified mundane events.[7] I divided Hatch's yearly count by 811, the maximum count in a single year (1952), producing an indicator of sightings with a maximum value of 1.0.

The *New York Times* is the nation's leading newspaper, an agenda setter for other news organs, and the best indexed newspaper during the postwar decades. I tabulated the number of articles about flying saucers/UFOs in the annual *New York Times Index* from 1947 to 2004 and divided each year's coverage by the amount in 1966, the year of maximum coverage, producing again an indicator with a maximum value of 1.0. *Times* coverage correlates highly (r = .78) with yearly counts of magazine articles about UFOs listed in *Readers' Guide to Periodical Literature*, adequately indicating years of high and low journalistic attention across the nation (also see Hickman et al. 1996).

UFO sightings and *Times* coverage, both graphed in figure 10.1, are correlated from year to year (r = .62), rising and falling in concert.[8] After the burst of saucer sightings and news coverage in early summer of 1947 there was relative quiet in 1948-51, then a sharply defined burst in 1952, and a return to relative quiet in 1953-65. Both indicators again peaked nearly simultaneously in 1966-67 and 1973. These variations are consistent with years of high and low activity as judged more qualitatively by Peebles (1995; also see Denzler 2001).

Does increased publicity in the mass media drive UFO sightings upward? To appraise this possibility, it is worth looking closer at the peak

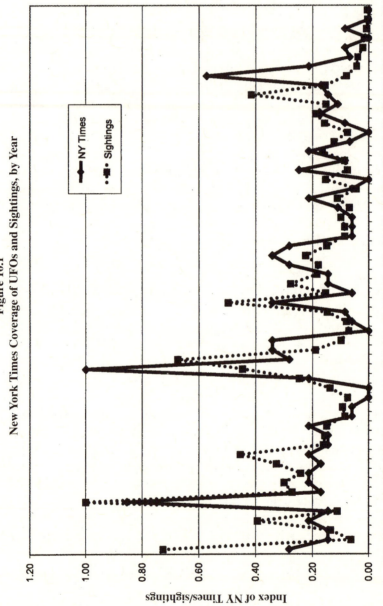

Figure 10.1
New York Times Coverage of UFOs and Sightings, by Year

Figure 10.2
Monthly UFO Sightings, 1950-55

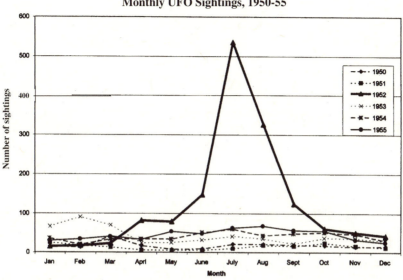

periods of sighting, called "flaps" by ufologists. Surely the 1947 flap was driven at least partly by that summer's spectacular press reports, set off by Kenneth Arnold's experience near Mount Rainier. Observers across the nation, whatever they saw, or thought they saw, or pretended they saw, used the peculiar name "flying saucer," confirming the importance of media imagery in the fad-like contagion.

By Hatch's count, the greatest number of sightings for one year occurred in 1952. This rise is timed more precisely in figure 10.2, which displays Blue Book's raw monthly counts for the years 1950 through 1955. Comparing 1952 with the other years, we see an unusual increase in saucer sightings beginning in April '52, skyrocketing in July, and abruptly falling at the end of summer. No single cause for this flap can be identified with certainty, but there are good candidates.

In March 1952 the Air Force consolidated its previous UFO inquiries into Project Blue Book, enlisting intelligence officers at all Air Force facilities to assess and report saucer sightings. This improvement in data collection may account for increased sightings in April and May but seems insufficient to explain the dramatic upturn during the summer.

The news media are another candidate. The Air Force's invigorated UFO inquiry was the lead-in for a highly influential story in *Life* magazine of April 7.[9] Titled "Have We Visitors from Space?," *Life's* answer was essentially "yes." Some 350 newspapers quoted the piece within days of its release (Condon 1968: 515). Media attention rose more sharply in July. The *New York Times*, for example, averaged only three UFO articles per month during the spring of 1952, but ran 17 articles in July, another 37 in August, and then by September nearly dropped the story.[10]

The movies are another candidate. UFOs first reached mainstream motion picture theaters in 1951, and perhaps their novelty encouraged sightings the following summer. *The Day the Earth Stood Still*, directed by Robert Wise, is the paradigm of saucer films, establishing standard themes of the genre. A flying saucer lands on the mall in Washington, D.C. Its commander is Klaatu, an emissary to earth, played by Michael Rennie with no modification to his human appearance. He is accompanied by Gort, a large silvery robot, unaggressive but capable of shooting lethal rays. Klaatu's mission is to warn us that nuclear weaponry will destroy humanity, and that we must learn to live in peace. Released in September 1951, the film was still in theaters the following year.[11]

The best known sightings of 1952, sometimes called "the invasion of Washington," occurred in July when personnel at the capital's National Airport, three miles from Klaatu's landing site, saw on two successive Saturdays (July 19 and 26) a tremendous number of UFOs and unidentified blips on their radar screens. Doubts about the reality of these objects arose when scrambled planes could not make visual contact with most of the targets shown on ground radars, nor could they locate them on airborne radar, nor did different ground radars agree on the tracks of the targets. Nonetheless, they made a terrific summer news story. The *Washington Post*, which had carried saucer stories only days before the flap (July 16 and 18), ran a front-page banner headline on July 22: "Radar Spots Air Mystery Objects Here." The *Post* editorialized on July 25 that the radar must have picked up real objects, but the next Sunday's edition (July 27) included *Parade* magazine warning, "Beware of Fake 'Flying Saucers.'" On Monday, July 28, after the second weekend of sightings, the *Post* ran another front-page banner: "'Saucer' Outruns Plane, Pilot Says." Half of July's articles in the *New York Times* were about the capital sightings. With heightened publicity came more sightings, more speculation, and more debunking. The UFOs at National Airport were later attributed to misidentified meteors or stars, and anomalous radar echoes from temperature inversions in the atmosphere (Condon 1968: 158; Peebles 1995).

The last three months of 1957 saw another flap, especially in November. Blue Book attributed many of these sightings to misidentifications of Venus. No increase in UFO news articles accompanied this peak, perhaps because journalists were focused on Sputnik 1, launched by the Soviet Union on October 4, and Sputnik 2 with the dog Laika on November 3. Headlines were plentiful, inducing people to watch the skies.

A plethora of UFO news began in March 1966 with repeated reports by many witnesses of glowing colored lights in two swampy areas near Ann Arbor, Michigan. Dr. Hynek, the Air Force consultant, thought these were visual effects of swamp gas or foxfire from rotting vegetation, producing a phosphorescent glow. Though scientifically reasonable, this "marsh gas" explanation was derided as a cover-up. Michigan congressman (later president) Gerald Ford called for a congressional investigation. House hearings in early April produced more news coverage. The publicity was a boon to the authors of some twenty-five books on UFOs published between 1965 and 1968 (Peebles 1995: 189). John Fuller, a columnist with *Saturday Review* magazine and a UFO believer, was the major beneficiary, fortuitously publishing two saucer books in 1966. Sightings rose apace with the publicity, peaking in 1967.

Sightings peaked again in fall 1973. This flap started in the southern states and might have gone unmentioned in *The New York Times* if Georgia Governor Jimmy Carter had not commented that he once saw a UFO (September 14). In mid-October the *Times* reported that a UFO seen by thousands of South Carolinians turned out to be the work of an artist who launched the object as an experimental sculpture. About the same time two shipyard workers from Mississippi, while fishing on the Pascagoula River, were nabbed by hideous looking aliens, taken aboard the spacecraft for examination, and then released. A local lawyer, acting as the abductees' agent, sought payment for the Pascagoula story. The men appeared repeatedly on network television despite the transparency of their hoax (detailed in Klass 1976). By this time there were sightings around the nation.

Traditional reporting of UFOs in the sky entered a period of quiescence after 1973. Figure 10.1 shows an anomalous peak of sightings in 1995, unaccompanied by news coverage. Mr. Hatch, responding to my inquiry, suggests this is an artifact, the result of a hiatus that year, due to difficult personal circumstances, in his customary filtering out of weak cases. If it is a real peak, I have no explanation for it.

After 1973 news reporters ignored UFOs except for a brief but intense return in 1997.[12] There were two big saucer stories that year. In March the bodies of 39 members of a millennial sect called Heaven's Gate were found at a wealthy estate in California, victims of a mass suicide intended to remove them from their earthly bodies so they could join a spaceship lurking behind the Hale-Bopp comet, then passing near earth. In a lighter vein, many thousands of partiers gathered at Roswell, New Mexico on the Fourth of July for the fiftieth anniversary of the crash of a flying saucer containing alien bodies – not all dead – that are still held in secret storage by the Air Force.

The seed for the Roswell story was the crash of a government balloon on a nearby ranch in early July 1947. This was barely a week into the media frenzy set off by Kenneth Arnold's "saucer" sighting near Mount Rainier. The rancher who found the wreckage notified the sheriff, who contacted Roswell Army Air Field, which picked up the debris. The base's zealous public information officer, Lieutenant Walter Haut, wrote a press release saying that the Army had retrieved the wreckage of one of the rumored flying discs. The *Roswell Daily Record* ran the story under the headline, "RAAF Captures Flying Saucer on Ranch in Roswell Region." By the following day, higher ups in the Army identified the wreckage as a weather balloon, but that was not completely true. In 1994 the Air Force revealed that what crashed at Roswell was a 600-foot long train of weather balloons and radar targets then being tested for Project Mogul, a top secret attempt to detect sound generated by Soviet nuclear-bomb tests.

What is most remarkable about the Roswell crash is that it was virtually a non-event for four decades. I found barely a mention of Roswell in my perusal of UFO literature prior to 1990. The exception was a book called *The Roswell Incident* (Berlitz and Moore 1980), but its absurdities (e.g., President Eisenhower lacked sufficient security clearance to be told about the downed saucer) gave it little credibility even among UFO believers. Roswell was reinvigorated in the early 1990s as new books promoted theories about one or more crashed saucers, recovered bodies, perhaps a survivor, and of course a cover-up. In 1995 the FOX-TV network ran in prime time a feature called *Alien Autopsy: (Fact or Fiction?)*. Produced by Ray Santilli, a London-based acolyte of P.T. Barnum, it shows footage of the medical autopsy performed on an ET from the crashed vehicle. Among the interviewees intended to lend some credence to the film is ex-Lieutenant Haut, recalling that a flying saucer really did crash at Roswell.[13]

Recapping, we see that UFO flaps generally occur when the mass media focus people's attention on objects in the sky. Correlation does not imply causation, but it does suggest that publicity is the primary driving force behind waves of misidentified objects and hoaxes. The general decline in UFO sightings since 1973 (possibly excepting 1995) may be the result of a loss of journalistic coverage as well as to Air Force disinterest, to the CIA's cessation (so far as we know) of spy plane flights over North America, and to people's familiarity with artificial satellites. There may have been as well a growing boredom with mysterious lights overhead. Perhaps as a result, the UFO movement returned to the more emotionally engaging domain of the contactee, bringing aliens into closer encounters with humans – much closer.

Aliens Abduction in the Mass Media

The Day the Earth Stood Still in 1951 was the first popular movie to show an alien abduction. Near its climax, the powerful robot Gort carries a fearful Patricia Neal into the saucer. Gort performs a medical procedure on the ship's operating table, not to Neal but to alien emissary Klaatu, who was shot by a human. The robot restores his master's life while the imprisoned Neal watches in amazement. By film's end there is a strong rapport between Klaatu and the earthling Neal, but with no sexual inference.

Humans are abducted again in *Invaders from Mars* (1953), directed by William Cameron Menzies. The boy at the center of this story is awakened one night by bright lights from a flying saucer landing behind his house and burying itself by a rail fence. His pajama-clad father, going out to investigate, is trapped by the aliens and taken into their saucer where a controlling device is implanted in his brain. Zombie-like, the father returns home. Others in town venture behind the house and receive the same treatment. The Menzies aliens -- obviously humans in costume -- had no lasting impact on the imagination of viewers, but his plot and certain scenes were highly influential.[14] Stephen Spielberg, in his blockbuster *ET* (1982), shows the same rail fence near the saucer landing site.

The alien abductors in *Earth vs. the Flying Saucers* (1956) come from a disintegrated solar system, intent on subjugating Earth with their death rays. Looking humanoid with hairless white heads and large eyes, they imprison humans in one of their saucers, extracting knowledge from their brains and turning them into zombies.

During these early years, few people in real life reported meeting aliens or riding in flying saucers. Psychoanalyst C. G. Jung wrote of George Adamski, adding to his fame as someone claiming to have made a brief trip around the moon, seeing that the side always turned away from earth contains an atmosphere, water, forests, and settlements (1959: 26; also see Peeble 1995). These were the people whom ufologists referred to as saucerians or contactees or, to use astronomer Hynek's unkind term, kooks.

Real-life accounts of actually being *kidnapped* by aliens were not well known prior to 1962. Apparently Betty and Barney Hill were the first Americans to describe such an experience, recalling it under hypnosis in 1963 and retrospectively dating the incident to 1961. The Hill episode blossomed to public awareness in 1966 and probably seeded all subsequent abduction reports.

The Hills were an interracial couple, newly married after both had left prior marriages. For Barney, a black man sensitive to racial prejudice, his remarriage meant a new life in Betty's white neighborhood of Portsmouth, New Hampshire. It was a stressful situation, with Barney suffering anxiety, ulcers, and high blood pressure. As the story was later told, on the night of September 19, 1961, the Hills were returning to Portsmouth from Montreal. Driving through the White Mountains, they sighted a flying saucer – Betty was already a believer. Fearing the saucer was following their car, Barney tried to elude it by driving side roads, finally arriving home two hours later than expected.

The next morning Betty called her sister, another believer. At her sister's suggestion, Betty used a compass to test if the car had been irradiated (*sic*) and concluded, from the needle's movement, that it had been. In the next days Betty read *The Flying Saucer Conspiracy*, by UFO believer Donald Keyhoe, and reported her sighting to his organization, though without mentioning abduction. Soon Betty was having nightmares in which she and Barney were kidnapped and taken aboard a flying saucer. She wrote down the details.

In 1962 Barney's physician suggested that he seek psychiatric help. By this time Betty was lecturing locally about the UFO incident and her dreams of abduction. In 1963 both Hills began psychotherapy with a prominent Boston psychiatrist, Dr. Ben Simon, exploring problems arising from their interracial marriage as well as their UFO encounter. Under time-regression hypnosis, Betty and Barney told Dr. Simon of being taken that night in 1961, against their wills, into the saucer, where they were undressed and examined by an alien doctor. They were prodded with a variety of instruments, one a long needle inserted into Betty's belly through her navel to test for pregnancy. Betty calmly recalled to Dr. Simon her initial discomfort with the forced examination, but she also remembered a pleasant conversation with the alien doctor and their cordial farewell. The aliens returned the Hills to their car, blocking memories of the two "lost" hours.

Betty's hypnotic account matched the notes she had written about her nightmares two years earlier. Barney's story under hypnosis was consistent in content with Betty's, but his sessions were marked by fearful agitation. He reported that aliens with "wraparound eyes" took a sample of his sperm.[15] After seven months of treatment, Dr. Simon, who regarded the abduction a shared fantasy, decided that neither patient was psychotic, that they were sincere in their beliefs, and that both had benefited from therapy.

By 1965 the Hills had attracted enough attention to be featured in a series of articles on UFO abduction in a Boston newspaper. *Saturday Review* columnist John Fuller was developing their story for a two-part article for *Look* magazine (Oct. 4 and 18, 1966) and for his book, *The Interrupted Journey* (1966). In 1975, NBC-TV showed a prime-time movie, *The UFO Incident*, based on Fuller's book. James Earl Jones starred as Barney. The film's aliens were short and slightly built, with hairless heads and big black eyes. Barney described their skin as grayish in color, giving rise to the label "gray" for this type of ET and suggesting a symbolic offspring of the Hills' mixed marriage. A spate of alien abductions occurred shortly after the TV film (Sheaffer 1998: 75-77).[16]

No one contributed more to alien iconography than Steven Spielberg. In *Close Encounters of the Third Kind* (1977) and *ET: The Extra-Terrestrial* (1982), the saucers are huge round ships, surrounded by lights, landing and leaving at night. There are three kinds of aliens in *Close Encounters*, most resembling "grays" with slight bodies, hairless oblong heads, and large eyes. Most of Spielberg's contactees are seduced rather than kidnapped, the result of telepathically implanting in their minds an obsessive attraction to Devils Tower, Wyoming, the depot for departure.

During the mid-1980s, several sensational books, presented as nonfiction, explicated the phenomenon of alien abduction, including intrusive medical examinations and the extraction from unwilling donors of sperm and ova, to be used in fertility experiments. There were accounts of hybrid fetuses taken from pregnant women, and of hybrid children shown briefly to their human mothers but kept by the aliens (Strieber 1987; Hopkins 1981, 1987; Jacobs 1992; Mack 1994). According to this literature, abduction and hybridization are commonplace, but since the aliens induce amnesia, contactees are barely aware of their encounters until memories are restored under hypnosis. The most commercially successful of these books, leading the *New York Times* bestseller list by May 1987, was *Communion* by Whitney Strieber, a well-known author of horror fiction, who wrote of his own abduction and traumatic medical examination by aliens.

A movie version of *Communion*, starring Christopher Walken, followed in 1989, and following that was a wave of reported abductions.[17]

Harvard's Dr. Mack

In 1994 the abduction phenomenon got an enormous boost from the trade publication of *Abduction: Human Encounters with Aliens*, by Dr. John E. Mack, a long-time professor of psychiatry at Harvard Medical School, and winner of a Pulitzer Prize in 1977 for a biography of T. E. Lawrence. Mack had been introduced to the abduction phenomenon in January 1990 by Budd Hopkins, an accomplished artist and amateur hypnotist who had worked with abductees for over a decade. In 1987 Hopkins had published *Intruders*, a book on the reality of alien abduction. By 1992, after *Intruders* was reshaped as a fictional TV movie, the lead character was a Mack-like psychiatrist (played by Richard Crenna) working with abductees. Both Mack and Hopkins were consultants on the film.

Dr. Mack provided a level of credibility that could not be approached by the likes of Hopkins or any other UFO believer. He provoked a storm of controversy at Harvard, including a Medical School investigation of his work with abductees, but tenure and the spirit of academic freedom preserved him from serious censure. In the paperback edition of his book, Mack slightly moderated the sensationalism of the original hardback, stating that he did not presume that everything abductees told him to be literally true. Still, he vigorously defended the credibility of abduction experiences until his death in 2004, struck by a bus in London. It remains puzzling why a physician of Mack's stature would espouse so implausible a phenomenon. He did have a history of flirting with dubious practices like Werner Erhard's EST and Stanislav Grof's "holotropic breathwork," a technique that allegedly accesses extraordinary states of consciousness (Neimark 1994). Whatever his motives, the Harvard professor and the mass media carried alien abduction a long way from the fabulous tale of Barney and Betty Hill.

There is no physical evidence associated with alien visitation or abduction that cannot be explained in ordinary terms. What we have is testimony from people like the Hills who insist that they personally experienced these events. Most do not suffer severe psychopathology (Clancy 2005). In the clinical laboratory, when their supposed abductions are brought to mind, these claimants show physiological signs of stress that are consistent with recall of a trauma (McNally et al. 2004). Apparently most of them truly believe they were kidnapped and sexual molested by extraterrestrials.

The major argument given to support the reality of alien abduction is that the stories told by unrelated abductees have a high degree of consistency on specific details. What are the broad commonalities? Most abduction occurs at night when the abductee is alone, usually in bed or asleep. Abductees often feel paralyzed while they are being taken. Some encounters happen while driving a lonely road in a remote area. Here are excerpts from Dr. Mack's description of common features:

> [First] is an unexplained intense blue or white light that floods the bedroom, an odd buzzing or humming sound, unexplained apprehension, the sense of an unusual presence or even the direct sighting of one or more humanoid beings in the room, and, of course, the close-up sighting of a strange craft.... [T]he beam of light seems to serve as an energy source or "ramp" for transporting the abductee from the place where the abduction starts to a waiting vehicle. Usually the experience is accompanied by one, two, or more humanoid beings who guide them to the ship.... When abductions begin in the bedroom, the experiencer may not initially see the spacecraft, which is the source of the light and is outside the house.... They are described as silvery or metallic and cigar-, or saucer-, or dome-shaped. Strong white, blue, orange, or red light emanates from the bottom of the craft...and also from porthole-like openings that that ring its outer edge.... Once inside...they are taken into one or more larger rooms where the various procedures will occur. These rooms are brightly lit, with a hazy luminosity from indirect light.... Computer-like consoles and other equipment and instruments line the sides of the rooms, which may have balconies and various levels and alcoves.... The ambiance is generally sterile and cold, mechanistic and hospital-like....
>
> Inside the ships the abductees usually witness more alien beings...of several sorts. They appear as tall or short luminous entities that may be translucent, or at least not altogether solid.... By far the most common entity observed are the small... humanoid beings three to four feet in height.... The leader is usually felt to be [larger and] male.... Gender difference is not determined so much anatomically as by an intuitive feeling that abductees find difficult to put into words.
>
> The small [aliens] have large, pear-shaped heads that protrude in the back, long arms with three or four long fingers, a thin torso, and spindly legs.... The beings are hairless with no ears, have rudimentary nostril holes, and a thin slit for a mouth which rarely opens or is expressive of emotion. By far the most prominent features are huge, black eyes which curve upward and are more rounded toward the center of the head and pointed at the outer edge.... In addition to boots, the aliens usually wear a form-fitting, single-piece, tuniclike garment, which is sparsely adorned.... Communication between the aliens and humans is experienced as telepathic, mind to mind or thought to thought....
>
> The abductee is usually undressed and is forced [onto a] table where the procedures occur.... Extensive surgical-like procedures done inside the head have been described.... The most common, and evidently most important procedures, involve the reproductive system. Instruments that penetrate the abdomen or involve the genital organs themselves are used to take sperm samples from men and to remove or fertilize eggs of the female. Abductees report being impregnated by the alien beings and later having an alien-human or human-human pregnancy removed. They see the little fetuses being put into containers on the ships, and during subsequent abductions may see incubators where the hybrid babies are being raised....

> The other important, related aspect of the abduction phenomenon has to do with the...alteration of consciousness of the abductees.... [This] concerns the fate of the earth and human responsibility for the destructive activities that are taking place on it.... [T]elevision monitor-like screens on the ships [show]...scenes of the earth devastated by a nuclear holocaust, [and] vast panoramas of lifeless polluted landscapes and waters... (18-24).

How, psychiatrist Mack asks, could there be so much agreement about the abduction experience "told by individuals who had not been in communication with each other" if they had not actually been abducted?

Referring to the seventy-six abductees he studied from mid-1990 to early 1993, Mack writes, "[M]ost of the specific information that the abductees provided about the means of transport to and from spaceships, the descriptions of the insides of the ships themselves, and the procedures carried out by the aliens during the reported abductions had not been written about or shown in the media" (1-2). But later Mack (1994: 23) discredits his own argument, acknowledging that detailed information *was* easily available: "The procedures that occur on the [space] ships have been described in great detail in the literature on abductions (Bullard 1987; Hopkins 1981, 1987; Jacobs 1992)." Many if not all of Mack's patients had plenty of opportunity, before they met him, to personally share details with other UFO believers. Some patients were referred to him through the UFO network; some had relatives who were abductees. In all thirteen cases that Mack describes in detail, the subject associated with other believers or read abduction literature before meeting the psychiatrist. Once subjects became patients, many joined other abductees in group support sessions. Dr. Mack was disingenuous in claiming their stories were derived independently.

Even if abductees were isolated from other believers, and had never read the believer literature, they share the popular images of aliens, spaceships, and abductions that were by 1990 part of contemporary American culture. Their message about the sorrowful fate of the earth, unless humans correct their behavior, is a distant echo of *The Day the Earth Stood Still*. Their common memory of television screens on alien craft, showing scenes of the earth devastated by a nuclear holocaust, and panoramas of destroyed landscapes, comes from the finale of director James Cameron's titanic motion picture, *The Abyss* (1989), starring Ed Harris, which was playing only months before Mack started hypnotizing abductees. These images are so widely available that people who make no claim to abduction produce similar scenarios when asked to imagine they had been kidnapped by aliens (Clancy 2005: 102).

Abduction believers exaggerate the extent to which the accounts are consistent. Emphasizing their *discrepancies*, psychologist Susan Clancy writes (2005: 82-83):

> They vary enormously in details such as how people get "taken" (through walls; sucked up by beams of light; ushered into UFOs), what the aliens look like (tall; short; pads on their fingers; suction cups on their fingers; webbed hands; nonwebbed hands), what they wear (nothing; orange overalls; silver track suits; black scarf and cap), what type of examination is done (needles stuck in nose; intestines pulled out; anal "nubbins" inserted; feet examined with manicure scissors), what type of sexual activity ensues ("he mounted me"; "a rotating ball massaged me"; "my eggs were taken"; "she was beautiful, with cherry-red pubic hair"; "sperm was sucked from my penis by a machine"), what the purpose of the abduction is (human colonization; hybridization; education; communication; world destruction; world peace), why people get chosen ("I'm very intuitive"; "we're all abducted"; "I'm the chosen one"; "they wouldn't tell me").

Given the choice between a commonplace explanation and a fantastic explanation for the provenance of abduction images, why do so many people believe the fantastic option? Or do they? Surely some tellers of these tales know they are fibbing. There is a strong profit motive and the lure of celebrity if you can create a sensation, appear on TV, sell your story to a publisher, and be portrayed in a movie. John Mack, Whitney Strieber, and Barney and Betty Hill attained all these rewards. Strieber is by profession a best-selling writer of fantasy literature. Some abductees may be motivated simply by the fun of a gag or a desire for attention.

Leaving aside fraudulent claimants and hoaxers, abductees tend to be troubled and impressionable people who are open to mystical beliefs, prone to fantasy and memory distortion, and are hypnotizable (Clancy 2005). Indeed, it is nearly always under hypnosis or a similar technique that they discover they were abducted. Some regression hypnotists blatantly lead their clients to this end, so let us look more closely at John Mack, a professionally trained psychiatrist of high repute.

On first contacting Dr. Mack, many patients had only vague notions of possibly being abducted, perhaps because of flash memories or hours of time unaccounted for. After an initial interview, Mack used hypnosis or relaxation methods to regress the memory of patients back to the suspected abductions, on the theory that suppressed details could be brought to consciousness. Some recalled only a single encounter but usually they remembered recurrent encounters, often beginning in childhood or infancy, and in at least one case – Eva – from a prior life when she was a rich merchant living in Morocco during the thirteenth century (p. 252).

Hypnosis is not fully understood but generally requires a relaxed patient who willingly defers to the hypnotist and complies with his suggestions, whether given explicitly or implicitly. Mack insisted that he did not bias his patients, but occasionally he admitted directing their past-life regressions (1994: 186, 190). His known sympathy for the reality of UFO abduction could by itself have biased subjects. Sometimes another abductee or guest was present during hypnosis (p. 266). Mack sent articles about aliens to at least one perspective subject before their first session. This woman, a writer named Donna Bassett, was a poseur who under hypnosis told Mack preposterous stories about meeting Nikita Khrushchev and John Kennedy on a flying saucer. Mack never detected her fakery (Willwerth 1994). Imaginative patients and biased or gullible hypnotists easily transform ordinary memories into exotic fantasies.

Ed is a technician of tradition Catholic upbringing who is interested in science and technology, practices meditation, studied Eastern philosophy "in his struggle to find his authentic path," feels he can "talk to plants," and is interested in alien intelligence. During the summer of 1989, after a visit to the Maine coast, Ed had "flashback" memories of an earlier visit to the coast in 1961 when he was in high school. While attending a UFO conference, other conferees suggested Ed contact Dr. Mack.

At their initial session, Ed recounted one night during his 1961 visit to Maine. He and a boyfriend were going to sleep in their car by the coast, talking about how "horny" they were and speculating about great encounters they would have at the beach. The next thing he knew, he was naked in a glass-bubbled "pod."

> With Ed in the pod was a small, slight female figure with long, straight, thin silvery-blond hair.... The female entity had a small mouth and nose, intense large dark eyes, and a "sort of "triangular" shaped head with a "largish" forehead.... He found her "attractively unusual" and felt "a little self-conscious." The figure, perhaps sensing this, "gave me some sort of blanket or big towel or something..." Ed was sexually excited, and the female being "sensed my horniness." Although he was "hazy" as to how this came about, Ed said, "we had intercourse." According to Ed this act was "similar" to human sexual intercourse with "fondling of the breasts," insertion of the penis in the vagina, and active participation by both individuals. Interestingly, although Ed was a virgin at this time, he did not recall this experience and still felt himself to be a virgin when he had sexual intercourse some time later (Mack 1994: 39).

Afterward the female imparted to Ed some information about the "heavily destructive" path humans were taking on the earth.

Eleven weeks later, using hypnotic relaxation, Dr. Mack regressed Ed to that night in 1961. Now he recalls seeing one or two figures through the car windows, a "couple of human sort of things, but cripes, their eyes are big!" Ed feels himself drifting out of the car, floating toward and into a luminescent domelike pod. He is in a surgery theater where there are observers. The head doctor is the sexy female with silvery hair and large black eyes without pupils. She fills his mind with erotic escapades, forcing his arousal. But this time, she refuses him intercourse, telling Ed that they need his sperm to create special babies. A tube is placed over Ed's penis. Relaxed, he experiences a rubbing sensation – perhaps her hand -- and ejaculates. The female doctor congratulates Ed on giving a good sample. Afterward, the female imparts information about the apocalyptic future of the earth because of human stupidity.

How do we interpret Ed's stories? For Mack, they are recollections of a real abduction. Ed's second version, under hypnosis, is stranger and fuller in detail but also inconsistent with the first version about whether or not he had intercourse with the sexy alien. In Mack's view, "the information recalled painstakingly under hypnosis is more reliable than the consciously recalled story" (54).

But perhaps the teenage Ed simply had a wet dream, later reified under the influence of UFO believers and embellished with media images. His story is remarkably like one in the popular science magazine *Omni,* about a young Brazilian man, Jocelino de Mattos, who sighted a hovering UFO and lost consciousness.

> On the hypnotist's couch, Jocelino soon remembered boarding the UFO. "The aliens asked me to lie down, and as I did so, they examined me.... Then, after the examination, they collected sperm (through a tube). They made me sit down on a kind of a table.... After some minutes a woman arrived in the room. She touched me. She caressed me, and it excited me. Then we started to make love."
>
> The woman looked human, the young abductee added, and he was able to complete the act. The aliens released him sometime later, after explaining...that they had come on a mission of peace (Rogo 1984).[18]

Sometimes the conflation of abduction memories with mass media images is so blatant that it is hard to believe the psychiatrist could miss it. Free-spirited Catherine, a twenty-two-year-old music student and nightclub receptionist, was in a career crisis. Leaving work, she took a midnight drive and on returning home thought there was a forty-five-minute period for which she could not account. The next day's news told of a UFO seen the previous night in the area where she had driven. Her mother was a UFO believer and perhaps they discussed the coincidence. Catherine called Dr. Mack, by then known for his work with abductees, and told him of the puzzling episode. He noted of their original conversation that "she had recently been reading about UFOs and [she said] 'halfway hoping to see one and halfway hoping I don't'" (1994: 130).

In May 1992 Catherine watched the television movie *Intruders*, in which Richard Crenna plays the Mack-like psychiatrist.[19] Shortly afterward, Catherine and Mack began eight months of hypnosis and relaxation sessions. Around this time she read David Jacobs's book, *Secret Lives*, on alien abduction (Mack 1994: 134, 149, 154). Her early images are reminiscent of *Close Encounters of the Third Kind*: a huge discus-like craft with lights around its rim, the presence of small glowing aliens, ascending a 45-degree ramp to enter the spaceship. Later sessions are darker as Catherine seemingly attributes to herself events portrayed in *Intruders* by the television film's two fictional female abductees. Everything in the following paragraph is reported by Mack as Catherine's memories, and all of it appears explicitly in *Intruders*:

> At age seven she is brought into a flying ship where an alien cuts her with a medical-like instrument, drawing blood. By adulthood she has been abducted repeatedly, placed on a table in a spaceship, and examined by terrifying large-eyed doctors who are taller than other aliens. Overcoming her resistance, they spread her legs and examine her genitals. In one instance a long instrument is placed into her vagina, in another instance an instrument is inserted through her nostril, later evidenced by a nosebleed. The examiners are either taking samples or implanting something. In one episode she is brought into a room where cases are stacked in rows, floor to ceiling, each containing a baby creature, suspended in liquid. The place is an incubatorium where hybrid fetuses are nourished. In the climactic episode, an extractor is inserted in her vagina to withdraw an unusually well-developed fetus that has gestated three or four months. The examiner informs the mother that she should be proud. As finale, an alien nurse shows a hybrid child to the abductee. At this end point we have a difference between Mack's real-life patient and the television film. Catherine is repulsed by the baby. The abductee in Intruders realizes that the child is her own and embraces it lovingly (Mack 1994: 130-166).

Granted that alien encounters have recurrent themes, and there are common media images in virtually all abduction accounts, the correlation here is extraordinary. A drawing by Catherine, depicting her experience, seems a composite of *Close Encounters* and *Intruders* (Figure 10-3). Her multi-tiered incubatorium is as shown in the movie, the babies in each case "all in liquid.... The heads are large and in the same proportion to the bodies as the alien figures themselves" (Mack 1994: 131, 148). Could Mack have been oblivious to the coincidence between her hypnotic tales and a film she had seen only weeks earlier, on which he was a consultant and the model for its lead character?

Why do People Believe They were Abducted?

In chapter 12 we will examine the "default assumption" of socialization

Figure 10.3
Catherine's drawing (middle) resembles scenes from *Close Encounters of the Third Kind* (bottom) and *Intruders* (top)

-- that people tend to believe whatever they have been taught as children to be credible, including the existence of UFOs and the occurrence of alien contact. Psychiatrist Mack comments that abduction experiences run in families, sometimes over three or more generations (1994:14). In nine of the thirteen cases he presents in detail, there is explicit mention of a parent or older relative who was a UFO experiencer or believer.[20] Susan Clancy comments in passing that some parents of her abductee subjects are believers (2005: 111-115).

Parents with New Age or other mystical beliefs may raise children who are relatively uncritical of kindred notions and therefore susceptible to UFO mythology. Most subjects whom Mack describes in detail have New Age orientations. Psychologists McNally (2003) and Clancy (2005: 134) also note the prevalence of New Age beliefs among their abductees.

Everyone studying abductees emphasizes that they are *not* generally psychopathic, but I would add that they are not generally untroubled individuals or hard-nosed rationalists either. Many seem "eccentric or odd" (Slater, quoted in Klass 1989: 112). Clancy writes of her abductee subjects, "If I compare them to the well-educated readers of university press books like this one, then the abductees are about 1.5 standard deviations from the norm, on a continuum I'll tentatively label 'weirdness'" (2005: 106; also see Newman and Baumeister 1996). As a group, Clancy's subjects scored high on a construct called "schizotypy," a tendency to look and think eccentrically and a proneness to "magical" thinking and odd beliefs, such as certain numbers having special powers (2005: 129). Mack's detailed cases reveal severe emotional problems, and he was struck by how many abductees came from broken homes or had one or more alcoholic parents (1974: 5). People who report extreme abduction experiences are fantasy-prone and subject to memory distortion (Spanos et al. 1993; Nickell 1996; Clancy et al. 2002; Clancy 2005: 132; but see Rodeghier et al. 1991 for equivocal results). They are highly impressionable and amenable to social influence, as best indicated by their susceptibility to hypnosis. If typical rationalist readers of this book think "there is no way I would ever believe I was abducted by aliens," they are probably correct.

Troubled individuals who uncritically entertain fantastical and otherworldly experiences, who have been exposed to alien images, and who are socially malleable, are ripe for abduction. Add to this mix a hypnotist or other therapist who (perhaps unwittingly) encourages subjects to imagine themselves in fictional actions. Such scenarios, discussed with a spouse or friends or authority figures who believe in UFOs, become validated as genuine memories. Like most conversions, it is a gradual process changing fantasy into actuality. These are the necessary components for abduction, but additional elements may come into play.

Most abduction memories begin with the victims in bed, either asleep or nearly asleep. The encounter starts with an awareness of unusual light or the feel an alien presence. William James discussed this "sense of presence" in *The Varieties of Religious Experience*, quoting one of his intimate friends:

> It was about September, 1884, when I had the first experience. On the previous night I had had, after getting into bed at my rooms in College, a vivid tactile hallucination of being grasped by the arm, which made me get up and search the room for an intruder; the sense of presence properly so called came on the next night. After I had got into bed and blown out the candle, I lay awake awhile thinking on the previous night's experience, when suddenly I *felt* something come into the room and stay close to my bed.... I did not recognize it by any ordinary sense, and yet there was a horribly unpleasant "sensation" connected with it. It stirred something more at the roots of my being than any ordinary perception (1985: 56).

Depending on the cultural setting and the predisposition of the person in bed, this presence may be Satan, a witch or incubus, a missing loved one, or an alien:

> What I felt that night was...overwhelming...terrifying.... There was something in the room with me. All I can say is that it happened to me... I felt them. Aliens (quoted in Clancy 2005: 47).

The nighttime sense of presence is often accompanied by a feeling of physical immobility:

> I would wake up in the middle of the night terrified, like I'd been having a nightmare.... I tried to yell for help, but I couldn't because I couldn't move.... I felt like something was in the room watching me, but all I could see was the gray shapes (quoted in Clancy 2005: 54).

This too is a known phenomenon at the boundary that separates sleeping from being awake. During REM (rapid eye movement) sleep, when dreaming usually occurs, the body becomes inert.[21] Even automatic reflexes, like kicking when the knee is tapped, are inactivated. Normally body movement returns as soon as REM sleep ends. Occasionally there is poor coordination, producing a brief period of wakefulness while the limbs are still immobilized. Called "sleep paralysis," this fairly common experience is conducive to imagining that malevolent beings have control over one's body.

Sleep paralysis is an addendum, not a full explanation. Obviously it is irrelevant if someone is fully awake, as Barney and Betty Hill were during their imagined abductions. A nighttime episode of dream-like paralysis might plant the seed of an alien encounter, but most full blown memories do not emerge until they are fertilized by a therapist (Clancy 2005: 57-59).

Notes

1. "The Invaders," by Richard Matheson, January 27, 1961, http://tzone.the-croc.com/twilight1.html.
2. Orson Welles became famous, getting the opportunity to make *Citizen Kane*, often regarded the greatest movie of all time.
3. See Peebles (1995) for a thorough history of the UFO movement.
4. See Moseley and Pflock (2002) for a first-hand account of UFO activists, their activities, hoaxes, promotions, and general weirdness.
5. The entire Blue Book file, numbering some 80,000 pages, was made conveniently available for public access only in 2005 (Rios 2005). See http://www.blueboo-karchive.org/.
6. A passage in Hynek (1974: 30) suggests he was outside the intelligence loop.
7. Since Hatch's pre-1970 counts are partly derived from Blue Book counts, it is unsurprising that the two are highly correlated (r = .77) for the period 1948-68. After 1969, with the Blue Book registry gone, the collection of UFO reports may have been less effective, contributing to the subsequent appearance of generally lower counts. This downward counting bias, if it exists, should not affect the detection of post-1969 years with extremely high or low sighting activity.
8. Larry Hatch learned of some sightings from news reports, raising the possibility that the indicators are correlated as an artifact of joint measurement. However, since most sightings are not reported in the national news, and most national news stories are not about particular sightings, any methodological conflation must be slight.
9. This issue otherwise commanded attention for its alluring cover photograph of starlet Marilyn Monroe. A year later, Monroe's far more famous nude photo would appear in the new *Playboy* magazine.
10. Online newspaper archives for the *Washington Post* and *Chicago Tribune* show the same July-August peak.
11. Online newspaper archives show ads for *The Day the Earth Stood Still* in the *Washington Post* as late as July 3, 1952, and in the *Chicago Tribune* on November 3, 1952.
12. Online archives of the *Washington Post*, *Chicago Tribute*, and *Los Angeles Times* show the same peak of coverage in 1997.
13. Philip Klass (1997) has meticulously documented and debunked the Roswell myth, seemingly without effect.
14. Early imitators were *Invasion of the Body Snatchers* (1956, 1978) and *It Conquered the World* (1956).
15. Kottmeyer 1990) notes that similar looking aliens appeared twelve days prior to Barney's hypnosis session in an episode of the television series *The Outer Limits*.
16. Barney Hill died in 1969. Betty continued to see UFOs, having a favorite "landing site" in southern New Hampshire where she often went to watch them, sometimes bringing reporters and other observers along. Ufologist John Oswald once accompanied her and reported that Mrs. Hill was "seeing things that are not UFOs and calling them UFOs." Once, according to Oswald, she was unable to "distinguish between a landed UFO and a streetlight" (quoted in Sheaffer 1998: 74). Betty continued having paranormal experiences until her death in 2004.
17. Strieber continued publishing books in a fantastic genre, including *The Day After Tomorrow*, a highly successful novel about the sudden coming of a new ice age brought on by global warming; it became a major motion picture, released in 2004. Given Strieber's prolific career of fantasy writing, it is a hard guess

11

Astrology

The sun and moon surely affect us, producing the repetition of days, months and years, the changing seasons, and ocean tides. Astrology presumes additionally that there is a close correspondence between celestial events and people's lives, and that this correspondence can be calculated with systematic rules. These ideas were present in the early civilizations of Babylonia, China, and Mesoamerica. We do not know if they were independently invented in each region or diffused from a common prehistoric beginning. Astrology is one of several ancient methods for divining the future, along with examining internal organs of sacrificed animals, consulting oracles, and casting or cracking bones. Its distinct method is the horoscope, showing the arrangement of planets and constellations at one moment in time. Long-established rules for interpreting horoscopes are based on analogies between heavenly bodies and worldly affairs, and on thousands of years of observation. Like Aristotelian physics, Hippocratic medicine, alchemy, and the anatomy of Galen, contemporary scholars had no difficulty matching the theory to reality.

Traditional astrology predicted the weather, harvests, epidemics, and war; answered questions of immediate interest; and advised on propitious timing for an event or activity. Most of today's practice, and the focus of this chapter, is *natal astrology*, the prediction of an individual's personality and life course from the time and place of birth.

History

Astrology as practiced in modern Europe and America is descended from Babylonia, home of the sexagesimal (base 60) numbering system, which eventually produced the 360 degrees in a circle, twenty-four hours in a day, and twelve signs of the zodiac, and which remains the basis for calculating horoscopes. During the first millennium BCE, astrology spread from Babylonia to Egypt, then Greece and later to the Hellenistic and Roman worlds.

The great codifier was Ptolemy of Alexandria (100 CE -178), who recognized a distinction between astrology, which was concerned with human affairs, and astronomy, which was not. In the *Almagest*, Ptolemy gave astronomy a geocentric model whose predictions of planetary positions remained unsurpassed for the next fourteen centuries. In the *Tetrabiblos*, he codified the astrological rules as understood in his day; and this work remains the ultimate authority for today's astrology, with variations including modifications for newly discovered planets. Despite his separate treatments, Ptolemy regarded the two fields as valid and intertwined, as did most scholars of antiquity.

The Bible, written during the centuries when astrology flourished, is rich in allusions to celestial signs and omens, most famously the Star of Bethlehem. Genesis opens with God creating lights in the dome of the sky partly to "be for signs" (1:14). Psalm 19 explains that "night to night [the dome of the sky] declares knowledge." God emphasized man's puny power by pointedly asking Job,

> Can you bind the chains of the Pleiades, or loose the cords of Orion?

> Can you lead forth the Mazzaroth [constellations of the zodiac] in their season, or can you guide the Bear with its children?

> Do you know the ordinances of the heavens? Can you establish their rule on the earth?" (38: 31-33).

According to the Jewish historian Josephus (37 CE – ca. 100), the twelve precious stones adorning the breastplate of Aaron, the high priest, are associated with the zodiac, and the seven branches of the Temple menorah with the seven planets (*Antiquities of the Jews*, book III, chapter 7-7).

The Passover seder, occasion for Christ's Last Supper, is set by the first full moon after the vernal equinox. Easter is normally the next Sunday. The Jewish New Year, Rosh Hashanah, starts at sunset of the day of the new moon closest to the autumnal equinox. Hanukkah begins with the new moon in Capricorn, Purim with the full moon in Pisces. Prehistoric temples of diverse faiths often align with the direction to an equinox or solstice. The Church celebrates Christ's unknown birth date at the winter solstice, a time of preexisting pagan rites. The Muslim holy month of Ramadan commences when the new moon is in Libra. The Vietnamese New Year, Tet, begins with the first full moon after the sun enters Aquarius (Bobrick 2005).

Despite astrology's prominence in scripture, St. Augustine (354-430) thought a fate determined by the stars was in conflict with free will and devotion to God. Under Augustine's influence, the Roman Church turned officially against astrology. Along with most other Greek learning, astrology disappeared from Europe during the Dark Ages but was preserved and developed by the more enlightened scholarship of the Arab world. Around the twelfth century, Greek works were reintroduced into Europe through Moorish Spain. By the Renaissance, astrology and much else of Greek philosophy was widely accepted by Christian scholars and taught in Europe's universities. Tycho Brahe (1546-1601) and Johannes Kepler (1571-1630), whose astronomical discoveries were crucial to Isaac Newton, were practicing astrologers. Even Galileo dabbled. Astrological motifs are plentiful in the paintings of Raphael, Botticelli, Michelangelo, Tintoretto, Dürer, and Rubens, and in the writings of Chaucer, Dante, and. Rabelais. Shakespeare's "star-cross'd lovers" are among more than 200 allusions to astrology in his plays.

The Scientific Revolution, begun when Copernicus placed the sun at the center of the universe, and culminating in Newton's gravitational synthesis of celestial and terrestrial mechanics, overwhelmed the earth-centered universe of the ancients. Ptolemy's authority collapsed. If his *Almagest* was wrong, why trust his *Tetrabiblos*? With its physical basis and traditional legitimacy destroyed, astrology was wholly discredited among educated Europeans and lost much of its mass following too. Dr. Johnson, in his 1755 *Dictionary of the English Language*, defined astrology as "the practice of foretelling things by the knowledge of the stars; an art now generally exploded as irrational and false."

Its revival began in early nineteenth century England with the publication of various popular almanacs and the increasing frequency in periodicals of predictions about love, marriage, travel, and business—forerunners of today's horoscope columns. By late century astrology was enmeshed with the Theosophy movement of Madame Blavatsky and moved with her to the United States. The art's greatest American champion was Evangeline Adams (1868-1932), a claimed relation of the two presidents Adams. In 1914 Ms. Adams was tried for practicing astrology, which by then was illegal in New York State as a form of fraud. She so impressed the judge with a horoscope reading of his son, that he ruled in her favor, declaring Adams had "raised astrology to the dignity of an exact science." In her New York studio Adams mixed astrology with palmistry, catering to King Edward VII of England, Enrico Caruso, Lillian Russell, Charlie Chaplin, and J. P. Morgan, the latter valuing her views on investment. In

1930 she became the first astrologer to host a radio show (Adams 1926). By then astrology had attracted prominent artists, writers, composers, and theater figures, including Arnold Schoenberg, Paul Klee, Piet Mondrian, Walter Gropius, William Butler Yeats, Henry Miller, H. G. Wells, Aldous Huxley, Katherine Anne Porter, Fanny Brice, John Barrymore, and Isadora Duncan (Bobrick 2005). Emulating these models, mysticism became a staple in the artistic and bohemian neighborhoods of Europe and America.

Ancient Astronomy

There are roughly 1,500 stars visible to the unaided eye, and anyone watching the sky regularly can see that their juxtaposition is unvarying. Imaginative viewers named familiar constellations, often for animals or mythological figures. A few heavenly characteristics like the Pleiades or Orion's Belt – certainly the Milky Way—are so salient and distinctive they were noted in different cultures. In the Northern Hemisphere the whole arrangement seems today to revolve around the North Star (Polaris), a truer guide to navigation than the magnetic compass. The constellations rise slightly earlier (nearly four minutes) each night, offering different views for each season in a cycle that repeats every year.[1] Amidst the otherwise constant background, a few points of light, the planets, continually change position and brightness. Venus is the most obvious, sometimes shining so vividly at dawn or dusk that it is mistaken for a UFO. The ancients counted seven "planets" (wanderers), including the sun and moon.

Today we understand that the stars move across the sky from east to west because the earth makes one eastward revolution daily. Greek astronomers understood this geometrically but regarded a rapidly revolving earth as physically implausible because it would produce a strong wind blowing constantly toward the west, and because objects would fly off the surface of a spinning world. Seeing neither of these effects, they preferred to think of a stationary earth as the center of the universe, and of the stars as embedded in a celestial sphere that rotated once daily about a polar axis running through the North Star and the center of the earth. Observationally, it makes no difference if we take the earth or the sun as the center of the universe. Either way, the *celestial equator* is defined as the unique plane that is perpendicular to the axis of rotation and cuts the earth at its center.[2]

A patient observer of the moon would see that it remains within a limited belt of heaven, regularly passing the same constellations while never approaching others. If you could see the sun against its celestial background, you would notice the brilliant disk creeping eastward among the fixed stars, following a slightly different path than the moon. The glare of sunlight prevents this, but by watching sunrises and sunsets, an observer can identify the closest constellation to the sun at any time of year. The sun's apparent orbit around the earth is called the "ecliptic," and it lies on a plane that is tilted 23½° from the equator. The planets, too, are always seen near the constellations of the ecliptic.[3]

Figure 11.1 shows the equator, the ecliptic, and the earth's polar axis. During half the year, the sun – in its yearly trip around the ecliptic – is "above" the equator, bathing the Northern Hemisphere in sunlight, producing the long days and greater warmth of spring and summer. The other half of the year the sun is "below" the equator, producing the shorter days of fall and winter in the Northern Hemisphere.

On the first day of Northern Hemisphere's spring (about March 21), the sun moves northward across the equator; on the first day of fall (about September 21), the sun again crosses the equator, now moving southward. These cross points are called the "vernal equinox" and the "autumnal equinox," names reflecting the equal duration (twelve hours) of daylight and night on these two days. The shortest and longest days of the year occur when the sun is at its southernmost and northernmost positions on the ecliptic. These dates are called the "winter solstice" (December 21) and the "summer solstice" (June 21). Ancient civilizations knew these dates, and many built monuments (e.g., Stonehenge) that align with the rising or setting sun at these special days. They observed holidays at these times. Since the date of Christ's birth is unknown, Christmas was placed in late December to correspond with preexisting pagan festivals celebrating the winter solstice.

Perhaps no divination of ancient oracles was more impressive than the accurate prediction of eclipses. Columbus's ability to forecast a lunar eclipse amazed Native Americans (Bobrick 2005). During a total eclipse of the sun, stars become visible against a black sky, and animals settle to sleep. It is an awesome experience even to modern observers who understand the phenomenon. Whatever prayers or alleviative actions are taken to restore the sun, they always work because darkness never exceeds eight minutes.

There *would* be two eclipses each month *if* the moon always remained on the ecliptic. If that were true, then when the sun and moon were on the same side of the earth, and the three bodies aligned, the moon would block out the sun. Half a month later, with the moon and sun on opposite

Figure 11.1
Earth-centered Spherical Astronomy

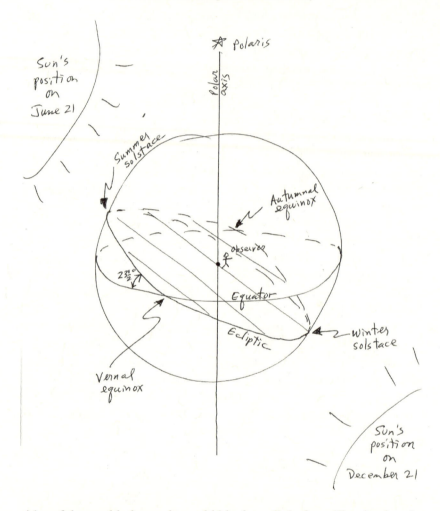

sides of the world, the earth would block sunlight from illuminating the lunar surface.[4]

In fact, as the Greeks knew, the moon's orbit is slanted 5½° from the ecliptic. As a result, only about two eclipses occur per year, and none is fully visible around the world. For an eclipse to occur, the three bodies must be aligned, and this can happen only when the moon crosses the ecliptic plane, twice a month. If the sun happens to be at the right place during one of these bimonthly transits, there is an eclipse. When the alignment is perfect there is a total eclipse. Usually the alignment is not perfect so there is a partial eclipse, not so magical but still impressive.

Ancient astrologers, knowing the 5½° angle between the moon's orbit and the ecliptic, and being able to calculate the position of each body in its orbit, could foretell when the earth, sun, and moon would align. Their ability to accurately predict eclipses must have given astrologers enormous legitimacy.

Concepts of Astrology

The ancients knew that the sun, moon, and planets appeared to circle the earth, always staying near the ecliptic. This narrow belt around the sky, obviously important, was named the "zodiac." It is divided into twelve sectors, also called "signs," each of 30°. Both the sector and the most prominent constellation in it were usually named for animals: Aries (ram), Taurus (bull), Gemini (twins), Cancer (crab), Leo (lion), and so on. (*Zodiac* is derived from the Greek for circle of animals.) The first sector, Aries, begins at the vernal equinox, which is the position of the sun on the first day of spring. The division of the zodiac into twelve sectors is an arbitrary invention of the Babylonians. Egyptians used thirty-six divisions.

A person's *sun sign* is the sector occupied by the sun at birth. For example, any person born between April 20 and May 20, when the sun is in the Taurus sector, is a Taurus. What is the significance of being a Taurus as opposed to, say, a Virgo? To answer this, astrology depends importantly on analogies, or correspondences, between named constellations and personality traits. Taurus, the bull, suggests endurance, plodding, and stubbornness, so a Taurus personality tends toward those traits. Virgo, the virgin, suggests reticence, modesty, submissiveness. Leo, the lion, is regal, proud, a born leader (table 11.1).

It may seem like splitting hairs, but it is worth distinguishing two ways of determining sun signs. One way, already noted, is to use the twelve geometric *sectors* of the zodiac (referenced to the vernal equinox). A second way uses the twelve named *constellations* of the zodiac. This made no difference when Ptolemy codified the system because named constellations were properly aligned with their sectors, e.g., the constellation Aries was in the Aries sector. But things changed.

The earth slowly wobbles. Like the precession of a gyroscope, the polar axis slowly reorients, as if carving a cone in space, completing one cycle every 26,000 years. As a result, the vernal equinox and with it the zodiacal sectors move westward with respect to the starry background.

Table 11.1
Signs of the Zodiac and Analogous Human Characteristics

Signs and Dates	Namesake	Human Characteristics
Aries (20 March-19 April)	ram	forceful, impulsive, quick-tempered, courageous
Taurus (20 April-20 May)	bull	endurance, plodding, patient, stubborn
Gemini (21 May-20 June)	twins	multi-faceted, duplicity, vacillating, two-faced
Cancer (21 June-22 July)	crab	clinging, protective exterior, tenacity
Leo (23 July-22 August)	lion	regal, proud, forceful, born leader
Virgo (23 August-22 September)	virgin	reticent, modesty, purity, submissive
Libra (23 September-22 October)	scales	just, harmonious, balanced, indecisive
Scorpio (23 October-21 November)	scorpion	suspicious, secretive, troublesome, aggressive
Sagittarius (22 November-21 December)	archer	active, aims for target, seeker, optimism
Capricorn (22 December-20 January)	goat	consolidation, tenacious, prudent
Aquarius (21 January-18 February)	water carrier	serving humankind, dispassion
Pisces (19 February-19 March)	fish	attracted to sea and alcohol, vacillation

Sources: Jerome 1977: 72; Hall 2005.

This drift has come to nearly 30°, or one whole sector, during the two millennia of Christianity. The sector Aries no longer holds the constellation Aries, but now holds the constellation Pisces. Soon the vernal equinox will have moved all the way past Pisces and into the constellation Aquarius. The coming of the Age of Aquarius is eagerly awaited by New Age devotees.

Precession presents a dilemma for astrologers. Should a person's sun sign be determined by the sun's nearest *constellation* on the day of birth? One would expect so, if the stars influence our lives. Or should one's sun sign be determined by the *sector* in which the sun lies on the day of birth? Most Western astrologers, following Ptolemy, use the sector, which once held its namesake constellation but no longer does. This is the basis for our *tropical* astrology. In India and other parts of the East, astrologers practice *sidereal* astrology, basing the sun sign on the constellation. Thus, East and West have different astrologies, producing different and sometimes inconsistent predictions from the same facts, yet all practitioners insist on the validity of their art.[5]

The constellations, by the way, are not groups of stars actually clustered together. The stars in a particular constellation may vary enormously in their distances from earth. They appear contiguous only because we view them in two dimensions. Like the signs of the zodiac, the constellations and their names are arbitrary, varying from one civilization to another.

Special importance is accorded the zodiacal sign that is *ascendant*, that is, about to rise on the eastern horizon at the time of birth. My astronomy professor in college, George O. Abell, used to declare himself a Pisces with Scorpio rising, which means that he was born when the sun was in the Pisces sector, at a location (Los Angeles) where Scorpio was then rising on the eastern horizon. Professor Abell was not unique in this. People born an hour earlier or later, and hundreds of miles away, might say the same thing.

Because of precession, it was the *sector* Scorpio that was rising, not the *constellation* Scorpio. The constellation rising at Professor Abell's birth was Libra. The skeptical professor commented, "there was nothing particularly special about the stars that were either just rising or just passing overhead at the moment of my birth, and none of them had anything to do with [the constellations] Pisces or Scorpio" (1981: 72). Nonetheless, those who believe in astrology believe Pisces and Scorpio were the two most important influences on Abell's character and life.

The positions of the planets are also important. Still reasoning by analogy, each planet conveys to humans the characteristics of its visual appearance, or of the god whose name it carries. Mars, named for the god of war, looks red in the night sky, suggesting blood, war, and aggressive behavior. A person born with Mars in ascendancy is aggressive, impatient, and has a fighting instinct. Venus, the brightest, most lovely planet at dawn and dusk, is named for the goddess of love. Being born with Venus in ascendance foretells beauty, sensitivity, and sexuality. Mercury, close to the sun, moves rapidly and is difficult to view; it is named for the fleet messenger of the gods. Someone born with Mercury in ascendance is communicative, perceptive, and travels. Not all correspondences make sense to the modern mind, but the general principle is clear.

Ptolemy also attributed characteristics based on his (erroneous) understanding of planetary positions with respect to the sun. For example,

"The nature of Mars is chiefly to dry and to burn, in conformity with his fiery colour and by reason of his nearness to the sun, for the sun's sphere lies just below him...." (For a translation of the *Tetrabiblos* see http://penelope.uchicago.edu/Thayer/E/Roman/Texts/Ptolemy/Tetrabiblos/home.html.) Planets discovered with the telescope – Uranus (1781), Neptune (1846), Pluto (1930) – have astrological influences in accord with the ancient gods for whom they are named.[6]

Quite apart from the twelve signs of the zodiac, astrology also has twelve *houses*. These were not used by the Greeks as they are today, but seem to date from Arab astrology of the Middle Ages. Houses are based on the daily rotation of the celestial sphere around the stationary earth, causing stars and planets to rise on the eastern horizon and set in the west. Two observers at widely distant locations, each watching their local horizon at the same time, will see different stars and planets rising. By attributing influences to whatever signs and planets are crossing the horizon at birth, astrology individualizes horoscopes to the location of birth along with the time of birth.

To visualize the houses, imagine that the celestial sphere, rotating overhead, is divided into twelve imaginary wedges, each wedge being a house. Each house has a special significance for one's life. The first house is that wedge immediately below the eastern horizon at the moment of birth, containing those stars and planets that will rise within approximately the next two hours. It is concerned with outward personality. The second wedge, or house, rises next and is concerned with worldly wealth. The third house is concerned with siblings, and so on. Depending on what stars or planets are in each house, the outlook for the infant can be good or bad, or foretell general attributes. A planet in the eighth house, which is concerned with death, may indicate how the infant will eventually die. In a twenty-four-hour period, the twelve houses (and the stars and planets they contain) rise successively on the infant's eastern horizon.

Horoscopes

A horoscope is a kind of map of the heavens at the time of the subject's birth. It juxtaposes the birth positions of zodiacal signs, planets, and houses, plus additional details that need not detain us. By compressing the universe into two dimensions, the ingenious graphical design shows all data needed to chart a life. Newspaper horoscopes using only sun signs, without regard even to the subject's ascendant, are not taken seriously by real astrologers.

The casting of horoscopes is mathematically objective. When calculated by hand, the work is laborious, subject to error, and depends on approximations. Today's horoscopes are computer generated and easily obtained on the web by inputting the time and place of birth. An ephemeris, which gives the coordinates of celestial bodies at any given time, is programmed into the computer. Generally speaking, the result is more accurate and error free, although charts produced by different websites are not exactly identical.

The top chart in figure 11.2 is the horoscope Professor Abell's published in 1981 for his own birth in Los Angeles at 10:50 P.M. on March 1, 1927. I recently ran the lower left-hand chart for the same birth information by computer.[7] Despite superficial differences in design, the basic formats are the same. The earth is at the center of each chart, surrounded by the celestial sphere. The horizontal bisector represents the local horizon at the time and place of birth (east at the left, west at the right). In the outer circle are the twelve symbols of the zodiac, rotated so the ascendant sign (Scorpio = ♏) is at the left (eastern) horizon. The pie-shaped wedges (numbered 1 to 12) are the houses. The first house, representing personality, is rising on the left (eastern) horizon. Inside the house-wedges are symbols for the sun, moon, and planets, placed around the zodiac in the positions they occupied at birth. The sun symbol ☉ is in Pisces, Professor Abell's sun sign.

Since the locations of celestial bodies are objectively real, and with today's instruments they are accurately measured, the ten planetary positions shown in these charts, as seen from George Abell's birthplace, should be exactly the same. They nearly are, but visual comparison shows slight deviations. For example, in houses 4 and 5 the computer has planets clustered more tightly than in Abell's hand-calculated chart. We leave unresolved whether astronomer Abell or the website is more accurate.

In ancient times, it would have been impossible, even meaningless, to time a birth to the nearest minute. Pre-modern astrologers necessarily made relatively crude estimates of the signs and planets in ascendance. It was not a critical matter because the *exact* timing and location of one person's birth does not importantly differentiate one horoscope from another. If we move Professor Abell's birthplace from Los Angeles to San Francisco, 400 miles to the northwest, and round his delivery time to 11:00 P.M., the computer provides a nearly identical horoscope (lower right-hand chart).[8]

By the way, computers cannot cast charts for anyone born in Lapland or the far north of Russia, Canada, or Alaska. Important as rising signs

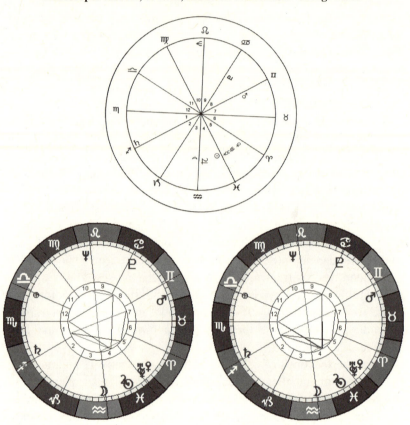

Figure 11.2
Horoscopes cast for, or near, the birth of Professor George Abell

and planets are for astrologers practicing their art in middle latitudes, they are meaningless above the Arctic Circle, where the sun, stars, and planets do not rise and set each day, and where houses do not pass overhead. Ancient astrologers were ignorant of this lacuna in their cosmology, and modern astrologers ignore it.

Interpreting the Horoscope

The casting of a horoscope is objectively precise, but its interpretation – its meaning to the subject's life – is flexible, and therein lays the art of astrology. There are many rules for interpreting horoscopes, many traceable to Ptolemy, others to Arab and Renaissance astrologers, and still others that are modern, such as those for the newly discovered planets.[9] There is no complete consensus about these rules, even on a matter so important as whether one's sun sign at is determined by the zodiacal sector (tropical astrology) or the actual constellation (sidereal astrology). A complete horoscope consists of many separate elements: twelve zodiac signs, as many as ten planets (including the sun and moon), the ascendant, plus esoteric features not discussed here including the descendant, mid-heaven, angular planetary aspects, and cusps. There may be a hundred elements in a subject's horoscope, and it is a firm tradition that no element can be interpreted in isolation from the others. This gives the astrologer enormous latitude to emphasize or countermand any single element in order to justify or reject one conclusion rather than another. Beethoven's chart can be interpreted to show musical genius, Hitler's to show consummate evil, but each can also be interpreted to show the absence of these salient qualities (Eysenck and Nias 1982: 31).

Interpretations are not wholly arbitrary because traditional rules are embedded in the art. For example, the planets indicate basic qualities, and the houses show where these qualities are expressed. If the horoscope shows Mars in the first house, which governs personality, the subject might be foretold to be forceful. While trained astrologers analyzing the horoscope of the same person may offer confliction opinions, there will also be some agreement. Professor Abell's horoscope was analyzed by nearly twenty different astrologers, and most said he had a penchant for a career in medicine, that his first marriage was at age twenty-four, and that he had a talent for communication (1981: 83). He was married at twenty-four, and I can vouch that he was a talented communicator. Any canny astrologer, informed that Professor Abell did not pursue a career in medicine, could reinterpret his chart accordingly.

Time of Birth (Astral Twins)

The great astronomer-astrologer Johannes Kepler was born on December 27 at 2:20 p.m. after a pregnancy lasting 224 days, nine hours, and fifty-three minutes from his conception at 4:37 in the morning of May 16, 1571. These times are recorded in the horoscope Kepler cast for himself (Koestler 1960). No doubt his precision was the result of calculation, not direct measurement. His inclusion of both dates reflects the longstanding uncertainty among astrologers whether it is the point of conception or of birth that matters most.

Despite the romantic notion that the stars seal one's fate at the instant of creation, this is difficult to determine with sexually active parents. There is no mistaking when a newborn clears the birth canal, so practicality wins, but even that was difficult to time before the existence of accurate clocks, unless an acute observer was watching the night sky. This could not have been true for Kepler, born in the afternoon. Ancient astrologers could not calculate horoscopes for the exact minute of birth, nor did they think in such small units of time. Even today, one should not take too literally the recorded minute of one's birth.

The Roman senator and orator Cicero was skeptical of astrology and raised an argument that has bedeviled the art ever since. How could twins, born at the same time and place, and therefore having the same horoscope charts, have different personalities and destinies?[10]

This is not an insurmountable objection. In his fine history of astrology, Benson Bobrick puts the rejoinder, "no adept would have supposed their [the twins'] charts identical in the first place. In the course of just four minutes, a new degree (and therefore possibly a new decan, subruler-ship, fixed star, and so on) can rise above the horizon, and give a wholly different cast to a child's fate" (2005: 94).

Most twins are indeed born more than four minutes apart.[11] However, as already noted, the timing of a birth to a precision of a few minutes was rarely available to pre-nineteenth-century astrologers. In theory, twins born four minutes apart might have very different destinies, but in practice the pre-modern astrologer casting their horoscopes would not have known the moment of either twin's emergence to that level of accuracy. Turning Bobrick's rejoinder on its head, any horoscope that is off by four minutes in its presumed time of birth is irrelevant to the subject's life.

Astrologers deemphasize the problem of hereditary twins while emphasizing the importance of "astral twins," two *unrelated* people born at the same time in nearby locations, who have remarkably similar lives. Historian Bobrick relates this famous example (without citing his source):

> On June 4, 1738, in the parish of St. Martins-in-the-Fields, two boys were born less than a minute apart. One was William Frederick, later crowned George III, King of England; the other, James [*sic*] Hemmings, an ironmonger's son. Widely separated by class, yet bound to a parallel fate, these two men, each in his own social sphere, lived out the edict of his stars. In October 1760, when George III succeeded his fa-ther on the throne, thereby fulfilling the purpose to which he was born, Hemmings took over his father's business. Both men were married on September 8, 1761, fa-thered the same number of children (even, weirdly, the same number of boys and girls), suffered the same accidents, succumbed to the same diseases, and died within less than an hour of each other on Saturday, January 29, 1820 (Bobrick 2005: 305).

How would anyone know that George and James (or Samuel in some versions) were born less than a minute apart? Accurate pendulum clocks with minute hands had been invented nearly seventy years earlier, and no doubt there was one in the palace. To credit the story, we must assume that a comparably accurate clock was available to time the birth of the ironmonger's son, that its minute hand was set identically to the minute hand on the palace clock, that both births were accurately recorded to the minute, and that someone was privy to both records in order to match the times.

It is puzzling that an historian as competent as Bobrick repeats the story without inquiring into its authenticity or genesis. Patrick Curry (1992) did inquire, finding it in the 1828 book, *A Manual of Astrology*, by Robert Cross Smith, who wrote under the penname Raphael (after the angel):

> In the newspapers of February, 1820, the death of Mr. Samuel [*sic*] Hemmings was noticed. It was stated that he had been an ironmonger and prosperous in trade – that he was born on the 4th of June 1738, at nearly the same moment as his late majesty, George III, and in the same parish of St. Martin's-in-the-Fields; that he went into business for himself in October, 1760, when his late majesty came to the throne; that he married on the 8th of September 1761, the same day as the king; and finally, after other events of his life had resembled those which happened to the late king, that he died on Saturday, January 29th, 1820, on the same day and nearly the same hour as his late majesty (Raphael 1828: xvi).

The pseudonymous astrologer Sepharial (Walter Gom Old) embellished the story in his 1910 *A Manual of Occultism*:

> The case of John Hemming [*sic*] the ironmonger's son, who was born at the same time and in the same parish of St. Martins-in-the-Fields as King George III, proves that planetary influence is more significant than heredity. For John Hemming's father died, and he succeeded to the business at the same time that George II died and George III came to the throne. They were both similarly afflicted by temporary loss of mental faculty, they had the same number of children, and they died on the same day and nearly at the same hour.

Pioneering American astrologer Evangeline Adams repeated Raphael's version in her 1926 autobiography (pp. 179-80). I have found it on numerous astrology websites, one giving the birth at precisely 7:48 A.M. Skeptic Geoffrey Dean (1994), checking contemporary records, could verify only the simultaneous dates of death.[12]

Even if the story of the king and the ironmonger were true in its essentials, we may ask if one can find a few coincidences between a monarch's life and the life of *any* commoner. Reading a biography of George III (Hibbert 1998), I learned that the king religiously intermarried a woman of German-Lutheran aristocratic descent, that they first met in London only months before the marriage, and that one of the bride's parents died days before the ceremony. These are also facts of my marriage.[13]

Today the problem of hereditary twins is far more serious for astrology than it was in Cicero's time. Using genetic tests, we can accurately distinguish monozygotic twins, who have identical DNA, from dizygotic twins who, like any two siblings, share 50 percent of their DNA.[14] A large body of modern psychological research on twins shows that monozygotic twins are very similar on IQ, major personality factors, and diverse traits, even when they are separated at birth and raised apart. But dizygotic twins, raised in the same family, are little more similar to one another than they are to their other siblings, born at different times (Bouchard and McGue 2003). Astrology provides no explanation for this stark difference between monozygotic and dizygotic twins, but genetics does.

Statistical Tests

Mathematical statistics grew to maturity during World War II and the years afterward. Coinciding with the postwar vogue of astrology in Europe and American, there was a flurry of statistical studies, attempts to test the validity of astrological forecasts. All of these were problematic because it was necessary to deduce simple, unambiguous statements that could be tested on samples of people. Given the flexibility of traditional interpretation, and the ever present potential in any individual's horoscope for one element to contradict another, many serious astrologers dismissed the value of such studies, arguing that hard-nosed statistics was antithetical to the art, and that no proof was needed in view of the validation provided by millennia of experience. Nonetheless, the statisticians proceeded to seek correlations between, for example, sun sign and occupation or personality, to see if those born under Aries really tend toward assertiveness, Taurians toward stubbornness, Leos toward pride, Virgos toward modesty, and so on. If true, these main effects should appear in a large population. Other inquiries compared the horoscopes of couples who divorced with those who remained married, or examined planetary associations with criminal activity (Mars with violence) or mental illness (the full moon and lunacy). Some early studies did seem to support traditional suppositions, however they were based on small samples, lacked control groups, or used fallacious statistical reasoning. As more competent attempts were made to replicate these findings, using larger samples, control groups, and proper statistical tests, the confirmatory findings were dismissed (Eysenck and Nias 1982; Dean et al. 1997; Abdel-Khalek and Lester 2006; Hartmann et al. 2006).

An unusually careful test was conducted by Shawn Carlson (1985), who avoided simplistic sun-sign predictions and guarded against biases that had crept into earlier work. The proposition tested in his double-blind study was that the full natal horoscope determines the subject's general personality traits. Carlson enlisted the support of the National Council for Geocosmic Research (NCGR), an organization widely respected by astrologers. NCGR nominated astrologers who consented to advise or participate in the study. These advisers reviewed the experimental design and made suggestions for improvement, as did skeptical advisers. Eventually, both camps were satisfied that the test was fair.

Volunteer subjects provided their time and place of birth from which horoscopes were calculated by computer. The subjects also completed a well-known psychological assessment instrument, the California Personality Inventory (CPI), which consists of 480 true-false questions that measure eighteen personality scales (dominance, passivity, femininity, etc.). Some twenty participating astrologers were each given the horoscopes of several randomly-drawn target subjects. For each target subject, three sets of CPI scores were also supplied, one for the target subject and two chosen at random from the subject pool. The astrologers were asked to select which of the three CPI sets best matched the target subject's horoscope.[15] The astrologers predicted beforehand that they could match at least half the horoscopes to correct CPI results. Of 116 horoscopes evaluated, the astrologers correctly matched 33 percent to CPI scores, just what would be expected by chance.

The most enduring "positive" result to come from this activity, the so-called "Mars effect," is attributed to the French psychologist Michel Gauquelin who, ironically, led a decades-long series of studies that continually undermined precepts of traditional astrology. Toward the end of this program Gauquelin firmly asserted, "No law of classical astrology has been demonstrated statistically by astrologers or scientists" (1979). What Gauquelin did claim to show was a non-classical and previously unanticipated relationship – a tendency of certain planets to occupy or avoid two sectors of the sky at the time of birth of very successful professionals. Mars, in particular, was reported to occupy these two sectors at the birth of sports champions but not at the birth of less eminent athletes. Gauquelin based his studies on large samples and included control groups. This earned the approval of respected psychologist Hans Eysenck in his otherwise negative overview of statistical tests of astrology. Eysenck was not much bothered by the small magnitude of Gauquelin's effects, or that the statistical significance of his results was not as impressive as presented because tests were applied to ad hoc findings rather than to a priori hypotheses.

Despite Gauquelin's repeated insistence that his results offered no support for traditional astrology, many astrologers view them as consistent with the general tenor of a heavenly connection to our lives, and I agree with them. The relevant question is whether Gauquelin's findings are valid? Using a subset of Gauquelin's own data on sports champions, statistician Marvin Zelen, Paul Kurtz, and George Abell confirmed that the Mars effect was marginally significant (at the .04 level) but that it became insignificant if athletes born in Paris were eliminated from the sample. The Mars effect did not appear at all for sports champions born in Belgium. It also failed to appear in an independent sample of several hundred sports champions born in the United States (Abell 1981). After re-examining the original data, Nienhuys (1997) made a strong case that the Mars effect is a methodological artifact, produced – perhaps inadvertently – by Gauquelin's biased selection of subjects for inclusion in his data set. The Mars effect lives on in astrology sites on the internet, but it seems no longer a topic worthy of new empirical investigation.

Why do People Believe in Astrology?

After the assassination attempt on President Ronald Reagan in 1981, entertainer Merv Griffin told his friend Nancy Reagan of an astrologer in San Francisco named Joan Quigley. The Reagans had dealt with astrologers for years. Nancy Reagan, now anxious for her husband's safety, began consulting Quigley about opportune times for the president's activities, including his famous speech at Bitburg, Germany, and signing with Soviet General Secretary Mikhail Gorbachev a treaty to limit nuclear weapons. According to Donald Regan, who was privy to the president's activities at that time, "Virtually every move and decision the Reagans made during my time as White House chief of staff was cleared in advance by a woman in San Francisco who drew up horoscopes to make certain that the planets were in a favorable alignment for the enterprise." Regan wrote about a multicolored calendar on his desk for bad and good days, judgments made by astrologer Quigley. After Regan made this public, the president was asked at a press conference if he believed in astrology. Reagan answered, "I don't guide my life by it, but I won't answer the question the other way because I don't know enough about it to say is there something to it or not" (Reeves 2005: 455).

Believing in astrology defies every criterion for implausibility (Chapter 10). The astrologer's claim to expertise, based on folk wisdom, is unsubstantiated—and substantially contradicted—by modern science. There is no known law of nature by which distant planets and stars can importantly influence human affairs. Astrology is founded on the ancient misunderstanding of the universe as geocentric, with the stars and planets revolving daily on a celestial sphere.

The lynchpin of the whole astrological system is the zodiac. In early Babylonian astrology, the zodiacal signs represented actual patterns of stars along the ecliptic, and the tradition, as it later developed, was based on the powers believed to reside in these constellations. By now, the precession of the equinoxes has caused the signs of the zodiac (referenced to the vernal equinox) to move away from the constellations with which they were originally associated. The inference from this is clear: either the astrological tradition became obsolete as soon as precession began to misalign the signs and their constellations, or else the qualities attributed to the signs are not connected with the stars at all.

The modern-day dilemma caused by the precession of the equinoxes is best seen by comparing today's tropical astrology, as practiced in the West, with the sidereal astrology that is practiced in the East. In tropical astrology, popular in the United States, one's sun sign is determined by the zodiacal sector in which the sun lies at birth. But this is inconsistent with sidereal astrology, where one's sun sign is determined by the constellation that *used to* occupy the zodiacal sector in Ptolemy's time. Both systems cannot be correct because that would imply a logical contradiction. Choosing one system over the other is like identifying the one true faith.

The connection between our horoscopes and our lives is explained by analogies with the imagined attributes of gods for whom planets and constellations were named. Planets not known before the invention of the telescope became relevant afterward. The system of houses, passing daily overhead, is meaningless for people born above the Arctic Circle.

Another important but nonsensical concept in astrological theory is that of planetary aspects. These are the apparent angles between pairs of planets, as seen from earth. They are based wholly on geometrical patterns formed on a sheet of paper, and are not related in any way to modifications of the planetary forces brought about by changes in relative position. (The triangles at the center of the horoscopes in figure 11.2, b and c, are planetary aspects.) Furthermore, the traditional astrologer, when calculating planetary positions, makes no allowance for the velocity of light. Taking Neptune as an example, the light coming from its surface takes two to three hours to reach earth, so Neptune's apparent position, as seen from earth, is roughly thirty degrees different from its actual position.

Competent statistical studies give no support to astrological forecasts. Since ancient times, as Cicero cogently argued, astrology has failed even the simple test of twin siblings having similar fates. (The time interval between twin births is small compared to the precision with which any birth was recorded prior to the nineteenth century.) So why does any intelligent person in the modern world believe in astrology?

As in explaining other implausible beliefs, we must register the caveat that many "believers" in astrology have barely entertained the option of disbelief, and if pressed would deny that they give strong credence to astrological forecasts. Reading one's daily horoscope, like working the morning crossword puzzle, may be nothing more than an amusing distraction, a brief respite from the day's chores. Nancy Reagan's belief is a far stronger one, as is that of patrons who pay considerable sums for astrological advice, now obtainable via internet to anyone with a credit card. ·

Being superstitious, gullible, unintelligent, or having low education may predispose some people to accept astrology (Mazur 2004; Glendinning and Bruce 2006), but there is little research on the matter. I have seen no suggestion that believers in astrology are mentally aberrant. To explain their acceptance of this implausible lore, I propose the usual default assumption, that sincere believers in astrology were raised in families or communities that fostered this and other New Age views, or they were later converted to astrology through the usual process of social influence from a spouse or friends. Unfortunately, this default hypothesis remains untested. While we have many surveys of individuals' beliefs about astrology, we lack studies that relate them to the beliefs of their parents, spouses, and friends.

Ronald and Nancy Reagan, a devotedly loving couple, disagreed on very little. The president's acceptance of his wife's astrology, if distressing in view of his high office, is nonetheless explicable as an instance of spousal convergence, especially considering their pre-political background in the astrology-believing entertainment community.

People predisposed toward astrology easily see validity in its claims about their lives. The tendency for people to identify themselves with personality descriptions of a general and vague nature is called the "Barnum effect" and has been demonstrated in a large number of studies, the earliest by Forer (1949), who gave personalities tests to 39 students and a week later returned fake results. All students were given the same personality profile consisting of thirteen statements taken from a sun sign book. The students were asked to indicate for each statement whether they considered it a true description of themselves. Most students saw the whole profile as applying to themselves. Nearly everyone accepted these items:

You have a tendency to be critical of yourself.

Disciplined and self-controlled outside, you tend to be worrisome and insecure inside.

At times you have serious doubts as to whether you have made the right decision or done the right thing.

You prefer a certain amount of change and variety and become dissatisfied when hemmed in by restrictions and limitations.

You have found it unwise to be too frank in revealing yourself to others.

I invite readers to check all of the above items that apply to themselves.

Once predisposed toward astrology, whether through childhood socialization, social conversion, the Barnum effect, or other inducements, there is a general tendency to interpret later readings in a positive light. *Confirmation bias* is perhaps the best known and most widely studied inferential error in the literature of human reasoning. When examining evidence relevant to a given belief, people usually see what they expect to see, and conclude what they hope to conclude. Consider, for example, experiences that might maintain one's belief that "the phone always rings when I'm in the shower." If the phone does ring while showering, it will stand out as a salient confirmation. If the phone does not ring while showering, that absence is unlikely to register as an event in memory (Gilovich 1991). Believers in astrology emphasize and remember horoscope readings that ring true while ignoring or forgetting readings that are off base (Evans 1989; Nickerson 1998).

Glick and his colleagues illustrated confirmation effects in a study that compared two groups of students, one group comprising believers in astrology, the other composed of skeptics. Each student was given a horoscope and told (deceptively) that it had been prepared especially for them by a professional astrology service. In fact, the horoscopes were not individualized at all. Half the students in each group received the same horoscope, one generally positive in tone, describing the subject as sympathetic, dependable, and sociable. The other half of each group received a version that was negative in tone, describing the student as undependable, unrealistic, and overly sensitive. Later, when student were asked how accurate the horoscopes were, those in the believers' group said is was very accurate (regardless of whether they received the positive or negative version). Skeptics who received the negative version said it was inaccurate, as expected from the confirmation bias. However skeptics who received the positive version were more likely to accord it accuracy, as if seduced by the Barnum effect. When believing and skeptical subjects were asked to interview another student and to evaluate the accuracy of that person's horoscope, the believers were more likely than skeptics to conclude that it was correct (Glick and Snyder 1986; Glick et al. 1989; Vyse 1997). In astrology, as in other domains of knowledge, we stain evidence through filters of prior beliefs.

Notes

1. Ancient societies knew the yearly cycle of seasons took 365 days. This is easily learned by watching the point on the horizon where the sun sets each day. In the Northern Hemisphere, the sun sets farthest north at the height of summer, and farthest south at the depth of winter. An observer tallying the days for the sun to return to one of these extreme points would count 365 days.
2. Earth's equator, or 0° latitude, is simply the intersection of the plane of the celestial equator with our planet's surface.
3. Today we understand that the orbits of all the planets (except the former planet Pluto) lie nearly in the plane of the ecliptic.
4. The Greeks inferred that the moon is closer than the sun from three observations. First, one can see details on the moon – it looks closer. Second, the moon moves across the starry background more quickly than other wanderers, a characteristic of close objects. Third, during a solar eclipse, one can observe the sun progressively occluded by the unlit lunar disk, indicating that the moon is "in front."
5. An advantage of the tropical system is that the zodiacal signs regularly accompany the seasons.
6. According to astrologer Judy Hall, Uranus, named for the primeval god who sired the monstrous titans, "is the great mover and shaker, symbolizing change or chaos;" Neptune, named for the ruler of the oceans, moves from the highest spiritual awareness "to the depths" of deception; Pluto, named for the god of the underworld, embodies the drive to confront "all that is deepest and darkest" in the psyche (2005: 203, 209, 215).
7. I used the site http://www.eugenialast.com/ maintained by syndicated astrologer Eugenia Last.
8. The planets (excepting the sun and moon) move so slowly against the starry background that the naked eye does not discern changes from one day to the next. It is the daily rotation of the earth, or to the ancients the daily rotation of the celestial sphere, that produces more rapid variation in horoscopes by altering the direction of the sun and moon, and by the rising of houses over the eastern horizon.
9. We need not go into the complications that arose with the discovery of each new planet that was unknown to the ancients, or with the recent demotion of Pluto from full planetary status.

10. Cicero also wondered how mass killings, such as Hannibal's slaughter of Roman soldiers at the battle Cannae in 216 BCE, were consistent with the diversity of birth times and places among those who died that day.

11. A study of 115 American women having live-born twins of 34 or more weeks' gestation, showed the mean interval between vaginal deliveries ranged from one to 134 minutes, with a mean of 21 minutes. The interval was more than 15 minutes in 39 percent of cases (Rayburn et al. 1984).

12. Pursuing the matter further, Dean and Kelly (2003) studied 2,101 people born in London from March 3 to 9, 1958, each delivered within several minutes of another person in the sample. The average recorded time between "astral births" was 4.8 minutes, and it was less than five minutes in 73 percent of pairings. Repeating over one hundred measurements when the subjects were ages 11, 16, and 23, including intelligence and school achievement, physical characteristics, personality traits, and interests, they found no more similarity between "twins" than would be expected by chance.

13. George III and I were each the second child of our parents, born after two grandparents were dead, a third died within a few years, and the surviving grandparent was emotionally distant. We grew up in bilingual families where English and a German dialect were spoken. We each had two children within two years of the marriage ceremony. We each named a daughter Elizabeth.

14. Monozygotic twins are produced when a single fertilized egg splits and subsequently develops into two identical embryos. Dizygotic twins are produced when two eggs are fertilized at the same time, producing two genetically distinct embryos.

15. There is a presumption here that the astrologers could properly interpret CPI scores in terms that correspond to their horoscope interpretations.

Part 4

Why Do We Believe These Things?

12

Social Influence

Whether a belief is plausible or implausible, rational or irrational, benign or evil, is irrelevant from the sociologist's perspective because every person's beliefs are formed through the same processes, via interaction with their social milieu. Sociology has no laws as binding as those of physics, but it does have empirically robust principles that explain why people hold particular views.

Principle 1: Beliefs Reflect Their Time and Place in History

I begin with a statement so obvious that it could go unmentioned except that many Americans seem unaware that their religiosity is unusual. In 1998, the United States was one of twenty-nine nations participating in a survey of religious attitudes and behavior, coordinated by the International Social Survey Programme (ISSP), which was briefly described in chapter 3's comparison of national views on the evolution of species. The nations included Canada, most of the European Union, Russia, Israel, Australia, New Zealand, and two predominately Catholic nations of the third world: Chile and the Philippines. By every measure, the United States was more religious than most other nations in the survey.[1] Only the Philippines, Chile, and Poland consistently equaled or exceeded the U.S. in religious devotion.

Table 12.1 compares religious attitudes and practices in the United States with two nations that Americans regard as most akin: Great Britain, and Canada. Today's Britons, despite having an established national church, are so unobservant that an English colleague described his country as the first post-Christian society. Other nations of Northern and Central Europe are as impious as Britain (Lambert 2004). Even Canada, usually dominated by American culture, is religiously more like the United Kingdom than the United States.

Table 12.1

Religious Beliefs and Practices in the U.S., Britain, and Canada

	United States	Great Britain	Canada
I am extremely/very religious.	26%	7%	12%
God exists and I have no doubt about it.	63%	23%	39%
I definitely believe in religious miracles.	51%	14%	26%
I definitely believe in Heaven.	66%	23%	36%
I definitely believe in Hell.	55%	14%	26%
Prays once a day or more	47%	15%	19%
Participates in church activities nearly every week	18%	7%	9%

Source: ISSP 1998 (http://www.gesis.org/en/data_service/issp/data/1998_Religion_II.htm).

To measure fundamentalism, respondents in all nations were read statements about the Bible and asked to choose the one closest to their own feelings. One statement, "The Bible is the actual word of God and it is to be taken literally, word for word," is a good indicator of core fundamentalist belief.[2] Respondents in the Philippines and Chile lead all other nations in choosing this literalist response; the United States ranks seventh (figure 12.1). Americans are half as likely as Filipinos but three times more likely than Britons or most Europeans to believe the Bible is literally God's word. In the U.S., women are slightly more likely than men to take the Bible literally (38 percent vs. 28 percent).

There have been several suggestions why Americans are more devout than Europeans (Stark and Finke 1993; Noll 2001). The answer is not wholly settled, but we can say that the difference is nothing new. The French traveler Alexis de Tocqueville, famous for his observations of American society during a visit in 1831, wrote in a letter to a friend, "It's obvious there still remains here [in the United States] a greater foundation of Christianity than in any other country of the world to my knowledge" (Pierson 1938).

Principle 2: We Accept Beliefs in Which we are Raised; Those Who Deviate Do Not Deviate Far

The extent of Americans' fundamentalist beliefs may perplex those who regard the United States as the most scientifically advanced nation in the world. The conundrum is resolved by looking at child rearing. "The

Figure 12.1
**Percent Who Believe the Bible is the Actual Word of God and is to be
taken Literally, by Nation**

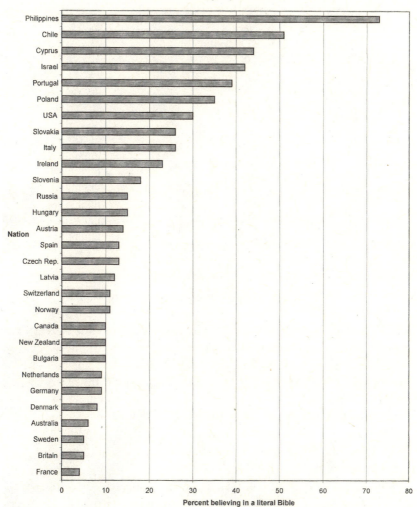

acorn does not fall far from the tree," says one piece of arboreal wisdom, and another goes, "As the twig is bent, so grows the tree."

Even in a nation as religiously free as the United States, with its many competing denominations, people reliably maintain the religious traditions of their parents. We see this in data from the General Social Surveys (GSS), which since 1972 has yearly or biennially asked random samples of U.S. adults about their religious identifications as well as omnibus attitudes and background information. If we include the various Prot-

Figure 12.2
Childhood Religion Determines Adult Religion

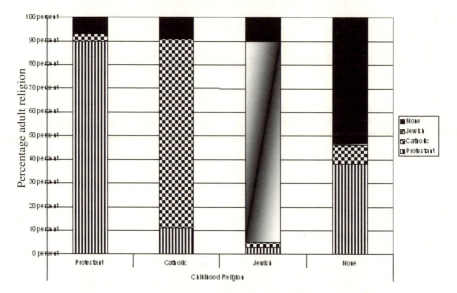

estant denominations under one umbrella, roughly 80 percent of adults continued to identify with the religion in which they were reared (figure 12.2). Of those people raised without religion, half remained irreligious as adults while roughly a third joined the nation's Protestant majority.

Americans are residentially mobile and commonly change the congregation they attend, even changing denominations, but they rarely stray very far from the basic religious orientation of their parents. Even within Protestantism, three-quarters of respondents who were raised fundamentalist remain in fundamentalist denominations as adults (figure 12.3). Of those raised as moderate or liberal Protestants, two-thirds retain those orientations as adults.[3]

Childhood socialization influences people's social affiliations as well as beliefs. We usually marry someone born into our own religion (figure 12.4). Even people reared without any religion disproportionately find mates who were raised non-religiously, though about half end up with Protestant spouses simply because most Americans of the opposite sex are Protestant. Among Protestants, nearly two-thirds of respondents who were raised as fundamentalists married someone also raised as a fundamentalist.

Endogamy conserves the traditions of childhood. When people reared in Genesis-believing families marry Genesis-believing spouses, they instill

Figure 12.3
Childhood Protestant Denomination Affects Adult Religion

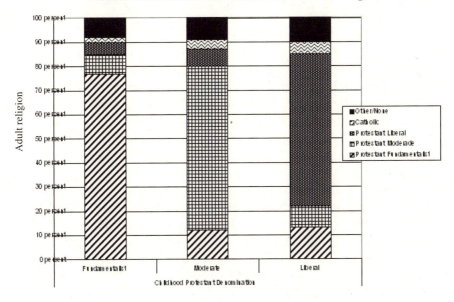

Figure 12.4
Childhood Religion Affects Marital Choice

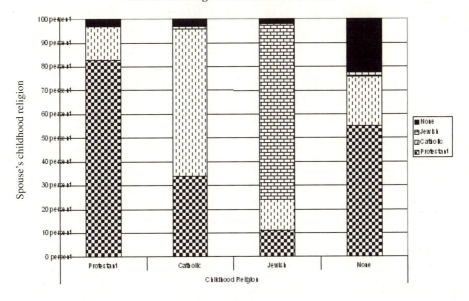

these ideas in their children. Usually they associate with Genesis-believing friends and a fundamentalist church, so their local community, perhaps even their local school, insulates them from contradictory forces.

The persistence of childhood tradition is impressively demonstrated by the Old Order Amish. These particular Amish, one of several Anabaptist groups in America, number about 100,000 and are concentrated in Pennsylvania, Ohio, and Indiana. Best known for their rural horse-and-buggy culture and their plain, archaic dress, the Amish remain isolated from the American mainstream, speaking a dialect of German. They oppose higher education, eschew modern technologies, and frown on many frivolities and forms of permissiveness common in U.S. culture.

Amish children learn to submit to the will of God and to the community. They dress to conform, not to impress or to differentiate themselves from their peers. If they express pride, they are criticized. Family socialization is fortified with the social resources of the community. When the Amish break the rules they may be asked to confess publicly on their knees before their neighbors. The Amish transgressor who does not confess might be excommunicated. If they remain in the community, they may be shunned. The Amish can speak to a shunned person, but cannot shake hands with them or accept anything from them. At a wedding the shunned person may be seated at a separate table.

Amish believe in adult baptism. This is supposed to be a free, informed choice, so older teenagers are allowed a few years of "running around." In recent decades this has taken the form of dressing like non-Amish teens, partying at dances with beer and live bands, installing CD players in their buggies, purchasing cars, and stronger forms of rebellion. At about age twenty, when it is time to decide about baptism, 90 percent of Amish youth commit to their childhood faith and community lifestyle (Kraybill 2001).

Amish success in holding their own may seem remarkable to participants in mainstream materialist culture, but this persistence follows from Principle 2. *Maintaining family beliefs and traditions is natural; it is the default option of childhood socialization, requiring no further explanation.* What requires explanation is the Amish youth who enters the material world, or the Genesis-raised college student who espouses Darwin. They are the exceptions, unaccounted for by the default option.

How do we reconcile the static implications of Principle 2 with the widely reported growth of fundamentalist Christianity in the United States since the 1970s? Today we have evangelical megachurches, "born again" televangelists, Christian radio, best-selling novels about the coming rapture, and elected officials promoting fundamentalist Christian precepts. But the appearance may be deceiving.

There was in the U.S. during the early to middle twentieth century a disproportionate increase in fundamentalist congregants relative to moderate mainline denominations, probably due to higher birth rates among the fundamentalists (Stark and Finke 1993; Noll 2001). Since 1972, according to GSS data, there has been little change in weekly attendance at religious services. Since 1983, when a prayer question was first asked in the survey, there has been little change in the frequency of personal prayer. Since 1984, when the GSS refined its classification of Protestant denominations (Smith 1987), there has been little change in the distribution of respondents among fundamentalist, moderate, and liberal denominations, except for brief fluctuations in the late 1980s (figure 12.5).

The media's exaggerated picture of fundamentalist growth is partly explained by the political ascendancy of the South due to population and

Figure 12.5
Percent of Fundamentalist, Moderate, and Liberal Protestants, by Year

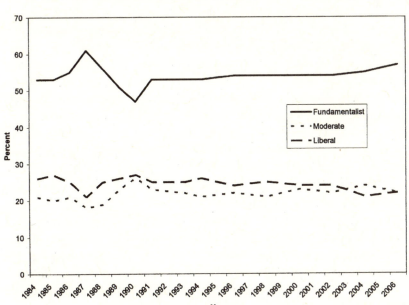

economic shifts away from the Northeast. This enabled the election of Jimmy Carter, the first southern president of modern times. Carter was a moderate Democrat but more importantly a born again Christian and a distinct break from the conventional Christianity of his predecessors. Bill Clinton of Arkansas, a Southern Baptist, and especially George W. Bush of Texas made the White House a venue for the kind of religiosity that had earlier seemed a backward feature of the remnant Confederacy. Media impressions notwithstanding, Americans have not departed much from the religious traditions of their parents.

Principle 3: Conversion is Seldom about Solitary Truth Seeking; It is Usually about Conforming to the Beliefs of a Spouse or Friends.

The famous epiphany of Saul of Tarsus on the road to Damascus was like a flash of lightning, individualistic and without portent (Acts 9:3). If true, Saul's experience was unusual. Sociologists Rodney Stark and Roger Finke (2000) compiled abundant evidence that conversion nearly always involves the intercession of another person and occurs gradually. Often converts "reconstruct" their conversion after the fact, attributing it to a self-conscious search for the truth or to sudden enlightenment, but in cases that are well studied, there is generally an intermediary—a friend or family member already in the new group—who facilitates an extended transition.[4]

The origin of the Church of Latter Day Saints, or Mormonism, illustrates the networking nature of conversion. In September 1823 in Upstate New York, an angel named Maroni appeared to Joseph Smith, Jr., revealing the hiding place of golden plates upon which were written an account of Christ's visit to the New World. Smith found the plates and translated their Egyptian script, producing the *Book of Mormon*.[5] His first converts were Smith's immediate family, and the first outside the family were Smith's longtime friend, Martin Harris, and Oliver Cowdery, a young schoolteacher who lived with Smith's parents. Cowdery showed the translation to his close friend David Whitmer. At the church's official founding in 1830, there were twenty-three Mormons including eleven Smiths (counting in-laws), ten Whitmers, Harris, and Cowdery. The next recruits included six members of the Jolly family, five Rockwells, seventeen Youngs, and many of Smith's distant relations. Smith in 1837 sent missionaries to Great Britain, where they had great success among three nonconformist churches whose pastors were a brother and two brothers-in-law of one of the missionaries. By 1840 the church counted nearly 17,000 members, its rapid recruitment still working along family and friendship lines (Arrington and Bitton 1979).

Today's Mormons are required to spend a period as missionaries, seeking new recruits. When they make cold calls, knocking on the doors of strangers, they obtain about one conversion per thousand attempts. When their first contact with a prospect is in the home of a Mormon friend or relative, the conversion rate is 50 percent. People rarely convert without a social mediator.[6]

The social process of conversion applies to politics as well as religion. In the first place, most Americans identify with the political party of their parents, holding similar political ideologies as liberals, moderates, or conservatives (Marcus et al. 1995; Zaller 1992; Kinder 2006).[7] When young adults do change their politics, usually it is through immersion in friendship, college, or work groups of the new political persuasion, or through marriage to someone with those views.

Psychologist Theodore Newcomb's classic study of Bennington College in the 1930s, then exclusively a women's school, illustrates how social milieu affects politics. At that time most of Bennington's students came from urban, economically privileged families whose social and political attitudes were conservative and Republican. The Bennington faculty, in contrast, was politically liberal, oriented to Franklin Roosevelt's New Deal policies. Most young ladies found at Bennington a political milieu quite different from home. During their college years, students who were socially integrated became more liberal. For example, during the 1936 presidential election, 62 percent of the freshmen but only 14 percent of the juniors and seniors "voted" for the Republican presidential candidate; 29 percent of the freshmen and 54 percent of the juniors and seniors "voted" for Roosevelt; and 9 percent of the freshmen and 30 percent of the juniors and seniors "voted" Socialist or Communist.

Twenty-five years later, Newcomb contacted these women to inquire about their lives and politics after college. He found that alumnae maintained or dropped the political views they held at graduation depending on the complexion of their social support – mainly from their husbands – over the ensuing years. Liberal graduates tended to marry liberal men, and these couples remained liberal. The young women who, at graduation, remained relatively conservative tended to marry conservative men, and these couples also maintained consistent political views. In those cases where spouses differed on political attitudes at marriage, the women usually changed their politics to conform to that of their husbands (Newcomb et al. 1967).[8]

Childhood Socialization versus Adult Conversion

With GSS data we can compare the importance of childhood socialization with that of adult conversion in sustaining a religious group. Figure 12.6 contains separate flow diagrams for Catholics, fundamentalist Protestants, moderate Protestants, liberal Protestants, Jews, and those with no religion. The number of GSS respondents *born in* to each of these groups is defined as its base = 100 percent. Most remain in the same group as adults, but some leave while others enter after childhood. In the Catholic diagram, for example, the 100 percent born into Catholicism are spit into 79 percent who remain Catholic and 21 percent who leave the religion. Another 12 percent were not Catholic as children but declare themselves Catholic as adults.[9] Adding those who enter to those who remain gives the percentage of current Catholics = 91 percent. Thus, over the last generation, American Catholics decreased by 9 percent (i.e., 100 percent - 91 percent = 9 percent).

The flow diagram for Protestant fundamentalists shows that most of today's fundamentalists were born into fundamentalist families. The 22 percent converting into fundamentalism (most raised as non-fundamentalist Protestants) nearly equals the 23 percent leaving fundamentalism, so the cross-generational percentage change is practically nil (100 percent - 99 percent = 1 percent). The conversion rate into fundamentalism is considerably smaller than the conversion rates to moderate (41 percent) or liberal (30 percent) Protestant denominations.

Nearly everyone who is Jewish was born Jewish. Few Christians become Jews, and few Jews become Christians.[10]

Figure 12.6
Flow Diagrams for Different US Religious Groups

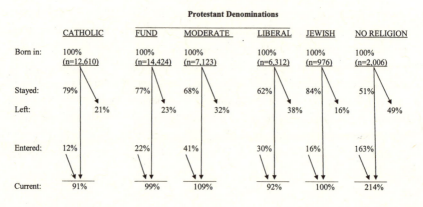

Protestant Denominations

	CATHOLIC	FUND	MODERATE	LIBERAL	JEWISH	NO RELIGION
Born in:	100% (n=12,610)	100% (n=14,424)	100% (n=7,123)	100% (n=6,312)	100% (n=976)	100% (n=2,006)
Stayed:	79%	77%	68%	62%	84%	51%
Left:	21%	23%	32%	38%	16%	49%
Entered:	12%	22%	41%	30%	16%	163%
Current:	91%	99%	109%	92%	100%	214%

Looking across figure 12.6, birth is far more important than conversion as a means of recruitment, with one exception. Respondent who say they have no religion are increasing three times faster from "conversion" than from child rearing (163 percent versus 51 percent). "No religion" is the fastest growing of the categories, perhaps signaling a departure from traditional American religiosity.

According to Principle 3, the few people who do convert are more likely to enter their new religion though conformity with a spouse or friends than by self-consciously searching out new beliefs. Among married converts to Catholicism, 84 percent wed someone born Catholic. Among married converts to Protestant fundamentalism, 56 percent wed someone born a fundamentalist. Among the married converts to Judaism, 63 percent married a born Jew. Forty-eight percent of those who converted to a moderate Protestant denomination wed someone born as a moderate Protestant; 51 percent of those who converted to a liberal Protestant denomination wed someone born a liberal Protestant. These rates of intermarriage among converts are far higher than would be expected by chance.[11] Almost certainly, in most of these cases, religious conversion was an accommodation to religious intermarriage.

A religion that depends wholly on conversion to sustain or increase its numbers will have a difficult time.[12] A small group of Shakers – named for their shaking during worship to rid themselves of evil—arrived from England in 1774 under the leadership of the charismatic Ann Lee. They were pious, pacifist, believed in sexual equality, and separation from the world. Industrious and inventive, their major legacy is Shaker furniture and architecture, known today for a spare but functional style.

The Shakers required their members to be celibate and discouraged marital bonds, strictures not unusual for monasteries or priests, but rare for an entire sect. Their rationale was that celibacy improves a person's chances for salvation, and the elimination of pair bonding fosters community solidarity. When married people joined, they were expected to end their intimate relationship. The Shakers took in orphans, some remaining with the community as adults. Despite the disincentive (for some) of celibacy, the movement grew in number to about 5,000 in 1840. But by the mid-nineteenth century the Shakers were in decline and very few remained by the late twentieth century (Foster 1984; Brewer 1986). Generally speaking, the best way to ensure the growth of a religion is a high birth rate.

Principle 4: We Coalesce around Group Identities, Especially If We are Members of Minority or Persecuted Groups, or During Stressful Conflict

Group identity is the tendency to sympathize more with members of one's own collectivity (whether a family, a community, a formal organization, a religious or ethnic group, or a nation) than with individuals outside that collectivity. Spectator sports demonstrate the ease with which we identify with "our" team, being joyful at its victories and sorrowful at its defeats.

Members of minority groups often share a sense of identification, vis-à-vis the majority, even when they are personally unacquainted. Every American who travels outside the country knows the experience of striking up a conversation with another American traveler, as if there were an invisible bond, especially in a setting where neither American speaks the local language. This may lead to a shared drink at the hotel bar, or a night out on the town, perhaps to a brief romance. When it is time to depart, there is an exchange of phone numbers and email addresses with promises of future contact, which rarely occurs because, once back on American soil, there is no longer any special connection or shared interest. Americans who belong to disadvantaged minority groups need not leave the country to experience this shared feeling of connectedness.

Stressful conflict reinforces group affiliation. The solidarity of comrades in arms who have survived battle is mythic. We "rally round the flag" to support our nation and its leaders against hostile foreign powers. During periods of heightened discrimination, members of persecuted minorities bond together in mutual support. Conversely, when prejudice against a religious group diminishes, as in the waning of American anti-Semitism, assimilation proceeds apace (Mazur 2005: 161-167).

Principle 5: Each Side to a Conflict has a Self-Justifying Account that is Inconsistent with the Other Side's Account.

Whenever religious, ethnic, or nationality groups are in conflict, the opposing sides give inconsistent and self-serving narratives of the situation. Each side explains the causes and events of the conflict so as to justify its own behavior while casting blame on its opponent. This occurs so reliably that social scientists call it the "Rashomon effect," after the classic Japanese movie *Rashomon*, by director Akira Kurosawa, which artistically illustrates the principle. Every day's newspaper carries examples of the Rashomon effect in articles about clashes between Israelis and Palestinians, or Sunnis and Shiites in Iraq, or Pakistanis and Indians over Kashmir, or disputes in the United States about abortion and stem cell research.

The Rashomon effect combines with the principle of group identity to predict how people choose sides in a conflict. Catholics and fundamentalist Protestants are far more likely than liberal Protestants and Jews to oppose abortion and research using embryonic stem cells. Americans of Irish descent, Catholic or Protestant, align with their coreligionists over arguments concerning Northern Ireland. Of course there are exceptions. Some Jews support the Palestinians against the Israelis, and some Arabs support Israel, but not many.

An example of the Rashomon effect that strikes close to home is President George W. Bush's consistently given account of September 11 and America's subsequent "war on terrorism," as in this excerpt from his address to Congress on September 7, 2003:

> Nearly two years ago, following deadly attacks on our country, we began a systematic campaign against terrorism... America and a broad coalition acted first in Afghanistan, by destroying the training camps of terror, and removing the regime that harbored al Qaeda... And we acted in Iraq, where the former regime sponsored terror, possessed and used weapons of mass destruction, and for 12 years defied the clear demands of the United Nations Security Council...
>
> For a generation leading up to September the 11th, 2001, terrorists and their radical allies attacked innocent people in the Middle East and beyond, without facing a sustained and serious response. The terrorists became convinced that free nations were decadent and weak. And they grew bolder, believing that history was on their side. Since America put out the fires of September the 11th, and mourned our dead, and went to war, history has taken a different turn. We have carried the fight to the enemy... Iraq is now the central front. Enemies of freedom are making a desperate stand there – and there they must be defeated.... We are active and resolute in our own defense. We are serving in freedom's cause – and that is the cause of all mankind.
>
> Thank you, and may God continue to bless America.

Compare this to Osama bin Laden's account, given in a videotape broadcast shortly before President Bush's re-election and released in translation by the Arab news agency Al Jazeera on November 1, 2004:

> Praise be to Allah who created the creation for his worship and commanded them to be just and permitted the wronged one to retaliate against the oppressor in kind...
>
> People of America, this talk of mine is for you and concerns the ideal way to prevent another Manhattan, and deals with the war and its causes and results.
>
> Before I begin, I say to you that security is an indispensable pillar of human life and that free men do not forfeit their security, contrary to Bush's claim that we hate freedom. If so, then let him explain to us why we don't strike for example — Sweden? And we know that freedom-haters don't possess defiant spirits like those of the nineteen [September 11th attackers] — may Allah have mercy on them.
>
> No, we fight because we are free men who don't sleep under oppression. We want to restore freedom to our nation. Just as you lay waste to our nation, so shall

we lay waste to yours…Bush is still engaged in distortion, deception and hiding from you the real causes. And thus, the reasons are still there for a repeat of what occurred…

The events that affected my soul in a direct way started in 1982 when America permitted the Israelis to invade Lebanon and the American Sixth Fleet helped them in that. This bombardment began and many were killed and injured and others were terrorized and displaced.

I couldn't forget those moving scenes, blood and severed limbs, women and children sprawled everywhere. Houses destroyed along with their occupants and high rises demolished over their residents, rockets raining down on our home without mercy…

In those difficult moments many hard-to-describe ideas bubbled in my soul, but in the end they produced an intense feeling of rejection of tyranny, and gave birth to a strong resolve to punish the oppressors. And as I looked at those demolished towers in Lebanon, it entered my mind that we should punish the oppressor in kind and that we should destroy towers in America in order that they taste some of what we tasted and so that they be deterred from killing our women and children.

When opponents or their supporters make contradictory factual claims, these may sometimes be deemed true or false on the basis of good evidence. Immediately after 9/11, some in the Arab-Muslim world doubted that bin Laden was behind the attacks. Instead they blamed the suicide mission on CIA or Israeli agents, acting as provocateurs. A corollary belief on the "Arab street" was that 4,000 Jews employed in the twin towers did not report for work on September 11 (Friedman 2002). These conspiracy theories were shown unequivocally false when Osama bin Laden acknowledged his role in the attack. On the other side, President Bush justified his 2003 order to invade Iraq by asserting that Saddam Hussein had weapons of mass destruction and was working cooperatively with bin Laden's terror network. These charges were also shown to be incorrect.

Many other contradictory claims cannot be objectively decided, even in principle. When adversaries differ on value judgments, on religious or political ideologies, these are subjective matters, not amenable to empirical evaluation. Who is the true "freedom fighter," George Bush or Osama bin Laden? To most readers of this book, and certainly to this author, bin Laden's posture and actions are indefensible. Still, we must try to understand his and other perspectives if we are to deal justly with the diverse peoples of the world. Ultimate Truth often lies in the eye of the beholder. Both George Bush and Osama bin Laden invoke the same God/Allah as their ally. Whose side is God truly on?

We see in religious conflict a persistent linkage between group identity and Rashomon effect. Without denying exceptions, there is a recognizably Catholic position on abortion, a Jewish position on Israel, and a Hindu position on Kashmir. Connections between religious membership and moral alignment are plentiful, and in extreme instances they become the basis for *jihad* – holy war.

One True Religion?

The foregoing principles explain how every society (or subgroup in a society) maintains its particular religion across generations, and why members of each religion coalesce to defend their particular beliefs against competing groups. Despite differences in mythology, rituals, taboos and prescriptions, all religions are based on the same social processes of transmission, coalescence, and rationalization. In this perspective, the religious traditions and beliefs are themselves epiphenomenal -- the surface reflections of deeper underlying social predispositions.

The arbitrariness of religious content is borne out by numerous instances when "one true" religion fractured into opposing factions. Christianity grew from Jewish roots and quickly became anti-Semitic. The gospel of John, for example, demonizes the Jews as having the devil for their father (8:44). The early Christians were themselves divided by bitter doctrinal differences. After Emperor Constantine established Christianity as the Roman Church, competing sects like the Gnostics were regarded as heretical and persecuted. The greatest schism came in 1054 when the Orthodox Church of Eastern Europe split from the Catholics of the West. Pope Leo IX in Rome and Patriarch Michael Cerularius in Constantinople excommunicated each other. Not until the twentieth century did their successors take a step toward reconciliation by lifting the mutual declarations of excommunication.

The Protestant Reformation is dated from 1517 when Martin Luther nailed his 95 theses to the door of Wittenberg Church, but the break from Rome did not produce a single Protestantism because competing denominations quickly proliferated and continue to do so. It is difficult to think of any religion that has escaped fragmentation. Within a generation of Muhammad's death, Islam split into hostile Sunni and Shiite branches, as well as other offshoots (Aslan 2005). There are numerous versions of Hinduism and Buddhism.

Enlightenment thinkers of eighteenth-century Europe and America were aware of the arbitrary content and political parochialism of religious institutions. Europe had been riven by the Thirty Years War, leaving France and the southern nations Catholic and still allied to Rome, while much of the north was Protestant of one brand or another. The various

German states were Catholic or Lutheran, depending on the preference of each ruler. Farther east, Russia was Orthodox, Turkey was Muslim. Across the Atlantic, the American colonies were settled largely by dissenters from the official Church of England: Puritans in Massachusetts, Quakers in Pennsylvania. Roger Williams founded Rhode Island on the notion that its residents could worship as they pleased. It required little sophistication to see that a person's religious beliefs, and his readiness to act in their defense, were determined by accident of birth.

Doctrinal differences that separated the various Christians were sometimes major but often seemed (to outsiders) picayune. Catholics claimed the road to heaven was through faith and good works. Lutherans insisted that faith alone was sufficient. Calvinists believed that each person's entry into heaven or hell was predetermined, that neither acts nor beliefs affected the outcome. The sacraments, according to Catholics, could be administered, and the Bible interpreted, only by priests ordained by the Church hierarchy at whose top sat the Pope. Martin Luther thought the Papacy rotten to the core, preaching that every believer has direct access to God and to scriptural understanding without need of priests. The Catholic Church insisted that the wine and wafer used in Communion changed literally into the blood and flesh of Christ, a chemical transmutation that Protestants thought was nonsense.

A common response of Enlightenment intellectuals was to discount idiosyncrasies that distinguished one religion from another, seeking instead their common denominator. The warring creeds at least agreed that a transcendent deity created the earth and gave meaning to human life. This resultant Deism was popular among America's founding fathers (Holmes 2006), later echoing in New England transcendentalism, and later still in the ecumenical philosophies of Gandhi and Martin Luther King, Jr.

The Human Frailty of Holy Institutions

Those more cynical rejected the entire religious enterprise. Its institutions were, after all, human organizations, sometimes righteous but at other times rife with sin and abuse. Even a cursory history of the papacy provides grist for anyone skeptical of the moral and religious infallibility of the office. Officially the papal succession begins with St. Peter (c.32-c.64), but Marcellinus (296-304) was the first bishop of Rome to use the title "pope" and the first known to renege on his vows of consecration, saving himself from martyrdom by surrendering the Bible for burning to Roman authorities. He was canonized anyway, as were all but two of the first fifty-four popes (Collins 2005).[13] Those failing to achieve sainthood were Liberius (352-66), who acquiesced to the Arian heresy that Jesus was subordinate to God, and Anastasius II (496-98), who accommodated to the Acacius heresy, thus earning himself a place in Hell in Dante's *Divine Comedy*.

For those accustomed to the orderliness of today's papal succession, some earlier machinations seem bizarre. Pope John VIII (872-882) was the first pope to be assassinated by disgruntled followers who initially tried poison, then clubbed him to death. Fourteen years later Pope Stephen VII (896-97) had the body of his predecessor, Formosus (891-96), exhumed, dressed in pontifical vestments, and brought to trial in the Lateran Palace. A sentence of damnation was passed, and all acts and edicts of his pontificate annulled. The fingers of the cadaver were cut off and the corpse thrown in the Tiber. Stephen himself was later thrown in prison and strangled by a Roman mob.

During the Middle Ages the papacy was blatantly political, nepotistic, corrupt – one could buy ecclesiastical offices or pardons (simony)—and sometimes brutal and scandalously sinful (McBrien 1997). Pope John XII (955-64), who apparently purchased the papal office at age eighteen and was accused of turning the residence into a brothel, made the Frankish King Otto the first Holy Roman Emperor in exchange for Otto's protection. Later the pope deserted Otto, who retaliated by deposing John and installing a new pope, Leo VIII (963-65). Rome did not recognize Leo and restored John. Such maneuvers between kings and popes had by the eleventh century established the abuse-laden Church as one of the leading political institutions of Europe.

Probably the papacy was strengthened by an encroaching Islam, which pushed the squabbling Christians into a coalition against the Muslim threat. Crusades decreed by medieval popes to free the Holy Land were in fact bloody adventures in slaughter, rape, and pillage. Pope Urban II (1088-99), urging Europe's soldiers to fight the Turks and Arabs, promised entry into heaven for those lost in the holy war:

> All who die by the way, whether by land or by sea, or in battle against the pagans, shall have immediate remission of sins. This I grant them through the power of God with which I am invested (quoted in Collins 2005: 103).

Today's Muslim suicide bombers pursue *jihad* on the same premise. A martyr's death brings immediate entry to paradise.

Popes have usually been Italian, but there were several French occupants during the fourteenth century when the holy office was located in the prosperous French town of Avignon. Rome, suffering from plague and the absence of Church wealth, became dilapidated. Eventually Pope Gregory XI (1370-78), prodded by the mystic St. Catherine of Siena, returned to Rome and there died. As a consequence, the conclave to elect his successor was convened in Rome. The cardinals, mostly French, correctly felt threatened by Romans clamoring for an Italian pope who would remain in their city. They elected Urban VI (1378-89), a simple and pious Italian of lowly birth and unassuming character. It was a choice immediately regretted. Upon his elevation, Urban became domineering, berating the cardinals for luxurious living, simony, lasciviousness, greed, and sloth, and he chose to rule from Rome rather than Avignon.

Within months the cardinals declared that their selection was made under duress and therefore invalid. The infuriated Urban excommunicated the cardinals, who moved to the safety of Naples and elected one of their number as Pope Clement VII (1378-94). Now there were two popes, each excommunicating the other and their respective supporters. Urban appointed new cardinals while others were imprisoned, tortured, or executed, and there were military actions. The monarchs of Europe had to decide which pope to support. Most of the northern countries picked Clement, and most of the southern countries backed Urban. Christians everywhere found themselves under threat of damnation for following the wrong pope. Since the split divided papal revenue in half, each side increasingly depended on simony and the selling of indulgences (Tuchman 1978).

Urban died in 1389, possibly by poisoning, and "his" cardinals elected as successor Boniface IX (1389-1404), infamous for his blatant nepotism and financial skullduggery, selling church offices to the highest bidder (McBrien 1997: 438). When Clement died five years later, "his" cardinals elected Benedict XIII (1417-23). Thus there were two papal successions, one based in Rome, the other in Avignon. Seemingly at an impasse, in 1409 a council declared the Holy See vacant and proceeded to elect as replacement Alexander V (1409-10), so there were then three rivals to the papal throne. We need not dwell on details, but in the mid-fifteenth century the number of popes was finally reduced back to one, and Rome was restored as the papal seat.

Unfortunately, this did not conclude the period of infamy. Pope Sixtus (1471-84) agreed to a request from the Spanish monarchs Ferdinand and Isabella to institute the Inquisition and appointed as grand inquisitor Tomás de Torquemada, who used hideous tortures to extract confessions from heretics, and to persuade them to name collaborators in sin. As many as 2,000 heretics were burned at the stake during the Spanish Inquisition (Collins 2005).

The Renaissance popes are a story in themselves. Nepotists, political intriguers, sires of illegitimate children, and profuse spenders, about the best we can say of them is that they sponsored marvelous art and architecture. Alexander VI (1492-1503), of the famous Borgia family, was the most notorious pope ever. He was responsible for – besides his own sins—the nefarious activities of his most infamous children, Cesare, whom he made a cardinal at age eighteen, and Lucrezia, rumored to be facile with poison. The next pope, Julius II (1503-13), hated the Borgias so much that he refused to occupy the apartments where Alexander and his family had lived. No saint himself, Julius fathered three illegitimate children, bribed his way into office, sold indulgences to release the souls of the dead from purgatory, and led armies against Italian cities. On the plus side, he was an unequaled patron of the arts, hiring Raphael and Bramante, and inducing Michelangelo to paint the ceiling of the Sistine Chapel. Julius laid the cornerstone of the present St. Peter's Basilica but did not live to see its completion.

Pope Paul IV (1555-59), an anti-Semite and strong supporter of the Inquisition, forced Rome's Jews to wear distinctive headgear and confined them within a walled section of the city, a *ghetto*. The practice soon expanded throughout the papal states.

I dwell on the Catholic Church because its abuses are so well documented, but some Protestants look no better. Martin Luther at first preached tolerance for Jews, hoping they would convert to Christianity as it was being reformed by the Protestant movement. When they did not, he published in 1543 a pamphlet, *Concerning the Jews and Their Lies*, asking,

> What then shall we Christians do with this damned, rejected race of Jews? Since they live among us and we know about their lying and blasphemy and cursing, we cannot tolerate them.... First, their synagogues...should be set on fire, and whatever does not burn up should be covered or spread over with dirt so that no one may ever be able to see a cinder or stone of it. Secondly, their homes should likewise be broken down and destroyed; ...their rabbis must be forbidden under the threat of death to teach any more.... All their cash and valuables of silver and gold ought to be taken from them and put aside for safekeeping.... [L]et the young Jews and Jewesses be given the flail, the ax, the hoe, the spade, the distaff and spindle, and let them earn their bread by the sweat of their noses....

Young King Henry the VIII of England was a devout Catholic until he asked Pope Clement VII (1523-34) for a divorce from the barren Catherine of Aragon in order to marry the beautiful and fecund Anne Boleyn. Clement could not comply because Catherine had as protector her nephew Charles V, rich with New World gold and the military backbone of the

Papacy. Henry's solution was to reject the pope's authority and establish his own Church of England with himself at its head. Henry's subordinate, the Archbishop of Canterbury, readily granted the divorce. Along the way Henry confiscated the wealth of England's Catholic churches and monasteries, and destroyed their irreplaceable religious art. This desecration is comparable to the destruction in 2001 by the Islamist Taliban government of Afghanistan of two massive Buddhas standing over a hundred feet high, carved out of cliffs in central Afghanistan, dating from the third and fifth centuries (Rathje 2001). The Taliban provoked vociferous condemnation in both the East and West and soon would become even more intolerable for its support of Osama bin Laden.

Henry VIII suffered no such downfall. He married Anne (with a final sum of six wives, of whom he beheaded two) and was succeeded by their daughter, Elizabeth I. All the while English Catholics could be imprisoned or executed for treasonous allegiance to the pope. Why, the cynic wonders, does a member of the Anglican Church, or of its American offshoot, the Episcopalian Church, give reverence to an institution begun under those sordid circumstances?

Luther, Henry VIII, some medieval and Renaissance popes—they are all skeletons in the religious closet. One might think that mendacity in the messenger would dilute the holiness of the message, but given the distance of a few generations, followers seem barely aware of these infelicities.

Changing Doctrines

Religious doctrine is malleable, not absolute. Prophets, popes, and charismatic leaders can alter practices and beliefs, or form wholly new doctrines, to suit their own interests or the tenor of the times. Even the Old Order Amish, seemingly fixed in the eighteenth century, have adjusted to modernity. They cannot drive cars but can ride in them. They use tractors in their barns to power farm equipment but not in their fields because that would put them on a slippery slope that leads to driving the tractor into town, then wanting a car, and so on. They do not use bicycles, but in-line skates are permissible. They cannot have a freezer in their home but can have one in the home of a non-Amish neighbor. They cannot use computers but calculators are alright. They do not use electricity from power lines but will use batteries and on-site generators, rationalizing that power lines would make them dependent on the outside world but batteries and on-site generators do not (Kraybill 2001).

Doctrines can turn on a dime. God revealed to Joseph Smith that polygamy, an Old Testament tradition, was proper for Latter Day Saints.

By 1852, when the Mormons were settled in Utah, they began practicing it openly. In 1862 the US Congress passed the Morrill Act prohibiting plural marriage in the territories and placing sanctions specifically on the Latter Day Saints, but distance and Washington's preoccupation with the Civil War ensured that the law was not immediately enforced. By the 1880s, a Supreme Court decision against the Mormons' claim to freedom of religion, plus additional legislation making polygamy a felony, brought the matter to a head. In 1890, Wilford Woodruff, then president of the Church, received a revelation from God that Mormon leaders should cease teaching the practice of plural marriage (Powell 1994).

There are still fundamentalist Mormons, mostly in southern Utah and northern Arizona, who regard the taking of multiple wives as a religious obligation. They are united as the breakaway Fundamentalist Church of Jesus Christ of Latter Day Saints, but this denomination is disavowed by the Salt Lake City establishment, which today excommunicates members who practice polygamy (Krakauer 2003).

Religious teachings can be flat wrong without wholly destroying their credibility. William Miller (1782-1849), like many Christians before, anticipated an imminent reappearance of Jesus on earth, which would signal the ascent of saints to heaven and the descent of sinners to hell. Unlike most others, Miller was specific about timing, having calculated from the Book of Daniel that the Advent would occur between March 21, 1843 and March 21, 1844. Over 50,000 Millerites from several Protestant denominations in New England and Upstate New York attended camp meetings in anticipation, comprising one of the most sensational movements of the day. When the period passed uneventfully, Miller endorsed a new date, October 22, 1844. When that too passed – it became known as "The Great Disappointment" –many left the movement, several joining the Shakers. But many others were steadfast and sought an explanation for the failure of October 22.

One popular hypothesis was that there had simply been an error in calculating the last day, and that the Advent was still imminent but at an unspecified time. A second hypothesis was that the Lord *had* come on October 22, not in the dramatically visible form expected, but Jesus appeared invisibly to judge who would be allowed into heaven and who would be excluded. The door to heaven was then shut for everyone who did not pass approval on October 22. Proponents of this position came together as the Seventh-Day Adventist Church, formally organized in 1863.[14]

An impediment to the Adventists' growth was their "shut door" doctrine, making it impossible for any new believers to reach salvation.

Eventually this position was revised, allowing recent recruits the privilege of conversion and entry into heaven (Cross 1950). In this, the Adventists were not uniquely inconstant. All religions evolve to survive.

Today's Judaism looks nothing like the ancient Israelite religion when a hereditary priesthood offered burnt sacrifices—animals and plants—to Yahweh. Rabbis and synagogues are "modern" innovations of the past 2,000 years. Reform and Conservative Judaism, the major denominations of America, originated in the nineteenth and twentieth centuries, respectively, each adopting superficial forms of worship and practice found among surrounding Gentiles. Even today's Orthodox Judaism differs considerably from Judaism's medieval forms.

Some regard Hasidic Jews as ultra-orthodox and historically authentic. If fact, Hasidism was an innovation of eighteenth century Poland and Russia, led by a charismatic known as the Ba'al Shem Tov (Master of the good name). His movement stressed emotional devotion over the scholarly rabbinic tradition. It featured ecstatic singing and dancing by the men during worship. Nearly obliterated by modernism and the Holocaust, Hasidism was barely present in the United States or Israel until its reinvigoration in the late-twentieth century.

When I was a child, American Catholics could not eat meat on Fridays, masses were said in Latin, and religious intermarriage was actively discouraged. These practices were eliminated during the 1960s as the U.S. hierarchy followed Vatican II liberalizations. None of these changes involved important doctrine, but they did affect the personal lives of Catholics, producing considerable dissonance. Some Catholics still refuse the vernacular mass, most famously the movie actor and director Mel Gibson.

In 1992 Pope John Paul II apologized for the repression of Galileo. The Vatican had insisted for centuries that the sun revolves around the earth, though nothing in the Bible requires that view.[15] It was adopted during the scholastic movement begun by Thomas Aquinas, who merged Greek and Hellenistic ideas with church doctrine. By the sixteenth century the geocentric universe was so well accepted that it was an affront to teach otherwise. Even Copernicus (or more likely, one of his friends) avoided that sin by penning a deathbed preface to *De Revolutionibus* (1543) claiming that his heliocentric model was a device for calculation, not a picture of the true universe. Galileo was less discreet in trumpeting that the earth truly moved around the sun, thereby forcing church fathers to shut him up. But science marches on, and Newton's synthesis was fully accepted during the eighteenth century, even before its stunning verification in 1846 by the discovery of the planet Neptune, exactly where it was predicted to be. It took another century and a half for the Vatican to admit its error. In 1996 John Paul II made another nod to science, acknowledging that evolution is "more than just a hypothesis."

Like all religions, Catholicism will continue to change and to rationalize those changes. Perhaps in the near future priests will be allowed to marry. The New Testament does not require priestly celibacy, the Catholic Church does not regard it as infallible dogma, and at least some of the apostles and early popes married (McBrien 1997). The requirement for sexual abstinence developed gradually, apparently from the Church's long association of sexuality with sin, and virginity with sanctity. St. Augustine (354-430), who greatly contributed to this tone, was well experienced with women before his conversion but later cited the inability of men to produce a timely erection, or to restrain one, as evidence that the body is not under control of the will. He wished it were possible to beget children without the mediation of lust (Woodward 1990). After the fourth century, marital restrictions were promoted erratically, in different places and under certain circumstances. Men who married before their ordination might be allowed to retain their wives, while marriages after ordination were proscribed. By the twelfth century, all conjugal relations by clergy of the Roman Catholic Church were reduced in canon law to concubinage, a position leading to full celibacy, but this may not be the final word. Given the present difficulty of recruiting priests in the United States, and scandals over pedophilia, a lifting of the celibacy requirement may be in the offing. The pope may at any time change the rules. Religions do adjust to the demands of their surrounding culture.

As I write this chapter, Western journalists are reporting the story of an Afghan man who went to court seeking custody of his children, and is now threatened by the court with execution for his conversion from Islam to Christianity. Muslim law regards it a grave sin to renounce the true faith, and the death penalty applies. According to news reports, President Bush is deeply troubled by the incident, and Secretary of State Condoleezza Rice called Afghanistan's President, Hamid Karzi, to urge a favorable resolution.

Like much in Islam, punishment for apostasy is derived from the Israelite tradition. Deuteronomy repeatedly condemns the worship of false gods, especially leading others along that path:

> If anyone secretly entices you – even if it is your brother, your father's son or your mother's son, or your own son or daughter, or the wife you embrace, or your most

intimate friend – saying, "Let us go worship other gods," whom neither you nor your ancestors have known,.... you must not yield to or heed any such persons. Show them no pity or compassion and do not shield them. But you shall surely kill them; your own hand shall be first against them to execute them.... Stone them to death for trying to turn you away from the LORD your God (13: 6-10).

Deuteronomy was the guiding text for the Inquisition and for the torture and execution of Christian heretics or witches at other times and places. The essential difference among the Abrahamic religions is that Judaism has disregarded this law for over two thousand years, and Christianity has ignored it for at least two centuries, but some Islamists still interpret it literally.

Holy writings can be complex and contradictory. By picking and choosing appropriate passages, ignoring others, perhaps also shading some meanings, we have wide latitude in deriving religious conclusions. The Vatican forbids ordination of women. Pope John Paul II affirmed in *Responsum Ad Dubium* of 1995 that this decision is infallible. The Episcopal Church, most Catholic-like of American Protestant denominations, using the same Bible, began ordaining women in 1976, and in 2006 elected a woman as presiding bishop, offending many who thought it a blatant disregard of scripture. Those who support female priests can cite Joel 2:28 or Galations 3:27-28:

I will pour out my Spirit upon all flesh; your sons and your daughters shall prophesy....

As many of you as were baptized into Christ have clothed yourselves with Christ. There is no longer Jew or Greek, there is no longer slave or free, there is no longer male and female; for all of you are one in Christ Jesus.

Those who oppose female ordination can cite 1 Timothy 2:12-14 or 1 Corinthians 14:34:

I permit no woman to teach or to have authority over a man; she is to keep silent.

Women should be silent in the churches. For they are not permitted to speak, but should be subordinate, as the law also says.

Of current relevance is Islam's prohibition against suicide. On this the Koran contains a single line: "Do not destroy yourselves" (4:29). Obviously there must be escape clauses because nearly every day a Muslim seeks entry into paradise by killing himself for the glory of Allah, while sending unbelievers to hell for eternity. Against the single admonition against suicide, the polemicist Sam Harris lists five pages of quotes from the Koran that vilify unbelievers and tell of the harshest consequences

(2005: 118-122). Among them, "God's curse be upon the infidels!" (2:89). "Those that deny God's revelations shall be sternly punished" (3:5). "If you should die or be slain in the cause of God, God's forgiveness and His mercy would surely be better than all the riches they amass" (3:156). "Those that suffered persecution for My sake and fought and were slain: I shall forgive them their sins and admit them to gardens watered by running streams, as a reward from God" ((3:195). "You will find that the most implacable of men in their enmity to the faithful are the Jews and the pagans, and that the nearest in affection to them are those who say: 'We are Christians'" (5:82). Harris concludes:

> Surely there are Muslim jurists who might say that suicide bombing is contrary to the tenets of Islam...and that suicide bombers are therefore not martyrs but fresh denizens of hell. Such a minority opinion, if it exists, cannot change the fact that suicide bombings have been rationalized by much of the Muslim world (where they are called "sacred explosions"). Indeed, such rationalization is remarkably easy, given the tenets of Islam.... The bottom line for the aspiring martyr seems to be this: as long as you are killing infidels or apostates "in defense of Islam," Allah doesn't care whether you kill yourself in the process or not (2005: 123-24).

One can find sufficient justification in sacred writing for nearly any policy. Abraham Lincoln, speaking to a nation pervaded by evangelical Protestantism but split by civil war, said in his second inaugural address, "Both [sides] read the same Bible, and pray to the same God; and each invokes His aid against the other. It may seem strange that any men should dare to ask a just God's assistance in wringing their bread from the sweat of other men's faces." Yet defenders of slavery, as well as abolitionists, proved that their cause was compatible with the Bible (e.g., Harper et al. 1852). "The justification of slavery relied heavily on a literal interpretation of the Scriptures. These biblical scholars argued that Old Testament patriarchs practiced a system of servitude much akin to U.S. slavery. These friends of the South also pointed out that nowhere in the New Testament did Christ condemn the slavery of his era" (McKivigan and Snay 1998: 8). In the decades prior to the war, the three major U.S. Protestant denominations—Methodist, Baptist, and Presbyterian—each split into northern and southern factions over the issue of slavery (Miller, Stout, and Wilson 1998).

Papal barges were manned by Muslim slaves until 1800. In 1888 the Vatican finally condemned slavery, after it was legally abolished in all Christian nations. A century later, Pope John Paul II called slavery an intrinsically evil, prohibited always and forever, and without exception (Noonan 2005).

Conclusion

Nearly everyone adheres more or less to their religion of upbringing. Relatively few people convert, and when they do it is normally to enter the tradition of a spouse or friends. Religious choice, for most of us, is an accident of birth or an act of conformity. Once our religious identity is determined, we coalesce with co-religionists, we see the world from our religion's viewpoint, and sometimes we fight to defend our religion and its institutions against people of other creeds.

These are robust findings of sociology, not seriously challenged within the discipline. There is considerable evidence that political beliefs are formed the same way as religious beliefs. No comparable research effort has been devoted to the provenance of beliefs in the paranormal, but there is no reason to think that these arise any differently. We may tentatively assign their origin to the usual social influences of family, spouse, friends, and social milieu, with some leavening from the mass media. The fragmentary evidence that is available on alien abductees, discussed in chapter 10, indicates that abduction runs in families or in predisposing social networks such as those oriented toward New Age views. In this particular case there is additionally the unusual but important intervention of hypnotists or other therapists who direct the "recovery" of memories of violation.

Religions and other belief systems inevitably evolve, fragmenting into competing sects, adapting to changing cultural environments. If there is among the plethora of denominations one that is uniquely correct, it would be difficult to objectively recognize it. If we do venture an identification, we need further pick a moment in time when the changing current of beliefs and practices was inerrant.

Whether or not God or gods are a social construct, holiness is mediated through human leaders and institutions that historically have faltered as paragons of truth and virtue. Barely a generation is required to camouflage, bury, or ignore clerical abuses or other foibles, to polish blemishes into a veneer of sanctity. The same may be said for leaders of paranormal sects.

These sociological conclusions do not undermine the potential value of a community or communities of faith. But they do put a strain on any claim that a particular interpretation of the special text of one privileged group is uniquely correct and infallible.

Notes

1. The survey covered religious beliefs about God, miracles, heaven and hell; frequency of worship; and participation in church activities (http://www.gesis.org/en/data_service/issp/data/1998_Religion_II.htm).

2. Other choices were "The Bible is the inspired word of God but not everything should be taken literally;" and "The Bible is an ancient book of fables, legends, history and moral precepts recorded by man."

3. The GSS classifies each Protestant denomination as fundamentalist, moderate, or liberal, based importantly on biblical inerrancy (Smith 1987).

4. Even mystical conversions, when exceptional individuals achieve a degree of spiritual intimacy with their particular holy spirit, setting them apart as extraordinary lovers of God, conform to specific expectations in the contemporary cultural milieu. What the Christian mystic experiences as an encounter with Jesus is similar to what the Hindu mystic experiences with Brahman, and the Muslim mystic with Allah. Among the most common are ecstasies and visions, prophecies, and physical stigmata. Just as some Christian mystics manifest on their bodies the wounds of the crucified Christ, so some Muslim mystics produce wounds similar to those suffered by Muhammad in battle (Katz 1983; Woodward 1990)

5. Proper names and other language in the *Book of Mormon* indicate that it was written in the 1820s or 1830s in western New York (Cross 1950: 144-46).

6. See Covington (1995) for a particularly exotic and detailed description of the two-year socially-mediated conversion of a *New York Times* reporter to snake-handling Penacostalism, though he soon lapsed.

7. The mistaken impression that teens and young adults commonly reject the views of their parents was prevalent in the 1950s and 60s with images of James Dean-like "rebels without a cause," and of campus radicals acting out against the values of their bourgeois parents. While such cases no doubt occur, the leftist campus activists of the 1960s more typically had politically liberal parents who were proud of their children's actions against the Vietnam War and in support of the civil rights movement (Keniston 1968). Far from rebelling, the student radicals were following social channels laid down by their parents.

8. In that era, politics was widely regarded as male business, giving husbands disproportionate influence in that area.

9. I use the number born into each group as the denominator of the percentage entering as adults.

10. Being Jewish is not fully comparable to being Christian because "Jewishness" is as likely to mean an ethnic identity as an acceptance of the Judaic religion. Indeed, many American (and Israeli) Jews are barely religious in terms of practices or beliefs, and some would declare themselves "Jewish atheists," a meaningless label to most Christians. For slightly different estimates see Green (2004).

11. According to the GSS, 26 percent of Americans are Catholic, 32 percent are fundamentalist Protestant, 2 percent are Jewish, 17 percent are moderate Protestants, 13 percent are liberal Protestants, and 10 percent have no religion. For slightly different estimates see Luo (2006).

12. Stark and Finke (2000) question the authenticity of most historic reports of mass conversions.

13. Methods of, and standards for, canonization have changed considerably. After 900 CE, few popes were named saints. In 1234 the right to canonize was officially reserved to the papacy alone. Mystics displaying stigmata or other wonders were once excellent candidates for sainthood but today are regarded with suspicion. Now virtually all accepted miracles are medical cures that are scien-

tifically inexplicable in the eyes of the Italian Catholic physicians who advise the Vatican's saint makers (Woodward 1990).

14.   The name "Seventh Day" refers to the practice of observing Sabbath on Saturday, not Sunday.

15.   In Joshua 10:12, Yahweh makes the sun stop in mid-heaven to give the Israelites more daylight in which to slaughter the Amorites. This passage is sometimes taken as support for the heliocentric view, but it can as well refer to the sun's apparent motion across the sky.

13

Personality

At the state mental hospital in Ypsilanti, Michigan, psychologist Milton Rokeach brought together three men, all paranoid schizophrenics, each claiming to be Jesus Christ. They met almost daily for two years. Rokeach's book, *The Three Christs of Ypsilanti* (1964), is a classic study of implausible belief:

Clyde, when asked to explain Joseph's and Leon's claims, replied: "They are really not alive. The machines in them are talking. Take the machines out of them and they won't talk anything. You can't kill the ones with machines in them. They're dead already." Somebody by the name of Nelly, he went on, had shot Leon, and Joseph had been shot by his wife. When I asked Clyde exactly where this machine was located, he replied by pointing to the right side of Joseph's stomach. I asked Joseph if he would mind unbuttoning his shirt, and with his permission Clyde tried to feel around for the machine. "Can you feel it?" I asked. "That's funny," Clyde replied. "It isn't there. It must have slipped down where you can't feel it..."

With a consistency that never varied, Joseph insisted that Clyde and Leon "can't be God or Jesus Christ or the Holy Spirit, by any means. There is only one God. I'm the only God. Clyde and...[Leon] are patients in a mental hospital, and their being patients proves they are insane."

Leon on the other hand gave several explanations, all of them differing from each other and from Clyde's and Joseph's. His companions claimed to be Christ, he said, to gain prestige, and because of prejudice, jealousy, hatred, negativism, duping, interferences, and electronic imposition. But, as he made clear, he did not deny that the other two were "hollowed-out instrumental gods with a small 'g'." Quoting from Psalm 82: "I have said ye are gods and all of you are children of the Most High," he added that, to their detriment, they were assuming a false personality. He maintained the he did not contest their beliefs because if he did he would be "stamped into shit, cosmically or physically." He too, he said, is an instrumental god, but he was the first one made and this automatically conferred certain privileges...

To the question "Why are you in this hospital?" Clyde continued to reply that he owned it and all adjacent lands and properties, and that he was in the hospital to look after them. Joseph sometimes said that he was "sick in the head but not insane..." As for Leon, his reply was usually that he is in a mental hospital because of prejudice, jealousy, duping, etc.; occasionally he said he was sent to the hospital by his uncle, the reincarnation of the Archangel Michael, to investigate conditions" (50-52).

Are True Believers Crazy?

Crazy people are often delusional, holding firmly to highly implausible ideas and sometimes acting on them. A gruesome case in the news at this writing concerns a woman diagnosed as paranoid schizophrenic, who heard the call of God to sacrifice her three small children, so she dropped them, one by one, to their deaths in San Francisco Bay (AP 2006).

What about the reverse proposition? Are people who firmly hold to highly implausible beliefs often crazy? That depends on what is meant by "crazy," an imprecise concept meaning different things in different contexts. In law, *insanity* refers to unsoundness of mind sufficient *in the judgment of a civil court* to render a person unfit to maintain a contractual obligation, or, in criminal cases, sufficient to prevent the accused from distinguishing if the act in question was right or wrong. Psychiatrists or psychologists are called as expert witnesses, but it is the court that judges if the defendant is insane. If so, the defendant may be committed to a mental hospital and otherwise escape punishment. Insanity is a legal, not a medical, designation. Few of those with whom we are concerned are ever tested in court.

In contrast to legal insanity is the medical diagnosis of mental disorders, which generally follows guidelines laid down, and occasionally revised, by the American Psychiatric Association in its *Diagnostic and Statistical Manual of Mental Disorders*.[1] Disorder classifications are based on prevailing contemporary opinion of mental health specialists and necessarily reflect changing cultural values. In the mid-twentieth century, homosexuality was listed as a mental disorder but is now regarded by most professionals as a normal sexual orientation. In Freud's day, hysteria was a common diagnosis for women but is no longer recognized as a category of mental disorder.

Psychosis is a generic psychiatric term for the most serious mental disorders in which rational thought and perception are severely impaired, preventing the sufferer from pursuing a normal life. (Lesser psychiatric problems include personality disorders, depression, anxiety, substance-abuse disorders, etc.) *Schizophrenia*, the most commonly diagnosed psychosis, eludes precise definition and may include a range of disorders. Typical symptoms are persistent delusions, hallucinations (sights or voices inaccessible to others), disorganized thinking and speech, and lack of affect and motivation. These produce severe social dysfunction. Onset of schizophrenia typically occurs in late adolescence or early adulthood.

Schizophrenia afflicts about 0.5 percent of the population at any given time (Goldner et al. 2002). Adding other forms of psychosis increases prevalence slightly, so we expect a few psychotics in any large group. There is no indication of much over-concentration of schizophrenia or other psychoses, or of other major personality abnormalities, among believers of implausibilities. Indeed, since about one-third of Americans are biblical literalists, it would severely strain the meaning of "abnormal" to characterize them as such. The question is more apt when inquiring about people with such unusual beliefs as having been abducted by space aliens. Possibly there is a small excess of psychotics among abductees, but researchers emphasize that most are not seriously abnormal by standard psychiatric criteria (Clancy 2005; Mack 1994).

We can firmly reject the notion that many believers in the implausible are crazy in the psychiatric sense of psychotic or the legal sense of insane. But that does not mean that psychosis or insanity is irrelevant.

Leadership

Every hierarchical social group, whether formally or informally or-ganized, has a relatively few people who know one another and handle leadership functions. This applies to cults, sects, and mass movements. The leadership clique may take the form of a council, an executive com-mittee, or simply an inner circle. If one person is recognized as overall head, or spiritual leader, or primary speaker, the inner circle comprises his or her closest associates. When no principle leader is acknowledged, a "first among equals" emerges from the core (Mazur 2005).

Although psychotic-like individuals are few in number, they can wield inordinate influence as leaders, even achieving sainthood. Joan of Arc (1412-1431), heroine of France, had symptoms of paranoid schizophrenia (Allen 1975). Always a pious girl, Joan was thirteen when she first saw angels and heard saintly voices. Their messages, recurring daily, were commands from God to rescue French forces besieged by the English at Orleans, and to have the Dauphin Charles crowned king of France. At age sixteen Joan presented herself to Charles, who accepted her mission and installed her near the command of his army. The young maid, clad in male attire with sword in hand, boosted French morale, quickly broke the siege, then led her troops to additional military successes and saw Charles crowned. She accomplished all this by the age of seventeen and should have returned home because her later battles were unsuccessful. She was wounded, captured by allies of England, and put on trial as a witch and heretic. The ungrateful King Charles did not bargain for her release. Joan burned at the stake, repeating the name of Jesus until the last. She was canonized in 1920 (Thurston 2005).

Against the claim that Joan was schizophrenic, which implies dysfunctionality, are contemporary reports that she functioned effectively on campaign and during most of her trial (Grundy 2006). Perhaps she was just extremely prone to fantasy, not itself a mental illness. Possibly she feigned the visions to emphasize her piety. The faithful believe she really communicated with heaven, which seems to imply that God preferred the French over the English, and especially favored the perfidious Charles.

It is a stretch from the maiden Joan to Reverend Jim Jones, but they have important commonalities. Both were true believers and charismatic leaders, both had symptoms of pathological paranoia, and both led ardent faith-filled followers to their deaths. Jones is no one's candidate for sainthood, but many thought him saintly while he was alive. How did this deranged man lead hundreds of followers to suicide?

Born 1931 in Indiana, Jim Jones was handsome and brilliant. While still in college he began his energetic career as a flamboyant but caring preacher, much taken with the race problem that was gaining national attention in the 1950s. He and wife Marceline adopted Korean and black children beside their birth son. In 1955 the Joneses established Peoples Temple in Indianapolis as an independent, racially integrated Pentecostal church espousing help for the poor, socialism, evangelism, speaking in tongues, healing by laying on hands, and abstinence from alcohol and drugs.

In 1965 Jim and Marceline relocated to northern California, bringing about ten families from Indiana. By 1973 they had purchased churches in San Francisco and Los Angeles, set up counseling services to help members with legal, medical, and financial problems, and with recruiting drives in black neighborhoods had swelled membership to over two thousand. Many more came to hear Jones's sermons and the vibrant interracial choir. Peoples Temple established communal houses, ran a fleet of buses for its members, and became active in electoral politics. A national interfaith organization listed Jones as one of the 100 outstanding clergymen of 1975; the *Los Angeles Times* named him Humanitarian of the Year in 1976; Jones was appointed to San Francisco's housing commission; the National Newspaper Publishers give their Freedom of the Press Award to Peoples Temple in 1977 (Stephenson 2005).

Debbie Layton, a troubled teenager with troubled parents, entered Peoples Temple through her older brother Larry, and in turn brought her mother into the fold. Like many recruits, they were impressed by Jim

Jones's charm and attentiveness, his advocacy for the disadvantaged, and the adoration of his followers, who called him "Father." These virtues, and his miracle healing, made believable Jones's claim to be the reincarnated Jesus and Lenin. Debbie came wholly under Jones's control after she joined the sheltered settlement in northern California. Jones achieved this through a mix of persuasion, coercion, peer pressure, humiliation, flattery, and exaggeration of external threats to the community. Those who stayed with the church displayed unquestioning obedience to Father. Debbie later claimed, in a memoir of unknown veracity, that on two occasions Jones insinuated himself upon her for sexual intercourse, which she accepted in ashamed passivity, too intimidated to repel his unwanted penetration, and too committed to question the man's integrity (1998).

Like many Americans during the 1970s, Jones was strongly critical of U.S. policies toward minorities and the war in Vietnam. Declaring himself a Marxist, he established a commune in Guyana and discussed the option of moving his people to the Soviet Union. Debbie, by this time a member of the inner circle, was entrusted with missions to Europe and Central America for the expansion of the church and its resources. But troubles were beginning for the organization.

A few followers had become disillusioned about strict disciplinary actions, excessive solicitation of members' assets, and about Jones's sexual involvement with members. In the mid-1970s these dissidents left the church, either taking or trying to take their relatives along. They complained to local news media, filed lawsuits, and sought government action against Jones. Reacting to the exposés and the beginning of an investigation, Peoples Temple transferred millions of dollars from the U.S. to international banks. In 1977 Jones moved to Guyana. Debbie and her cancer-stricken mother followed him to Jonestown, as the Guyanese settlement was called, now grown to over a thousand residents.

Soon Jones began staging defensive drills against feared military assaults on Jonestown. During these "White Nights," his security squad, acting as attackers, prowled the surrounding jungle, firing shots, while residents with machetes and sickles formed a protective cordon, believing a real attack was in progress. These exercises lasted for hours, sometimes all night, until Jones declared the danger passed. The predictable Rashomon effect, polarizing residents against their fictitious assailants, solidified the community around Jones. By 1978 the White Nights included practice in collective suicide.

We have a mixed picture of sentiment in the Guyanese community. There were hardships and dissatisfactions in settling so many people in undeveloped rain forest, under strict discipline and with a dearth of luxuries, but there was at the same time continued devotion to Jones and his mission. Some people wanted to leave, a difficult task without Jones providing the means and permission, which he did not extend to anyone suspected of disloyalty. For the infirm it was virtually impossible to walk out of the isolated jungle commune. It was emotionally wrenching to leave behind family and friends, and most importantly, departure meant defying Father.

Debbie Layton writes that her defection was precipitated by Jones's wrath at her ill mother over a slight rule infraction. The opportunity arose when Debbie was sent on community business to Georgetown, Guyana's capital. After considerable hesitation, she furtively informed American embassy officials that she wanted to return to the United States. This required an emergency passport, a cloak-and-dagger ruse, and a sprint to the airport, but Debbie's escape was effected, leaving her mother behind.

Back in California, Debbie circulated an affidavit detailing conditions at Jonestown, including the rehearsal for mass suicide. The *San Francisco Chronicle* and the Associated Press picked up her story. It helped induce U.S. Congressman Leo Ryan to make a fact-finding mission to Guyana, accompanied by journalists and dissidents hoping to retrieve their relatives. Jones regarded this unwelcome visit as an onslaught by racist and fascist forces, intent on kidnapping some of the children and destroying the settlement.

On November 17, 1978, a week after Debbie's mother died of her cancer, Ryan and his party flew into a small airstrip near Jonestown without any assurance of being received. After some negotiations they were allowed entry into the community, served supper and entertained, and given accommodations for the night. Ryan seemed to get a generally favorable impression except that several residents asked to leave with him, a prospect that upset Jones.

As the time for departure approached, one distraught resident attacked the congressman with a knife. The assailant was subdued without harming his target, but he did change the tenor of the visit. Now urgently, Ryan's party—including about twenty defectors and, suspiciously, Debbie's true-believing brother Larry—trucked back to the airstrip. As they began boarding, gunmen opened fire, killing the congressman, three journalists and a defector, and wounding several others. Larry Layton had joined the attackers.

The shooters, except Layton who was captured, returned to Jonestown. Jones called his followers together, telling them the airport attack extinguished all hope, and the only option was revolutionary suicide. As rehearsed, Flavor Aid was mixed with cyanide in a washtub and distributed in small cups. Parents gave it to their children, then drank themselves, huddling together to die. Those who could not or would not drink were injected with cyanide. Jones, dead from a gunshot to the head, was found with the bodies of Marceline and others of the inner circle. The day's toll was 918 dead. The only survivors among those present were members of the security squad, and one elderly lady who hid under her bed, emerging the next morning among the corpses.

Peoples Temple leaders purposively left records so historians would see that their course was correct. There is a tape of the final meeting with Father presiding. He credits the Jonestown security squad for "showing them justice" at the airport, and warns that authorities will soon come. Here is an abbreviated transcript of the ensuring discussion:

Jones: How very much I've tried my best to give you the good life. But in spite of all my trying, a handful of our people, with their lies, have made our life impossible. There's no way to detach ourselves from what's happened today. Not only are we in a compound situation, not only are there those who have left and committed the betrayal of the century, some have stolen children from others... We are sitting here waiting on a powder keg. I don't think it is what we want to do with our babies... It almost happened here... The congressman was nearly killed here. But you can't steal people's children...without expecting a violent reaction... If we can't live in peace, then let's die in peace. (*Applause*)....

Thank you... I've never lied to you... I know what's going to happen... So my opinion is that we be kind to children and be kind to seniors and take the potion like they used to take in ancient Greece, and step over quietly, because we are not committing suicide. It's a revolutionary act. We can't go back. They won't leave us alone. They're now going back to tell more lies, which means more congressmen. And there's no way, no way we can survive.

Anybody, anyone who has any dissenting opinion, please speak... Yes, Christine.

Christine Miller: Is it too late for Russia?

Jones: Here's why it's too late for Russia. They killed. They started to kill. That's why it makes it too late for Russia. Otherwise I'd say, Russia, you bet your life. But it's too late... I've always put my lot with you. If one of my people do something, it's me. And they say I don't have to take the blame for this, but I can't— ...I can't live that way..., and I'll die for all. (*Applause*) I've been living on a hope for a long time, Christine, and I appreciate—you've always been a very good agitator. I like agitation, because you have to see two sides of one issue, two sides of a question. But what those people are gonna get done, once they get through, will make our lives worse than hell....

Christine: Well, I say let's make an airlift to Russia. That's what I say. I don't think nothing is impossible if you believe it....

Jones: You think Russia's gonna want us with all this stigma? We had some value, but now we don't have any value.

Christine: Well, I don't see it like that. I mean I feel that as long as there's life, there's hope. That's my faith.

Jones: Well someday everybody dies. Someplace that hope runs out, because everybody dies. I haven't seen anybody yet didn't die. And I'd like to choose my own kind of death for a change. I'm tired of being tormented to hell, that's what I'm tired of. Tired of it. (*Applause*) Twelve hundred people's lives in my hands, and I certainly don't want your life in my hands. I'm going to tell you, Christine, without me, life has no meaning. (*Applause*) I'm the best thing you'll ever have... I'm standing with those people. They're part of me. I could detach myself. I really could detach myself. No, no, no, no, no, no. I never detach myself from any of your troubles... And I'm not going to change that now... (*Applause*) ...This is a revolution—it's a revolutionary suicide council...

Christine: But I look about at the babies and I think they deserve to live, you know?

Jones: I agree. But they—but don't they also deserve much more—they deserve peace.

People: Right....

Christine: ...I think we all have a right to our own destiny as individuals.

Jones: Right.

Christine: And I think I have a right to choose mine, and everybody else has a right to chose theirs....

Jim McElvane: Christine, you're only standing here because he was here in the first place. So I don't know what you're talking about—having an individual life. Your life has been extended to the day that you're standing there, because of him.

Jones: I guess she has as much right to speak as anybody else, too. What did you say, Ruby? Well, you'll regret that this very day if you don't die....

Woman: You must prepare to die....

Jones: ...I'm gonna lay down my burden. Down by the riverside. Shall we lay them down here in -- by Guyana? ...When they start parachuting out of the air, they'll shoot some of our innocent babies. I'm not lying.... But they gotta shoot me to get through to some of these people. I'm not letting them take your child. Can you let them take your child?

People: No, no, no, no....

Woman: You mean you want us to die—

Jones: I want to see—(*People shouting*) Please, please, please, please, please, please, please, please, please....

Man: We're all ready to go. If you tell us we have to give our lives now, we're ready—at least the rest of the sisters and brothers are with me.

Jones: Some months I've tried to keep this thing from happening. But I now see it's the will—it's the will of Sovereign Being that this happen to us. That we lay down our lives to protest in what's being done... They won't accept us. And I don't think we should sit here and take any more time for our children to be endangered. Because if they come after our children, and we give them our children, then our children will suffer forever....

Woman: At one time, I felt just like Christine felt. But after today, I don't feel anything....

Jones: It's all over. The congressman has been murdered. Well, it's all over, all over.... They invaded our privacy. They came into our home. They followed us six thousand miles away.... Please get us some medication. It's simple. It's simple. There's no convulsions with it. It's just simple. Just please get it. Before it's too late....

Woman: Now. Do it now!

Jones: Don't be afraid to die. You'll see, there'll be a few people land out here. They'll torture some of our children here. They'll torture our people. They'll torture our seniors. We cannot have this. Are you going to separate yourself from whoever shot the congressman? I don't know who shot him.

People: No. No. No....

Woman: I appreciate you for everything. You are the only—you are the only—you are the only. And I appreciate you.(*Applause*)

Jones: Please, can we hasten? Can we hasten with that medication? You don't know what you've done. And I tried. (*Applause*)....

Nurse: You have to move, and the people that are standing there in the aisles, go stand in the radio room yard. Everybody get behind the table and back this way, okay? There's nothing to worry about. Every – ever body keep calm and try to keep your children calm. And all those children that help, let the little children in and reassure them. They're not crying from pain. It's just a little bitter tasting. It's not –they're not crying out of any pain....

Jim McElvane:--things I used to do before I came here. So let me tell you about it. It might make a lot of you feel a little more comfortable... I used to be a therapist. And the kind of therapy that I did had to do with reincarnation in past life situations. And every time anybody had the experience of it... [they were] so happy when they made the stop to the other side.... If you have a body that's been crippled, suddenly you have the kind of body that you want to have.... It feels good. It never felt so good....

Woman: I just want to say something for everyone that I see that is standing around and--or crying. This is nothing to cry about. This is something we could all rejoice about.... I've been here one year and nine months. And I never felt better in my life. Not in San Francisco, but until I came to Jonestown. I had a very good life. I had a beautiful life. And I don't see nothing that I could be sorry about...(*Applause*)

Woman:...I just like to thank Dad [Jones], 'cause he was the only one that stood up for me when I needed him. And thank you, Dad.

Woman: I'm glad you're my brothers and sisters, and I'm glad to be here. Okay.

Jones: Please. For God's sake, let's get on with it....Let's be done with the agony of it. (*Applause*) ....This is a revolutionary suicide. This is not a self-destructive suicide.... They brought this upon us. And they'll pay for that.... If every body will relax. The best thing you can do is to relax, and you will have no problem....

Man:...I'd just like to thank Dad for giving us life and also death. And I appreciate the fact of the way our children are going. Because, like Dad said, when they come in, what they're gonna do to our children—they're gonna massacre our children. And also the ones that they take captured, they're gonna just let them grow up and be dummies like they want them to be. And not grow up to be a socialist like the one and only Jim Jones. So I'd like to thank Dad for the opportunity for letting Jonestown be, not what it could be, but what Jonestown is. Thank you, Dad. (*Applause*)

Jones: It's not to be feared. It is not to be feared. It's a friend. It's a friend—sitting there, show your love for one another. Let's get gone. Let's get gone. Let's get gone. (*Children crying*) We had nothing we could do.... Lay down your life with dignity. Don't lay down with tears and agony. There's nothing to teach. It's like Mac [Jim McElvane] said. It's just stepping over into another plane. Don't be this way. Stop the hysterics. This is not the way for people who are socialists or communists to die. No way for us to die. We must die with some dignity.... Look children, it's just something to put you to rest. Oh, God. (*Children crying*) Mother, mother, mother, mother, mother, please. Mother, please, please, please.... Lay down your life with your child....

Woman: We're doing all of this for you.

Jones: Free at last. Peace. Keep your emotions down…. Children, it will not hurt…. Adults, adults, adults. I call on you to stop this nonsense. I call on you to quit exciting your children, when all they're doing is going to a quiet rest. I call on you to stop this now, if you have any respect at all... All they're doing is...taking a drink. They take it to go to sleep. That's what death is, sleep. I'm tired of it all... Where's the vat, the vat, the vat? ….Bring the vat in. Please? Bring it here so the adults can begin.

Woman: Go on unto Zion, and thank you, Dad.

Heaven's Gate

Another probable psychotic led the largest mass suicide within U.S. borders. In March 1997, Marshall Herff Applewhite died alongside thirty-eight followers of his Heaven's Gate cult in a rented mansion near San Diego. A former member who had received farewell videos found the bodies, all with shaved heads, garbed in black athletic suits and shoes, lying on their backs on cots or cushions. Each wore a patch that said "Heaven's Gate Away Team." All but two had purple cloths folded in triangles like shrouds over their heads and shoulders. Beside each body was a small travel bag containing clothing and toiletries, as if in preparation for a short trip (Perkins and Jackson 1997; Bearak 1997; Balch 2002).

Evidence at the scene indicated they died over three or more days, probably fifteen at a time, aided by those who would follow. The procedure began with Dramamine, then tea and toast, and then alcohol mixed with Phenobarbital and chocolate pudding or applesauce. Some bodies had plastic bags over their heads, a painless means of suffocation. Autopsies revealed that Applewhite and seven other men were castrates.

Left behind were videotapes and a website explaining that Comet Hale-Bopp, then clearly visible in the night sky, was the marker they had been waiting for. A spaceship traveling in the comet's wake would take them to heaven, to the Level Above Human. In taped farewells, the cultists joyfully told of "shedding their containers [bodies]" and "leaving the planet" to return from whence they came because their task was done.

Cult leader Applewhite, son of a Presbyterian minister, was born in a small Texas town in 1931, where in high school he became president of the National Honor Society. After briefly studying for the ministry he changed course, becoming an opera singer and professor of music at a Catholic college in Houston. He married and had children but then divorced and followed a gay lifestyle. In 1972, a stressful time when Applewhite thought he was receiving private tutelage from God, he met Bonnie Nettles, an older registered nurse with three children and on the verge of her own divorce. Nettles, a born-again Christian, was also an astrologer and psychic who called on deceased souls. When Applewhite asked Nettles to do his astrological chart, they discovered they knew one another in previous lives. Together they opened the Christian Arts Center, specializing in astrology, mysticism, healing, and Theosophy.[2] Bonnie prepared horoscopes with help from a dead monk named Brother Francis. After the center faltered and Applewhite lost his teaching job, the pair departed Houston on New Year's Day 1973.

Traveling for months and ending on the Oregon coast, they formed a tight platonic relationship, conjuring visions of extraterrestrial experiences and a divine mission. They came to believe themselves the two prophets foretold in the Book of Revelations (11:3-12), destined to bear witness to the truth for 1,260 days, then to be killed and brought up to heaven in a cloud. They interpreted Revelation's cloud as a spaceship. Calling themselves Bo and Peep (later Do and Ti), they gathered over a hundred followers who expected an imminent departure via flying saucer from earth to "the next level." When no departure occurred, disaffected followers fell away as new entrants took their place.

During the 1970s weird cults were a popular media topic, and Bo and Peep were picked up as a fluff piece by the national media, including a cover story in the *New York Times Magazine* (February 29, 1976). Writer James Phelan emphasized the loony aspect of "The Two" and suggested they manifested what psychiatry calls *folie a deux*, where two closely related people share identical delusions, reinforcing each other's delusional misreading of reality. Their followers were drawn from believers in psychic phenomena and UFOs. Many had spent years trying to find themselves, seeking meaning in Scientology, yoga, Zen, offbeat cults, hallucinogens, hypnosis, tarot cards and astrology.

After their burst of national fame, the group – numbering perhaps 200 at its highest—fell out of sight. At first they lived in campgrounds across the West. As attrition brought the number to around forty, they rented houses. The Two elaborated a millenarian vision, warning that government, the wealthy, and "moral" leaders are under the control of evil space aliens. The coming apocalypse would destroy civilization, to be followed by a restoration. Nettles could not wait. In 1985 she died from cancer, leaving her bodily container and returning to the Next Level.

Between 1992 and 1994, Heaven's Gate, as the cult was then named, came out of seclusion to recruit publicly. It was during this period that some of the men began having themselves castrated to quench their sexual desires. By 1996 the group was living quietly in the rented mansion near San Diego. Housing twenty computers, it was the base for their new business of designing websites. One client later commented, "They definitely seemed odd. But living in California, odd is nothing strange to us. They seemed to me to be well within the norms of being able to handle society" (Purdum 3/28/97).

As with Jim Jones's followers at Jonestown, heavy demands had winnowed casual hangers-on, leaving a core of fervent believers. Some had followed Applewhite for over twenty years. Everyone in the mansion had forsworn material possessions, alcohol, tobacco, and sex. The cult had a nourishing quality for many, ridding them of addiction, depression, or loneliness. Members rarely contacted their families, remaining isolated from countervailing influences and committed to group solidarity. The day before the suicides commenced, all went to a restaurant for their last lunch, ordering thirty-nine identical meals of chicken pot pie, cheesecake, and iced tea.

Comet Hale-Bopp, first sighted in July 1995, had a peak visibility seen perhaps once every two centuries. UFO buffs spread a rumor that a spaceship followed the streaking light. In January 1997 two mansion residents purchased a $3,645 telescope to see the comet. How easily this fortuitous wanderer fit into the heavenly mythology of Applewhite and Nettles. Hale-Bopp's closest approach to Earth was March 22, about the date when the cultists started killing themselves.

In a newspaper interview afterward, a former member, the husband of a woman who died in the mansion, was morose at having missed the ascension, saying he would probably join them. Five weeks later, in a nearby motel, he died in a copycat suicide, with another former member unconscious in the same room (Purdum 5/7/97).

A Methodological Dilemma

It is tempting to call these people "crazy" in the legal sense of insanity or in the medical sense or psychosis, but that is not fully justified except in a few cases. The issue of legal insanity was raised (and rejected) only for Larry Layton, the one person brought to trial (and convicted) for the deaths at Jonestown. Two of Applewhite's followers are known to have had serious mental problems,[3] but it is not known whether others were ever examined psychiatrically. A diagnosis of psychosis is elusive even for Jones, Applewhite, and Nettles because none had a personal psychiatric evaluation, nor, obviously, did Joan of Arc. While many commentators label these leaders psychotic (specifically paranoid schizophrenic), there is in each case the counter-argument that they managed unusual lives in moderately effective ways, at least until the end. In that sense, they were not like the three Christs of Ypsilanti, unable to cope outside the institution.

Apart from legal insanity and medical psychosis, there is the layperson's commonsense notion of craziness as extremely odd, eccentric, or weird. From that lay perspective, it is oxymoronic to attribute normalcy to the deluded leader of a mass suicide, or to someone who believes they floated from their bed into a flying saucer, mated with a space alien, and created a hybrid baby. At some point beliefs or actions become sufficiently outlandish to compel most of us toward the conclusion that there is a mental disorder. There is no clear border to the outland, but neither is there precision in the legal or psychiatric definitions of insanity and psychosis.

The psychologist William James took extreme religious expressions by certain medieval figures as prima facie evidence of psychopathology. In his classic, *The Varieties of Religious Experience*, James quotes from the autobiography of a fourteenth century German mystic named Suso, who wrote of himself in the third person:

> He wore for a long time a hair shirt and an iron chain, until the blood ran from him; so that he was obliged to leave them off. He secretly caused an undergarment to be made for him; and in the undergarment he had strips of leather fixed, into which a hundred and fifty brass nails, pointed and filed sharp, were driven, and the points of the nails were always turned towards the flesh... In this he used to sleep (1985: 247).

Suso used this garment and performed other self-tortures for sixteen years, until he had a vision of a messenger from God who said it was enough. But then, to emulate the sorrows of his crucified Lord, he made a cross with thirty protruding nails, bearing this on his back day and night. William James comments:

> It is pleasant to know that after his fortieth year, God showed him by a series of visions that he had sufficiently broken down the natural man, and that he might leave these exercises off. His case is distinctly pathological, but he does not seem to have had the alleviation, which some ascetics have enjoyed, of an alteration of sensibility capable of actually turning torment into a perverse kind of pleasure. Of the founder of the Sacred Heart order, for example, we read that "Her love of pain and suffering was insatiable.... She said that she could cheerfully live till the day of judgment, provided she might always have matter for suffering for God; but that to live a single day without suffering would be intolerable" (1985: 249).

James might have also had in mind Saint Theresa of Avila (1515-1582), who famously wrote of her interlude with an angel:

> In his hands I saw a great golden spear and, at the iron tip, there appeared to be a point of fire. Then he plunged it into my heart several times, so that it penetrated

my entrails. When he pulled it out, I felt that he took them with it, and left me utterly consumed with the great love of God. The pain was so severe it made me utter several moans. The sweetness caused by this intense pain is so extreme that one cannot possibly wish it to cease, nor is one's soul then content with anything but God (Cohen 1957: 209).

Tempting as it may be, labeling unexamined individuals as "pathological" easily segues into unwarranted stigmatization of eccentric people as diseased. I have no solution to this slippery slope except to be wary of it. To abjure abnormal characterizations of people now dead, or otherwise unavailable for professional assessment, is to accord them normalcy by default. This has been a continual source of tension among psychologically-oriented political theorists.

Eric Hoffer (1951), on the one side, had no reluctance to label the earliest and most fanatic adherents to fascist and communist movements as alienated misfits and psychopaths with criminal tendencies. Perhaps true of certain individuals, it is incorrect as a generalization and reflects a bias against those to whom Hoffer was unsympathetic. It was in striking contrast to this view that Hannah Arendt (1963) commented, after the trial of Nazi Adolf Eichmann in Jerusalem, that the overseer of the "final solution" was an unimaginative but otherwise ordinary man who obeyed orders without critically thinking about his actions. The subsequent tendency of social psychologists has been to discount the importance of abnormal personality in explaining strange behavior, emphasizing instead the demands of abnormal situations, which might affect anyone.

Wary of Hoffer-like biases, modern researchers usually accept implicitly two methodological rules: First, a belief or action, however strange, cannot in itself be taken as evidence of a psychotic or of otherwise abnormal personality. If we were to accept a "crazy action" as sufficient evidence for a "crazy personality," then we would demonstrate nothing but a tautology. Second, personality has explanatory value only when it is assessed independently of the belief or action to be explained. The researcher must evaluate subjects using a psychiatric interview or pencil-and-paper personality tests, and then see if out-of-the-ordinary evaluations correlate with the strange belief of interest.

These are good rules, protecting against circular reasoning, and avoiding the stigmatization of people whose thinking seems exotic to academicians. But the rules do erect a strong burden of proof because relatively few true believers are accessible for academic study, and also because the means for measuring personality abnormality are crude. (The contradictory testimony of psychiatrists for opposing sides in a sanity hearing is notorious.) Perhaps for these reasons, there is only modest evidence that craziness *in the lay sense of personal weirdness* underlies unusual beliefs.

Conclusion

It is worth repeating that any implausible belief that is held by a large portion of the population cannot be explained by abnormal personality. To do so would contradict the meaning of "normal." Roughly a third of the population believes in the literal truth of the Bible and in the veracity of astrology. Common beliefs cannot have a generally abnormal etiology, even if they do contradict science and logic.

The question of personal "craziness" is meaningful only when asking about beliefs held by only a small portion of the population. Even fringe beliefs can usually be explained by normal social processes: Either the person was raised in a family of fringe believers, or later converted through the social influence of friends or a spouse on the fringe, or a particularly persuasive (charismatic) leader or guru or therapist. Normal people are especially susceptible to such conversions when they are lonely, distressed, confused, addicted to drugs, or seeking a deep meaning to life, and when the mass media give unusual attention to the topic.

This leaves little room, or need, to explain implausible belief as the result of craziness, however the term is defined. Legal insanity applies to hardly anyone discussed in this book. Psychosis, as determined by psychiatric evaluation, is rarely relevant because few people are evaluated and diagnosed as psychotic. If we loosen the diagnostic criteria, allowing distal (but hardly uncontroversial) evaluations of schizophrenic-like personalities – as in the cases of Joan of Arc, Jim Jones, and Marshall Applewhite – we still account for few believers in the implausible. The importance of such individuals is not in their number, which is surely small, but in the extraordinary influence they sometimes gain as leaders of cults or movements.

Rejecting medical psychosis as an explanation (except when clearly diagnosed) does not imply that a true believer is "normal" in the sense of being modal, well adjusted, or free of mental quirks. People within the "normal range" vary enormously, and no personality test is useful if it does not pick up wide variation. IQ tests, for example, distribute the population along a wide bell-shaped curve that has a mean defined as IQ = 100. Most people score between 85 and 115, but some score much higher or lower. Other personality traits, beside IQ, may predispose certain people toward more or less acceptance of implausible beliefs, to more or less critical examination of such claims, or to more or less susceptible to socially-mediated conversion.

This leaves as plausible the layperson's commonsense notion of craziness, that certain beliefs or actions are sufficiently weird that we presume the believer or actor is ipso facto mentally abnormal (even if not so extreme as to be psychotic or insane).[4] Temping as this explanation may be, it carries the danger of stigmatizing as mentally deranged any person who thinks or acts in ways that alienate our sympathies. Anyone espousing a "crazy" explanation should be certain that their target person is not adequately explained by the usual processes of socialization and conversion.

Notes

1. The most recent edition is the "text revision" of the fourth edition, published in 2000 and designated DSM-IV-TR.
2. Theosophy is a spiritualist philosophy originated by Madame Helena Blavatsky (1831-1891), who emigrated from Russia to New York in 1873 and was highly influential through her books and séances, channeling to masters in the other world. Theosophy retains followers today.
3. One had been collecting benefits for a "manic disorder" and another for schizophrenia (Perkins and Jackson 1997:43).
4. Many lay notions of craziness would fit psychiatric diagnostic categories in the *DSM* that indicate abnormality but are not so severe as psychosis.

14

Sincerely Irrational Convictions

Not all those who say they believe really do. Every paranormal venue has its hoaxers and jokesters, as well as sensationalizing distorters who walk the line between truthfulness and lying.[1] Some have criminal motives, some seek legal profit or celebrity, and some are just having fun. Many of the disingenuous are innocuous enough, like newspaper astrologers who do not even pretend that their daily horoscopes are more accurate than Chinese fortune cookies. Others are despicable, exploiting vulnerable innocents, sometimes ruining lives.

Frauds

Since M. Lamar Keene is a confessed liar, his autobiography as the fraudulently spiritualist pastor of a New Age church in 1960s Florida may not be wholly truthful. One hopes that the victims during his thirteen-year career were not as gullible as he claims, but perhaps they were. Keene's *The Psychic Mafia* (1976) is a classic of the debunking literature, explaining tricks of the trade and telling of hundreds of con artists like himself who profit from the private sorrows of sincere believers.

Raised a Baptist, the youthful Keene first considered entering the legitimate ministry. Led by a boyhood friend named Raoul, he instead ventured into séances, psychic healing, and ghostly apparitions. They joined Tampa's biggest spiritualist church as half-sincere believers. The eager acolytes were soon accepted as aides by the church's co-pastors, becoming privy to the reality beneath the appearances. Keene recalls, "from a psychological viewpoint I think that Raoul and I were healthier when we renounced our halfway position and became out-and-out frauds." The young partners bought a small church and with continued tutelage from the network of spiritualist frauds, built it into a thriving and profitable congregation. Keene's specialty was running séances in a darkened room where a mysterious ectoplasm would appear as a shimmering white haze, serving as a conduit for communication with the spirit world. (This was accomplished by swirling chiffon in the semi-darkness.) Another of his favorite devices was a bright, floating trumpet that amplified voices of the departed. (Dressed in head-to-toe black, Keene would speak through a second, black trumpet, creating the effect of a voice coming from the visibly suspended trumpet.)

After thirteen years, Keene had a bitter break with Raoul and turned whistleblower, becoming a pariah in the spiritualist community and a darling among debunkers. In his autobiography Keene ponders what compels a person, past all reason, to believe the unbelievable. "How can an otherwise sane individual become so enamored of a fantasy, an imposture, that even after it's exposed in the bright light of day he still clings to it – indeed, clings to it all the harder?"

UFO hoaxers have fooled sane but credulous believers since the term "flying saucer" was coined in 1947. Some deceptions were as simple as sailing plates in front of cameras. During the 1960s, a popular science magazine explained how to construct "fire balloons" from dry-cleaner bags, candles, and soda straws, which boys could launch at night to simulate UFOs. (See http://php.indiana.edu/ percent7Elrobins/candbal.htm.) Dyed-in-the-wool ufologists are among the most avid debunkers, hoping to separate dross from gold. Especially wary of government cover-ups, they were delighted in 1997 when the CIA finally admitted that during the late 1950s it encouraged the misidentification of secret spy planes as UFOs (Haines 1997).

In 1995 British video distributor Ray Santilli claimed to have original film showing the autopsy of one of the aliens that crashed at Roswell in 1947. Edited into a made-for-TV documentary titled *Alien Autopsy (Fact or Fiction?)*, it was shown in the United States on the Fox television network in prime time, first on August 28, 1995 and at least two more times. The telecast attracted enormous attention, its authenticity debated in and out of the mass media. Eventually the "documentary" was shown in over thirty nations. Released as a videotape, it reached the top twenty-five in U.S. video stores. (I bought one.) The *Times* of London estimates the autopsy has been seen by a billion people around the world.

Ufologist James Mosely comments on his first viewing,

> I couldn't believe anyone could take it seriously. For example, the "doctors" performing the autopsy were wearing unsealed protective suits. The alien itself obviously was a dummy, looking like a prop rejected by the director of a very bad 1950s science-fiction flick.... Worst of all was the ridiculous way the actors, uh, doctors handled the alien entrails, not to mention the entrails themselves. After cutting the dummy's, uh, alien's abdomen open, the quacks scooped out masses of dark, gloopy

stuff with their hands and dumped them into containers without performing the slightest examination (Mosely and Pflock 2002: 319).

Believers would also have to assume that the most important autopsy in history was conducted by two inept examiners in about two hours, and photographed with a single hand-held camera, in black-and-white with poorly focused close-ups. Some viewers may have been swayed by experts who seem impressed with the autopsy. Stan Winston, creature designer for *Aliens, Jurassic Park*, and *Terminator 2*, says in the documentary that he doesn't know how the autopsy could have been faked. But Winston later told *Time Magazine* that he "absolutely" thought it was a hoax (Corliss 1995).

Eleven years after the footage was first shown, British sculptor John Humphreys, who worked on social effects for the long-running sci-fi television series *Doctor Who*, admitted that he made the alien dummy and acted as the chief examiner. The film was shot in Camden, north London, in 1995. The bug-eyed dummy was filled with sheep brains, chicken entrails, and knuckle joints bought from a nearby meat market (Horne 2006). Santilli has not at this writing confessed, but he has produced a new film, *Alien Autopsy* (2006), which spoofs his original film, showing a similar autopsy on a similar dummy.

If we extrapolate from Keene and Santilli, the problem of implausible beliefs is one of dishonest promoters fooling gullible believers. That would be a gross exaggeration. Most religious leaders are genuine in their calling, and some promoters of the wackiest paranormal ideas really believe what they are promulgating. In these cases both leaders and followers are true believers. Now we turn to them, to people who sincerely believe the implausible. Where do they get their fantastic ideas, and why do they keep them, even when exposed to the light of reason?

Socializing True Believers

Most beliefs are adopted through social influence, first during childhood socialization; later from friends, spouse, and the surrounding community. It is not that people are thoughtless chameleons, but that our thinking is influenced importantly by those closest to us and secondarily by the broader social milieu, including the mass media. Each of us is capable of reaching conclusions by the purely cognitive exercise of our mind, apart from the constraints and pressures of society, but that is not the most frequent source of attitudes and beliefs.

Americans' values reflect the subcultures in which they are reared, at least initially. Political differences among ethnic groups are much discussed at election time. Southern white fundamentalists, for example, are more likely to vote Republican, to be politically conservative, and to oppose abortion than are blacks or Jews. Tastes can differ from group to group on any dimension. Southern white fundamentalists enjoy country and gospel music more than jazz or Broadway musicals; Jewish tastes are exactly opposite; blacks listen to gospel or jazz and do not care much for country singers.[2] These are median – not total – differences, and of course there are exceptions, so beware the pitfall of false stereotyping. Nonetheless, we truly are shaped by our upbringing.

Parents need not teach a particular belief but can instill a general orientation that predisposes the child toward later acceptance or rejection of that belief. No child during the twentieth century was instructed to oppose stem cell research, but many were taught that human life is sacred from the moment of conception, a tenet biasing them against stem cell research using human embryos. Fundamentalist Christians, accepting the reality of Satan, were a major constituency for the unsubstantiated myth circulating in the 1980s and 1990s that Satanic cults ritually mutilated and sacrificed infants (Victor 1993). Fundamentalist Muslims are susceptible to the belief that a suicide bombing of infidels will bring rewards in the sensual paradise described in the Koran (Harris 2005). Fundamentalist Jews are predisposed toward believing that Palestinians are intruders in the Promised Land.

Fringe beliefs, or fringe predispositions, can be acquired the same way as mainstream beliefs and predispositions. Meyer Baba (1894-1969) arrived in the United States from India in 1931 and became an icon of the 1960s counterculture, attracting celebrity converts including rock star Peter Townsend of The Who. Baba was by most accounts a nice man and a benevolent leader, but his teachings were as farfetched as those of Jim Jones or Marshall Applewhite. He professed to be the living God, literally the reincarnation of Jesus, Zoroaster, Rama, Krishna, Buddha, and Mohammed. Disciples called him the Avatar, the Infinite in human form, the God-Man, the Messiah (Mazur 2004). Decades after his death, I met one of the few remaining "Baba lovers," as followers are called. Inquiring about her continued devotion to a guru whose moment in the sun was long past, I found a simple answer. Her parents and grandmother had been devotees. She was raised in the faith, and she found continuing friendships and social support in the remaining community of worshippers. She was a Baba lover for the same reason that most Baptists are Baptist, and Catholics are Catholic.

The first generation of UFO believers was produced by the mass media, not by parents. Space visitors entered the public mind with Orson

Welles's 1938 radio broadcast of *War of the Worlds*, and they came on full bore during the flying saucer blitz of 1947. Hadley Cantril's 1940 study of Welles's listeners showed that believers were relatively less educated, more exposed to media sources, and less likely to assess the credibility of UFO reports against other sources of information. Also, perhaps, they were more likely than nonbelievers to mistake their own sightings of Venus or artificial satellites for UFOs. In any case, by the 1950s there existed a generation of parents telling their children about space visitors, with visual aids supplied by Hollywood and television.

Pollsters often measure the proportion of the population having one belief or another. Unfortunately polls do not inquire if the respondent's parents had similar beliefs. The General Social Surveys is unusual in asking the religion not only of the respondent but of the respondent's parents. We have no comparable parent-child data for astrology, UFOs, or other paranormal views. This is a serious gap that must be closed by future research.

There is piecemeal evidence that believers in the paranormal adopt their faith from parents or other older relatives. Professor Fred Frohock (2000), giving capsule biographies of thirteen modern psychics, notes in passing that eight have a psychic parent or grandparent. According to Harvard psychiatrist John Mack (1994), alien abductions run in families; over half of his published cases explicitly mention an older relative who was a UFO experiencer or believer. My own inquires often reveal a predisposing family background, for example, a professionally syndicated astrologer who learned her craft from her godfather, or a woman raised in a Christian Science family whom I met on her return from a psychic healer in Brazil.

If the default assumption is insufficient, the next simplest explanation is conversion—the believer came to his or her belief through the influence of friends or a spouse who holds that belief, or because of moving into a new social environment that fosters this belief. That is why, when Genesis-believer youths attend a secular university, their commitment often weakens, unless they encapsulate themselves in a fundamentalist circle on campus. If they make non-fundamentalist friends, or marry evolution-believing spouses, their conversion is likely to proceed toward Darwinism.

Peter Townsend and others who followed Meyer Baba during the 1960s were drawn in by friends and partners, and attracted by the celebrity status Baba had attained in the entertainment world and the press, and no doubt charmed by the man's considerable personal magnetism.

Also important at the time was the counterculture's emphasis on finding meaning and enlightenment through alternate forms of knowledge. With changing times and waning publicity, most converts moved elsewhere, but a few remain, keeping the faith alive.

Is the Mind Fully Integrated?

To appreciate how normal people can retain beliefs that are implausible by standards of logic and science, we must separate socially embedded ideas, especially those obtained during childhood, from beliefs that are not strongly tied to social allegiances. This bifurcation is most striking in conversations with people who are aware of their own inconsistencies. A chemist of my acquaintance, raised as a Seventh Day Adventist but now an atheist and an evolutionist, told me that she still believes at some level the Genesis stories of creation. When I asked how one reconciles these inconsistencies, she responded that she rarely thinks about them. They simply co-exist in her mind without critical examination. (Also see Dean 2007.)

Michael Faraday, the greatest experimental physicist of the nineteenth century, retained a well-known mental separation between his scientific thinking and the dictates of his Sanderman Protestantism, the literalist Scottish faith in which he was raised and followed all his life. Biographer Alan Hirshfeld tells an episode when the aging Faraday challenged church elders on a matter of scriptural interpretation: Can an individual forgive a transgressor, as Faraday maintained, or is that power vested solely in the church? Intensely disturbed by the threat of excommunication, Faraday recanted before the elders, acknowledging that false reasoning had brought him into error.

> Faraday's life was completely compartmentalized...he had erected a wall separating matters secular from those religious. One day he might stand tall in the arena of science or public affairs, asserting his independence before the weight of authority, yet the next, submit weakly to the reprimands of his church. The wonder is how he managed to occupy both sides of the wall simultaneously (Hirshfeld 2006: 204).

How *does* an immensely intelligent, empirically grounded person like Faraday simultaneously hold in mind inconsistent beliefs, or apply inconsistent modes of thinking, to these different domains? We do not understand the brain sufficiently well to answer this conclusively, but it is clear that mental inconsistency is a conundrum only if we assume that a normal person's mental processes are fully integrated, which probably is untrue.

The evolution of species is a conservative process (Mazur 2005). As new structures are added to a lineage, old ones may be modified considerably but they rarely disappear altogether. When some chordate evolved into a fish, fishlike behaviors were enabled by adding to the spinal cord and brain some olfactory bulbs, optic lobes, a cerebellum, hypothalamus and pituitary, and small cerebral hemispheres. As fish evolved into amphibians, then amphibians evolved into reptile-like amniotes, and then amniotes into birds and mammals, new forms of behavior were associated with new or modified brain parts. Rather than replacing old structures, new elements were figuratively stacked on top, forming an agglomerate brain.

There is neocortex in all mammalian brains and only in mammals. This structure is involved in perception, volition, memory and movement, reasoning and, in humans, language. The neocortex is especially large (relative to both body and brain mass) in primates. During embryonic development of apes and humans, the cerebral hemispheres fold as they grow, cramming a lot of neocortex into the skull, producing the convoluted walnut-like appearance of our brains. This voluminous neocortex—only about a third of it shows on the surface—engulfs older brain elements within the brain's hemispheres.

Some of these submerged structures are often designated the "limbic system." That term is much criticized, first because different authors disagree on the structures to be included, and second because "system" infers a functional unity that has never been demonstrated. Nonetheless, to a first approximation, conscious thoughts and actions depend primarily on the neocortex. The limbic structures are more concerned with emotions, motivation, and affective behavior (Brodal 1998).

Any conceptualization of the brain as an accretion of new structures atop ancient ones necessarily raises a question of how well these elements work together. Does the human brain operate as a fully integrated entity, or does it perform different functions in specialized modules that are not completely coordinated, for example, pitting our emotions against our cognitions?

That separate parts of the brain are capable of independent - even conflicting - thoughts and actions is illustrated in patients undergoing split-brain surgery for the control of epilepsy. In this operation the corpus collosum that connects the brain's two hemispheres is severed, thereby preventing the spread of abnormal nerve discharges from one hemisphere to the other, but at the same time halting normal communication between the hemispheres. Contrived laboratory tasks demonstrate independent operation of the two disconnected sides of the brain. For example, a patient can speak the name of an object held in the right hand, because the sensations of touch by the right hand go to the left hemisphere, where the speaking function is located; but the patient cannot say the name of an object held in the left hand since those sensations go to the right hemisphere, now severed from the speaking function on the left.

These patients manage well in everyday life because sights and sounds from the environment usually reach both hemispheres at the same time, but occasionally peculiar behaviors result from the disconnection. Neuroscientist Joseph LeDoux tells of seeing a patient several days after surgery who was pulling his pants down with this right hand and up with his left, as if the opposite sides of his brain had different aims and the normal means of reconciliation had been broken (2002: 305). Anyone who has resolved to diet and then gorged on cookies and ice cream, or tried to quite smoking and failed, or has had sex in a manner that –or with a person who—an hour earlier seemed a foolish choice, knows the appetites and emotions generated in one part of the brain may sharply contradict the good sense residing elsewhere. The joke that God gave man two gifts, a penis and a brain, but forbade him the use of both at the same time, carries enough truth to make the point but shows as well that it can be overstated.

When split-brain research appeared in the 1960s, it triggered a wave of extreme claims, never well supported, that each hemisphere specializes in certain kinds of mental processing—the left devoted to analytic, linguistic, rational, scientific, linear thought; the right to intuitive, non-linguistic, mystical, artistic, and holistic thought. With opposing halves vying like yin and yang, our personality was said to be determined by the dominant hemisphere.

This view is exaggerated, and it is worthwhile emphasizing the obvious but often overlooked point that split brains are anomalies. While they demonstrate the possibility of independent actions in different parts of our heads, they do not indicate this is normal operation. The pendulum of commentary is today swinging back, emphasizing that the emotional and cognitive parts of the brain, while in some ways separate, are on the whole highly connected and intensively interdependent. Brain scans made during diverse mental tasks typically show both hemispheres participating, if not in equally. Anatomically, there are dense connections among and between limbic elements and the neocortex. Emotional and cognition content are intertwined, as when depression comes with pessimistic thoughts, elation with optimistic plans (Dolan 2002). Information content in the form of bad news can make us feel down; good news cheers us up.

The connection of cognitions and emotions is illustrated by any escalating conflict between ethnic, religious, or nationalistic groups. Nearly every involved person's intellectual view of the conflict—how it started, whose fault it is, what solutions are just and unjust—is predictable from his emotional identification with one side or the other, whether Israeli against Palestinian, Pakistani against Indian, or Russian against Chechen. This alignment is so predictable that in chapter 10 we spoke of it as the *Rashomon* effect. It explains why the same suicide bomber or airplane hijacker is perceived as a terrorist by his enemies and as a freedom fighter or martyr by his allies.

Usually the mind's attitudes and beliefs are consistent with its feelings; there is an alignment of the neocortex and the limbic system. For this reason, our beliefs typically correspond with our social attachments of childhood, with our spouses and other loved ones, and with our friends and associates. This connection between limbic system and neocortex is the physiological basis for socially embedded beliefs. But it can also produce inconsistencies in thinking. If we are emotionally attached to Genesis-believing parents and, at the same time, to an evolution-believing spouse, we may hold both beliefs simultaneously.

Not all our ideas are socially embedded. The human mind is capable of rational thought, apart from any social attachment, whether the derivation of a mathematical theorem or the inductive conclusion from a body of evidence. This too may raise ideas that are inconsistent with our socially embedded beliefs. Unless we are strongly disposed toward ridding our thinking of all contradictions – hardly anyone is – then we easily accept inconsistent beliefs, perhaps giving one priority over the other without wholly expunging the subordinate notion, or we may simply avoid thinking about our mental inconsistencies.

Rationalizing Implausible Beliefs

Skeptic Michael Shermer asks, Why do even *smart* people believe weird things? His answer: *Smart people believe weird things because they are skilled at defending beliefs they arrived at for non-smart reasons.* (2002: 283). Possibly Shermer oversimplifies, but still his point is cogent. Socialization and socially mediated conversion are the usual "non-smart reasons" that an intelligent person accepts weird ideas. Socially derived beliefs have emotional attachments to the limbic system and are not easily changed by rational argumentation. The intelligent person employs his talented neocortex to verbalize a clever defense of his beliefs. If Thomas Aquinas were alive today, he could rationally parry every objection to the existence of God. Ptolemy was neither the first nor last astrologer to explain away failed predictions: "It should be remembered that these mistakes arise not from any deficiency or want of power in the science itself, but from the incompetence of unqualified persons who pretend to exercise it" (Bobrick 2005: 143).

True believers are so wedded to their explanation of an event that they reject far more plausible alternatives and doggedly defend their farfetched position. Psychologist Susan Clancy notes the resistance of her subjects – all alien abductees – to the suggestion that they experienced an episode of sleep paralysis rather than a true abduction by an extraterrestrial. In one instance Clancy overheard a cell phone call that the subject later made to a friend:

> I'm totally pissed. Can you believe the nerve of that girl? She comes to me, like, "Oh, I believe you've been abducted! Let me interview you to learn more about the phenomenon!" And then she brings up this sleep paralysis shit. "Oh, what really happened is sleep paralysis." Riiight! How the fuck does she know? Did she have it happen to her? I swear to God, if someone brings up sleep paralysis to me one more time I'm going to puke. There was something in the room that night! I was spinning. I blacked out. Something happened – it was terrifying. It was nothing normal. Do you understand? I wasn't sleeping. I was taken. I was violated, ripped apart – literally, figuratively, metaphorically, whatever you want to call it. Does she know that that's like? Fuck her! I'm out of here! (Clancy 2005: 50).

This defensive fervor and indignation recall the Rashomon effect, intensified by Clancy's assault on her subject's beliefs. Frontal argument, however cogent, rarely convinces a true believer. To the contrary, it deepens commitment.

Even when a belief is blatantly falsified, the true believer persists if fortified by the company of fellow believers. In the psychology classic, *When Prophecy Fails* (1956), Leon Festinger and his colleagues followed a tiny flying-saucer cult led by Mrs. Marian Keech, a housewife who received messages from Sanandra of the planet Clarion, predicting a great flood would end the world on a specific date. By proper devotion, Keech's followers would be rescued by a spaceship on the final day. When the day passed without event, Mrs. Keech predicted a new date, and then another. A few of her followers became disenchanted, but the majority who had gathered around their leader remained committed, finding an explanation for the failed prophecies in their own strong faith, which repeatedly deferred the cataclysm.

This is essentially the story of some of William Miller's followers in New York State after his mid-nineteenth-century predictions of the end to the world. While many did leave the movement after Miller's prophesies failed, others explained away these failures and remained unshaken. The Seventh-Day Adventist Church was created by some who remained true to Miller's movement.

Jehovah's Witnesses, a related sect, expected the destruction of the earth by fire, and the establishment of God's kingdom, in 1914, then 1915, 1918, and 1925. After World War II failed to end the world, 1975 seemed likely. There is no longer an official date. Some recent converts are unaware of earlier predictions. Membership in Jehovah's Witnesses, which grew before each prophetic date, fell afterward as the unfaithful were "cleansed" from the church, but each time revived with renewed proselytizing. Since 1990 the church has grown at about 3 percent per year worldwide (Watters 1990; http://www.jwic.com/stat.htm).

English Enlightenment philosopher Francis Bacon (1561-1626) described the rationalization of implausible belief nicely:

> The human understanding, when it has once adopted an opinion..., draws all things else to support and agree with it. And though there be a greater number and weight of instances to be found on the other side, yet these it either neglects and despises, or else by some distinction sets aside and rejects; in order that by this great and pernicious predetermination the authority of its former conclusions may remain inviolate.... And such is the way of all superstitions, whether in astrology, dreams, omens, divine judgments, or the like; wherein men, having a delight in such vanities, mark the events where they are fulfilled, but where they fail, although this happened much oftener, neglect, and pass them by.

Eccentric Personalities

Biblical literalism and denial of evolution are mainstream views in many American communities. Belief in UFOs is fairly common across the nation, and astrology is especially popular in New Age subcultures. It is natural for people raised and living in such communities and subcultures to hold these views. There is no reason to associate eccentric personalities with any belief that is commonly held.

The question of personality is more germane when explaining fringe beliefs, those incongruent with the social milieu. Are weird ideas held by weird people? Some theorists dismiss the connection, emphasizing the importance of abnormal situations rather than abnormal personalities. Ordinary people, faced with unusual crises, become anxious, depressed, lonely, or desperate. These feelings, if prolonged, motivate the sufferer to find succor in strange cults or by adopting arcane beliefs and practices. In this view, anyone might move in the strangest directions as a result of life's misfortunes.

Alien abduction, the most *outré* belief examined here, is a good test of the importance of personality. Few abductees are psychotic, but they do not cluster around the normal mode either. After interviewing about fifty people who claim they were abducted by space aliens, Susan Clancy (2005) described them as "1.5 standard deviations" from average on a scale of weirdness. While most are not seriously psychiatrically impaired, as a group they score high on schizotypy, a tendency to think eccentrically and to have "magical" ideas such as that certain numbers have special powers. They believe in telepathy and clairvoyance. They are daydreamers, highly imaginative, and prone to fantasy. They are loners. They are excellent hypnotic subjects. Apparently they are especially susceptible to sleep paralysis, which occurs with accompanying hallucinations in perhaps a fifth of the general population. Altogether, they are primed to "experience" visitations.

This kind of personality increases the likelihood of fantastic beliefs, but the content of these fantasies seems to be determined by the usual processes: childhood socialization and socially-mediated conversion. The importance of home socialization is indicated by Mack's comment that abduction runs in families, and Clancy's incidental descriptions of mothers of abductees who were either abducted or supported the notion of abduction. As adults, abductees live in settings that accept alternate realities:

> If you want to meet such people, I can tell you that they gravitate to certain professions – for instance, massage therapy, yoga instruction, the theater, the visual arts. You can find them in the New Age section of bookstores, at open-mike poetry readings, and in health food stores. They may well be dressed in purple or buying incense (Clancy 2005: 135).

Subjects almost never recall being abducted until they "recover" these memories through the mediation of a psychotherapist or ufologist using hypnosis or similar techniques. During this conversion, the subject and therapist jointly construct a fantasy scenario about flying saucers and hybrid insemination.

Reviewing personality studies of people with diverse superstitions, Professor Stuart Vyse of Connecticut College noted that results were often inconclusive but nonetheless drew a profile of common characteristics. Superstitious people are, according to Vyse, often female and often concentrated in particular occupations such as the theater and athletics. They tend toward lower intelligence and education; when they attend college they often major in the arts, humanities, or education. They score high on hypnotic suggestibility, alienation, neuroticism, depression, anxiety, and fear of death. They score low on ego strength and self esteem. They tend to see life's outcomes as determined more by chance or external forces than by their own efforts (1997: 24-58).

Vyse's profile overlaps Clancy's description of abductees, but there are important differences such as the fantasy proneness and sleep paralysis of abductees, and there is no suggestion that abductees are unintelligent. They usually are women, but gatherings of UFO enthusiasts are overwhelmingly male. The profile does not describe religious fundamentalists overall, though it may reflect people in fringe groups, such as snake handling Pentecostals. A general rule almost certainly valid is that the more commonly held a belief, the more normal the personality distribution of believers.

Deeper Explanations

Some readers will find superficial my explanation of implausible beliefs as the result of the ordinary processes of childhood socialization and socially-mediated conversion, with a dash of personality eccentricity. Simple explanations for strange phenomena can be unsatisfying. In his skeptical account of astrology, Lawrence Jerome writes, "Perhaps the reasons people want to believe in astrology and other occult 'sciences' lie deep within the psyche, within the psychological depths of the mind, an indication of the ceaseless struggles between id and ego, complex and archetype" (1997: 7). Carl Jung also found deep psychoanalytic meaning in people's fascination with astrology and UFOs. Religion, more than any other system of belief, is often said to emerge from the wellspring of the human spirit and to have evolved as a special feature of our species. This once revolutionary idea, propounded by French theologian and paleontologist Pierre Teilhard de Chardin (1965), has reemerged in the language of evolutionary psychology (Kurtz 1986; Atran 2002; Boyer 2002; Wilson 2003; Dennett 2006; Dawkins 2006).

No doubt there are important functions that may be served by implausible beliefs: giving meaning to our lives, assuaging our terror of death, defining our place in the chaotic cosmos, providing peak emotional experiences, sanctifying our existence, justifying our misfortunes, soothing our anxieties, making us more important than mere dots in infinite space, putting us in touch with the divine. They may be the ultimate reasons why we cling to beliefs that defy science, logic, or commonsense – clinging to them all the harder when they are exposed to the threatening light of disproof. Such profound speculations are worthy of reflection but difficult to test empirically, so perhaps we will never know if they are true or false.

Notes

1.   For a sampling of documented frauds see Abell and Singer (1981), Condon (1968), Gardner (1957, 1981), Klass (1983, 1989, 1997), Mosely and Pflock

(2002), Randi (1982), Shermer (2002), Sheaffer (1998), and the *Skeptical Inquirer* and the *Skeptic* magazines and websites.

2.   The General Social Surveys (Davis et al. 2001) verify these differences, for example, about 75 percent of Jewish respondents like musicals and jazz, but only about 25 percent like country or gospel. Among southern white fundamentalists, about 85 percent like country and gospel, and about 30 percent like jazz or musicals. Among blacks, 93 percent like gospel, 76 percent jazz, 54 percent musicals, and 42 percent country.

References

Abdel-Khalek, A. and D. Lester. 2006. "Astrological Signs and Personality in Kuwaitis and Americans." *Psychological Reports* 98: 602-607.

Abell, G. and B. Singer. 1981. *Science and the Paranormal*. New York: Charles Scribner's Sons.

Adams, E. 1926. The Bowl of Heaven. New York: Dodd & Mead.

Allard, W. 2006. "Solace at Surprise Creek." National Geographic (June): 120-147.

Allen, C. 1975. "The Schizophrenia of Joan of Arc." History of Medicine 6 (3-4): 4-9.

Anderson, B. 1966. *Understanding the Old Testament, 2nd Edition*. Englewood Cliffs, NJ: Prentice-Hall.

Associated Press. 2006. "Lawyer: 3 Kids Tossed in Bay as Sacrifice." CNN.com (May 24).

Arendt, H. 1963. Eichmann in Jerusalem. New York: Viking Press.

Arnold, K. 1948a. "I Did See the Flying Disks." FATE 1 (spring).

Arnold, K. 1948b. "Are Space Visitors Here?" FATE 1 (summer).

Arnold, K. and R. Palmer. 1952. The Coming of the Saucers. Amherst, WI: Amherst Press.

Arrington, L. and D. Bitton. 1979. The Mormon Experience: A History of the Latter-Day Saints. New York: Knopf.

Aslan, R. No god but God. New York: Random House.

Atran, S. 2002. In Gods We Trust: The Evolutionary Landscape of Religion. New York: Oxford University Press.

Avigad, N. 1974. "Jericho." Pp. 113-20 in Archaeology. Jerusalem: Keter.

Balch, R. 2002. "Making Sense of the Heaven's Gate Suicides." Pp. 209-228 in D.

Barker, R. 1990. They Call It Hypnosis. Buffalo, NY: Prometheus Books.

Barkun, M. 2003. A Culture of Conspiracy. Berkeley, CA: University of California Press.

Bartholomew, R. and G. Howard. 1998. UFOs and Alien Contact. Amherst, NY: Prometheus Press.

Bass, E. and L. Davis. 1988. The Courage to Heal: A Guide for Women Survivors of Child Sexual Abuse. New York: Harper and Row.

Bearak, B. 1997. "Odyssey to Suicide." New York Times (April 28): 1.

Beckmann, P. 1993. A History of Pi. New York: Barnes & Noble Books.

Berlitz, C. and W. Moore. 1980. The Roswell Incident.

Bernstein, M. 1956. The Search for Bridey Murphy. New York: Doubleday.

Blume, S. 1990. Secret Survivors: Recovering Incest and Its Aftereffects on Women. New York: Wiley.

Bobrick, B. 2005. The Fated Sky. New York: Simon & Schuster.

Bouchard, Jr., T. and M. McGue. 2003. "Tenetic and Environmental Influences on Human Psychological Differences." Wiley InterScience (www.interscience.wiley.com).

Boyarin, D. 1993. Carnal Israel. Berkeley CA: University of California Press.

Boyer, P. 2002. Religion Explained: The Evolutionary Origins of Religious Thought. New York: Basic Books.

Brainerd, C. and J. Reyna. 2005. The Science of False Memory. New York: Oxford University Press.

Brewer, P. 1986. Shaker Communities, Shaker Lives. University Press of New England.

Broad, W. 1997. "Air Force Details a New Theory of U.F.O. Case." New York Times (June 25): B-7.

Brodie, F. 1971. *No Man Knows My History: The Life of Joseph Smith*. New York: Random House.

Bromley and J. Melton (Eds.), Cults, Religion and Violence. New York: Cambridge University Press.

Brown, D. 2003. The Da Vinci Code. New York: Random House.

Brown, R. 1998. Manipulating the Ether. London: McFarland.

Brueggemann, W. 2003. *An Introduction to the Old Testament*. Louisville, KY: Westminster John Knox Press.

Bullard, T. 1987. UFO Abductions. Mt. Rainier, MD: Fund for UFO Research.

Campbell, A. and M. O'Brien. 1993. Sources of the Pentateuch. Minneapolis: Fortress Press.

Carlson, S. 1985. "A Double-blind Test of Astrology." Nature 318: 419-425.

Cantril, H. 1940. The Invasion from Mars. Princeton: Princeton University Press.

Carroll, R. 2003. The Skeptic's Dictionary. New York: Wiley.

Chotai, J., M. Lundberg, and R. Adolfsson. 2003. "Variations in Personality Traits among Adolescents and Adults according to their Season of Birth in the General Population: Further Evidence." Personality and Individual Differences 35L 897-908.

Clancy, S. 2005. Abducted. Cambridge, MA: Harvard University Press.

Clancy, S., R. McNally, D. Schacter, M. Lenzenweger, and R. Pitman. 2002. "Memory Distortion in People Reporting Abduction by Aliens." Journal of Abnormal Psychology 111: 455-461.

Clark, J. 2000. Pp. 122-140 in D. Jacobs (Ed.), UFOs and Abductions. Lawrence KS: University Press of Kansas.

Clute, J. 1995. Science Fiction. London: Dorling Kindersley.

Cohen, J. 1957. The Life of Saint Teresa. New York: Viking Penguin.

Collins, M. 2005. The Fisherman's Net. Mahwah, NJ: Paulist Press.

Condon, E. 1968. Scientific Study of Unidentified Flying Objects. New York: Bantam Books.

Corliss, R. 1995. "Autopsy or Fraud-topsy?" Time Magazine 146 (November 27).

Covington, D. 1995. Salvation on Sand Mountain. New York: Penguin.

Crews, F. 1995. The Memory Wars: Freud's Legacy in Dispute. New York: The New York Review of Books.

Cross, W. 1950. The Burned-Over District. New York: Harper & Row.

Darrach, Jr., J. and R. Ginna. 1952. "Have We Visitors from Space?" Life (April 7): 80-96.

Davis, J., T. Smith, and P. Marsden. 2001. General Social Surveys: 1972-2000: Cumulative Codebook. Chicago, NORC.

Dawkins, R. 2006. The God Delusion. Boston: Houghton Mifflin.

Dean, C. 2007. "Believing Scripture but Playing by Science's Rules." New York Times (February 12): 1.

Dean, G. 1994. "Samuel Hemmings and George III." Correlation 13 (2): 17-30 and 14 (2): 23-27.

Dean, G. and I. Kelly. 2003. "Is Astrology Relevant to Consciousness and Psi?" Journal of Consciousness Studies 10: 175-198.

Dean, G., D. Nias, and C. French. 1997. "Graphology, Astrology, and Parapsychology." PP. 511-542 in H. Nyborg (Ed.), The Scientific Study of Human Nature. Oxford: Elsevier Science Ltd.

Dennett, D. 2006. Breaking the Spell: Religion as a Natural Phenomenon. New York: Viking.

Denzler, B. 2001. The Lure of the Edge. Berkeley, CA: University of California Press.

Evans, J. 1989. Bias in Human Reasoning. Hillsdale NJ: Erlbaum.

Dever, W. 1997. "Is there any archaeological evidence for the exodus?" Pp. 67-86 in E. Frerichs and L. Lesko (Eds.) Exodus: The Egyptian Evidence. Winona Lake, IN: Eisenbauns.

Ehrman, B. 2005. Misquoting Jesus. New York: HarperCollins.

Ehrman, B. 2004. Truth and Fiction in The Da Vinci Code. New York: Oxford University Press.

Eurobarometer 55.2, Europeans, Science and Technology. Brussels: European Commission, 2001.

Eve, R. and F. Harrold, 1991. The Creationist Movement in Modern America. Boston: Twayne Publishers.

Festinger, L., J. Riecken, and S. Schachter. 1956. When Prophecy Fails. New York: Harper & Row.

Frerichs and L. Lesko (Eds.), Exodus: The Egyptian Evidence. Winona Lake, IN: Eisenbauns.

Elliott, A. 2006. "In Kabul, a Test for Shariah." The New York Times (March 26): 4.3

Eysenck, H. and D. Nias. 1982. New York: St. Martin's Press.

Farlow, J. and M. Brett-Surman. 1997. The Complete Dinosaur. Bloomington, IN: Indiana University Press.

Finkelstein, I. and N. Silberman. 2001. The Bible Unearthed. New York: Simon and Schuster.

Forer, B. 1949. "The Fallacy of Personal Validation." Journal of Abnormal and Social Psychology 44: 118-123.

Fortey, R. 1998. *Life: An Unauthorized Biography*. Flamingo.

Forrest, D. 1999. Hypnotism: A History. London: Penguin.

Foster, L. 1984. Religion and Sexuality. Urbana, IL: University of Illinois Press

Freedman, D. (Ed.). 1992. Anchor Bible Dictionary. New York: Doubleday.

Frerichs, E. and L. Lesko (Eds.). 1997. Exodus: The Egyptian Evidence. Winona Lake, IN: Eisenbauns.

Friedman, D. 1992. "Torah (Pentateuch)." Pp. 605-622 in D. Freedman (Ed.), Anchor Bible Dictionary. New York: Doubleday.

Friedman, R. 2003. *The Bible with Sources Revealed*. New York: Harper Collins.

Friedman, T. 2002. New York Times, January 23.

Frohock, F. 2000. Lives of the Psychics. Chicago: University of Chicago Press.

Gauquelin, M. 1979. Dreams and Illusions of Astrology. Buffalo: Prometheus.

Geraerts, E., J. Schooler, H. Merckelbach, M. Jelicic, B. Hauer, and Z. Ambadar. 2007. "The Reality of Recovered Memories." Psychological Science 18: 564-568.

Glendinning, T. and S. Bruce. 2006. "New Ways of Believing or Belonging: Is Religion Giving Way to Spirituality?" British Journal of Sociology 57: 399-414.

Goldstein, E. and K. Farmer. 1992. Confabulations. Boca Raton, FL: SIRS Books.

Harper, W., J. Hammond, D. Simms, and T. Dew. 1852 (1968). The Pro-Slavery Argument; as Maintained by the Most Distinguished Writers of the Southern States. New York: Negro Universities Press.

Fuller, J. 1966. Incident at Exeter. New York: G.P. Putnam's Sons.

Fuller, J. 1966. "Aboard a Fyling Saucer." Look (October 4): 45-56, and (October 18): 111-117.

Fuller, J. 1966. The Interrupted Journey. New York: Dial Press.

Gallup, G. 1947. "Nine out of Ten People Heard of Flying Saucers," Public Opinion News Service (August 15). Princeton, NJ.

Gardner, M. 1957. Fads and Fallacies in the Name of Science. New York: Dover.

Gardner, M. 1981. Science: Good, Bad, and Bogus. Buffalo, NY: Prometheus Press.

Gardner, M. 2006. The Memory Wars. Skeptical Inquirer 30: January:, 28-31, and March, 46-48.

Gerlach, L. and V. Hine. 1970. People, Power, Change: Movements of Social Transformation. Indianapolis: Bobbs-Merrill.

Gilovich, T. 1991. How We Know What Isn't So. New York: Free Press.

Glick, P. and M. Snyder. 1986. "Self-fulfilling Prophecy: The Psychology of Belief in Astrology." The Humanist 46: 20-35.

Glick, P., D. Gottesman, and J. Jolton. 1989. "The Fault is not in the Stars: Susceptibility of Skeptics and Believers in Astrology to the Barnum Effect." Personality and Social Psychology Bulletin 15: 572-583.

Goldner, E., L. Hsu, P. Waraich, and J. Somers. 2002. "Prevalence and Incidence Studies of Schizophrenic Disorders." Canadian Journal of Psychiatry 47: 833–43.

Grundy, J. 2006. "Joan of Arc Considered." http://www.stjoan-center.com/topics/jgrundy.html

Haines, G. 1997. "CIA's Role in the Study of UFOs, 1947-90." Studies in Intelligence: 67–84.

Hall, J. 2005. The Astrology Bible. New York: Sterling.

Hamer, D. 2004. The God Gene. New York: Doubleday.

Harris, S. 2005. The End of Faith. New York: Norton.

Hartmann, P., M. Reuter, and H. Nyborg. 2006. "The Relationship between Date of Birth and Individual Differences in Personality and General Intelligence: A Large-scale Study." Personality and Individual Differences 40: 1349-1362.

Hibbert, C. 1998. George III. New York: Basic Books.

Hickman, J., E. McConkey II, and M. Barrett. 1996. "Fewer Sightings in the National Press: A content Analysis of UFO News Coverage in The New York Times, 1947-1995." UFO Studies 6:213-225.

Hirshfeld, A. 2006. The Electric Life of Michael Faraday. New York: Walker.

Hoffer, E. 1951. The True Believer. New York: Harper and Row.

Hoffmeier, J. 1997. Israel in Egypt. New York: Oxford University Press.

Holden, K. and C. French. 2002. "Alien Abduction Experiences: Some Clues from Neuropsychology and Neuropsychiatry." Cognitive Neuropsychiatry 7: 163-178.

Holmes, D. 2006. The Faiths of the Founding Fathers. New York: Oxford University Press.

Hopkins, B. 1981. Missing Time: A Documented Study of UFO Abductions. New York: Richard Marek Publishers.

Hopkins, B. 1987. Intruders: The Incredible Visitations at Copley Woods. New York: Random House.

Horne, M. 2006. "Max Headroom Creator Made Roswell Alien." The Sunday Times (of London), April 16.

Hughes, D. 1966. "The War of the Worlds in the Yellow Press." Journalism Quarterly 53: 639-646.

Hume, D. 1758. An Enquiry Concerning Human Understanding. New York: Oxford University Press, 2000.

Humphries, C. 2003. The Miracles of Exodus. New York: HarperCollins.

Hynek, J. 1974. The UFO Experience: A Scientific Study. New York: Ballentine.

Jacobs, D. 1992. Secret Life: Firsthand Accounts of UFO Abductions. New York: Simon and Schuster.

James, W. 1985 (1902). The Varieties of Religious Experience. Cambridge, MA: Harvard University Press.

Jerome, L. 1977. Astrology Disproved. Buffalo, NY: Prometheus Press.

Jones III, J. 2005. Kitzmiller v. Dover Areas School District, et al. U.S. District Court for the Middle District of Pennsylvania.

Jung, C. 1959. Flying Saucers. New York: Harcourt Brace Javonovich.

Kasser, R., M. Meyer, and G. Wurst. 2006. The Gospel of Judas. Washington, DC: National Geographic.

Katz, S. 1983. Mysticism and Religious Traditions. New York: Oxford University Press.

Keene, M. 1976. *The Psychic Mafia*. New York: Dell.

Keniston, K. 1968. Young Radicals. New York: Harcourt, Brace, and World.

Keyhoe, D. 1950. "Flying Saucers are Real." True (January).

Keyhoe, D. 19--. The Flying Saucer Conspiracy.

Kinder, D. 2006. "Politics and the Life Cycle." Science 312: 1905-1908.

Kirsch, I. 1985. "Response Expectancies as a Determinant of Experience and Behavior." American Psychologist 11: 1189-1202.

Klass, P. 1976. UFOs Explained. Vintage Press.

Klass, P. 1983. UFOs: The Public Deceived. Amherst, NY: Prometheus Press.

Klass, P. 1989. UFO Abductions: A Dangerous Game. Buffalo, NY: Prometheus Books.

Klass, P. 1997. The Real Roswell Crashed-Saucer Coverup. Amherst, NY: Prometheus Press.

Kurtz, P. 1986. The Transcendental Temptation. Amherst, NY: Prometheus Books.

Koestler, A. 1960. The Watershed. Garden City, NY: Doubleday.

Köhler-Rollefson, I. 1996. "The one-humped camel in Asia: origin, utilization and mechanisms of dispersal. Pp. 282-294 in D. Harris (Ed.), The Origins and Spread of Agriculture and Pastoralism in Eurasia. Washington DC: Smithsonian Institution Press.

Kottmeyer, M. 1990. "Entirely Unpredisposed: The Cultureal Background of UFO Abductions." Magnolia (January).

Krakauer, J. 2003. Under the Banner of Heaven. Doubleday.

Kraybill, D. 2001. The Riddle of Amish Culture. Baltimore: Johns Hopkins University Press.

Lambert, Y. 2004. "A Turning Point in Religious Evolution in Europe." Journal of Contemporary Religion 19: 29-45.

Layton, D. 1998. Seductive Poison. New York: Random House.

Lehnert, E. and M. Perpich. 1982. "An attitude segmentation study of supermarket tabloid readers." Journalism Quarterly 59: 104-111.

Lind, M. and J. Heilbrun. 1995. "On Pat Robertson." The New York Review of Books (April 20): 71-76.

Loftus, E. 1993. The Reality of Repressed Memories. American Psychologist 48: 518-537.

Loftus, E. and J. Doyle. 1997. Eyewitness Testimony. Charlottesville, VA: Lexis Law Publications.

Losh, S, C. Tavani, R. Njoroge, R. Wilke and M. Mcauley. 2003. "What Does Education Really Do?" Speptical Inquirer 27 (Sept-Oct): 30-35.

Lowell, P. 1895. Mars.

Luo, M. 2006. "Evangelicals Debte the Meaning of 'Evangelical'." New York Times (April 16).

Mack, J. 1994. Abduction: Human Encounters with Aliens. New York: Ballantine Books.

Marcus, G., J. Sullivan, E. Theiss-Morse, and S. Wood. 1995. With Malace Toward Some. New York: Cambridge University Press.

Mazur, A. 2007a. "Disbelievers in Evolution." *Science* 315: 187.

Mazur, A. 2007b. "Bible Stories: A Sociologist Looks at Implausible Beliefs in Genesis." *Skeptical Inquirer*.

Mazur, A. 2007c. Global Social Problems. Boulder CO: Rowman & Littlefield.

Mazur, A. 2005. Biosociology of Dominance and Deference. Boulder CO: Rowman & Littlefield.

Mazur, A. 2004. "Believers and Disbelievers in Evolution." *Politics and the Life Sciences* 8 (November): 55-61.

Mazur, A. 1998. A Hazardous Inquiry: The Rashomon Effect at Love Canal. Cambridge MA: Harvard University Press.

Mazur, A. 1989. "Allegations of Dishonesty in Research and Their Treatment by American Universities," Minerva, Summer: 177-94.

Mazur, A. 1981. The Dynamics of Technical Controversy. Washington DC: Communications Press.

Mack, J. 1994. Abduction: Human Encounters with Aliens. New York: Schribner's.

McBrien, R. 1997. Lives of the Popen. New York: HarperCollins.

McCombs, Jr., M. and Shaw, D. (1972) Agenda-setting Function of the Mass Media. Public Opinion Quarterly 36: 176-87.

McIntosh, C. 1969. The Astrologers and their Creed. New York: Praeger.

McKivigan, J. and M. Snay. 1998. Religion and the Antebellum Debate over Slavery. Athens GA: University of Georgia Press.

McNally, R. 2003. Remembering Trauma. Cambridege,MA: Harvard University Press.

McNally, R., N. Lasko, S. Clancy, M. Macklin, R. Pitman and S. Orr. 2004. "Psychophysiological Responding During Script-driven Imagery in People Reporting Abduction by Space Aliens." Psychological Science 15: 493-497.

Mervis, J. 2006. "Judge Dones Defines Science – and Why Intelligent Design Isn't." Science 311 (6 January): 34.

Metzger, B. and M. Coogan. 1993. *The Oxford Companion to the Bible*. New York: Oxford University Press.

Michel, L and D. Herbeck. 2001. American Terrorist. New York: HarperCollins.

Miller, R., H. Stout, and C. Wilson (eds). 1998. Religion and the American Civil War. New York: Oxford University Press.

Milling, L., J. Reardon, and G. Carosella 2006. "Mediation and Moderation of Psychological Pain Treatments." Journal of Consulting and Clinical Psychology 74: 253-62.

Mooney, C. and M. Nisbet. 2005. "Undoing Darwin." Columbia Journalism Review (September/October): 1-14.

Moseley, J. and K. Pflock. 2002. Shockingly Close to the Truth! Amherst NY: Prometheus Books.

National Science Board. 2006. Science and Engineering Indicators 2006. Washington, DC: National Science Foundation.

Neimark, J. 1994. "The Harvard Professor and the UFOs." Psychology Today (March-April): 44-48, 74-90.

Nelkin, D. 1982. The Creation Controversy. Boston: Beacon Press, 1982.

Newberg, A. and M. Waldman. 2006. Why We Believe What We Believe. New York: Simon& Schuster.

Newcomb, T., K. Koonig, R. Flacks, and D. Warwick. 1967. Persistence and Change: Bennington College and its Students after Twenty-five Years. New York: Wiley.

Newman, L. and R. Baumeister. 1996. "Toward an Explanation of the UFO Abduction Phenomenon." Psychological Inquiry 7: 99-126.

Newport, T. 2004. "Third of Americans Say Evidence Has Supported Darwin's Evolution Theory," Gallup Poll News Service, November 19.

Nicholson, E. 1998. The Pentateuch in the Twentieth Century. New York: Oxford University Press.

Nickell, J. 1996. "A Study of Fantasy Proneness in the Thirteen Cases of Alleged Encounters in John Mack's Abduction." Skeptical Inquirer 20: 18-20.

Nickerson, R. 1998. "Confirmation Bias: A Ubiquitous Phenomenon in Many Guises." Review of General Psychology 2: 175-220.

Nienhuys, J. 1997. "The Mars Effect in Retrospect." Skeptical Inquirer 21 (6): 24-29.

Noll, M. 2001. The Old Religion in a New World. Grand Rapids, MI: Eerdmans.

Noonan, Jr., J. 2005. *A Church that Can and Cannot Change: The Development of Catholic Moral Teaching*. University of Notre Dame Press.

Ofshe, R. and E. Watters. 1999. Therapy's Delusions. Scribner.

Ofshe, R. and E. Watters. 1996. Making Monsters: False Memories, Psychotherapy, and Sexual Hysteria. Berkeley, CA: University of California Press.

Park, R. 2000. Voodoo Science. New York: Oxford University Press.

Peebles, C. 1995. Watch the Skies! New York: Berkley Books.

Perkins, R. and F. Jackson. 1997. Cosmic Suicide. Dallas: Pentaradial Press.

Phelan, J. 1976 "Looking for: The Next World." New York Times Magazine (February 29): 172.

Phillips, K. 2006. American Theocracy. New York: Viking.

Pennock, R. (Ed.), Intelligent Design Creationism and Its Critics. Cambridge MA: MIT Press, 2001.

Pierson, G. 1938. *Tocqueville and Beaumont in America*. Oxford: Oxford University Press.

Powell, A. 1994. Utah History Encyclopedia. Salt Lake City: University of Utah Press.

Purdum, T. 3/30/97/ "Death in a Cult: The Scene." New York Times (March 30): 1.

Purdum, T. 5/7/97. "Ex-cultist Dies in Suicide Pact; 2nd is Critical." New York Times (May 7): 1.

Randi, J. 1982. Flim-Flam! Buffalo, NY: Prometheus Press.

Raphael. 1828. A Manual of Astrology. London: C.S. Arnold.

Rathje, W. 2001. Why the Taliban and Destroying Buddhas. USA Today (March 22).

Rayburn, W., J. Lavin Jr., M. Miodovnik, and M. Varner. 1984. "Multiple Gestation: Time Interval between Deliver of the First and Second Twins." Obstetrics & Gynecology 63: 502-06.

Reeves, R. 2005. President Reagan. New York: Simon & Schuster.

Rice, M. 2003. Egypt's Making, Second Edition. London: Routledge.

Rios, D. 2005. "Still Believe in Flying Saucers? Air Force Files Now Open to You." Syracuse Post-Standard (August 17): A-5.

Robertson, P. 1991. The New World Order. Dallas: Word.

Rockeach, M. 1960. The Open and Closed Mind. New York: Basic Books.

Rokeach, M. 1964. The Three Christs of Ypsilanti. New York: Knopf.

Rodeghier, M., J. Goodpaster, and S. Blatterbauer. 1991. "Psychological Characteristics of Abductees." Journal of UFO Studies 3: 59-90.

Rofé, A. 1999. Introduction to the Composition of the Pentateuch. Sheffield, UK: Sheffield Academic Press.

Rogo, D. 1984. "Extraterrestrial Sex." Omni 6 (September): 111.

Rosenberg, D. and H. Bloom. 1990. The Book of J. New York: Grove Press.

Sagan, C. 1996. The Demon-Haunted World. New York: Ballantine Books.

Schick, Jr., T. and L. Vaughn. 2002. How to Think About Weird Things. Boston: McGraw Hill.

Schönborn, C. 2005. Finding Design in Nature. The New York Times (July 7): A27.

Schowalter, D. 1993. "Virgin Birth of Christ." Pp. 789-90 in B. Metzger and M. Coogan (eds.), The Oxford Companion to the Bible. New York: Oxford University Press.

Sepharial. 1972 (1910). A Manual of Occultism. London: Rider.

Shaw, I. 2004. Ancient Egypt. Oxford UK: Oxford University Press.

Sheaffer, R. 1998. UFO Sightings: The Evidence. Amherst NY: Prometheus Books.

Shermer, M. 2002. Why People Believe Weird Things. New York: Henry Holt.

Smith, T. 1987. "Classifying Protestant Denominations, Revised." GSS Methodological Report 43. Chicago: NORC.

Sokolove, M. 2005. "The Senator from a Place Called Faith." New York Times Magazine (May 22): 56-60.

Spanos, J., P. Cross, K. Dickson and S. DuBreuil. 1993. "Close Encounters: An Examination of UFO Experiences." Journal of Abnormal Psychology 102: 624-632.

Stark, R. and R. Finke. 1993. The Churching of America, 1776-1990. New Brunswick, NJ: Rutgers University Press.

Stark, R.and R. Finke. 2000. Acts of Faith. Berkeley CA: University of California Press.

Stephenson, D. (Ed.) 2005. Dear People: Remembering Jonestown. Berkeley: Heyday Books.

Sutherland, S. 1992. Irrationality: Why We Don't Think Straight! New Brunswick, NJ: Rutgers University Press.

Szasz, T. 19--. The Myth of Mental Illness.

Teilhard de Chardin, P. 1965. The Phenomenon of Man. New York: Harper & Row.

Thompson, R. and S. Madigan. 2005. Washington, DC: Joseph Henry Press.

Thurston, H. 2005. "St. Joan of Arc." The Catholic Encyclopedia. Online Edition. www.newadvent.org/cathen/08409c.htm.

Tuchman, B. 1978. A Distant Mirror. New York: Albert A. Knopf.

Tversky, A. and D. Kahneman 1974, Judgment under uncertainty, Science 185: 1124-31.

Victor, J. 1993. Panic: The Creation of a Contemporary Legend. Chicago: Open Court.

Vyse, S. 1997. Believing in Magic: The Psychology of Superstition. New York: Oxford University Press.

Waltke, B. 1992. "Torah (Pentateuch)." Pp. 932-940 in D. Freedman (Ed.), Anchor Bible Dictionary. New York: Doubleday.

Ward, W. 1997. "Summary and conclusions." Pp. 105-112 in E. Frerichs and L. Lesko (Eds.), Exodus: The Egyptian Evidence. Winona Lake, IN: Eisenbauns.

Watters, R. 1990. "When Prophecies Fail: A Sociological Perspective on Failed Expectation in the Watchtower Society." Bethel Ministries Newsletter (May/June); also http://www.freeminds.org/psych/propfail.htm .

Wells, H. G. 1898. War of the Worlds.

Wilgoren, J. 2005. "Seeing Creation and Evolution in Grand Canyon." New York Times (October 6): 1.

Willwerth, J. 1994. "The Man from Outer Space." Time (April 25): 74-75.

Wilson, D. 2003. Darwin's Cathedral. Chicago: University of Chicago Press.

Woodward, K. 1990. Making Saints. New York: Simon and Schuster.

Zaller, J. 1992. The Nature and Origins of Mass Opinion. New York: Cambridge University Press.

Zmuda, B. 1999. Andy Kaufman Revealed. Boston: Little, Brown and Company.

Index